THE WILDERNESS OF THE UPPER YUKON

Rams.
From a painting by Carl Rungius.

THE WILDERNESS OF THE UPPER YUKON

A HUNTER'S EXPLORATION FOR WILD SHEEP IN SUB-ARCTIC MOUNTAINS

BY

CHARLES SHELDON

ILLUSTRATED

BOONE AND CROCKETT CLUB

B&C CLASSICS

MISSOULA, MONTANA | 2014

WILDERNESS OF THE UPPER YUKON
BY CHARLES SHELDON

Originally published in 1911.
Reprinted in 2014 as part of Boone and Crockett Club's series, B&C Classics.

Paperback ISBN: 978-1-940860-08-4
eBook ISBN: 978-0-940864-98-6
Published April 2014

Published in the United States of America by the
Boone and Crockett Club
250 Station Drive, Missoula, Montana 59801
Phone (406) 542-1888
Fax (406) 542-0784
Toll-Free (888) 840-4868 (book orders only)
www.booneandcrockettclub.com

MESSAGE FROM THE PUBLISHER

THE Boone and Crockett Club was founded by Theodore Roosevelt and George Bird Grinnell in 1887. Two years earlier, Grinnell, then editor of *Forest and Stream,* wrote a critical review of Roosevelt's book, *Hunting Trips of a Ranchman*. Roosevelt paid him a visit to discuss the matter. During that meeting Grinnell presented a strong case about his concerns on the future of hunting and conservation. TR was in agreement, and thus began a lifelong friendship that led to the founding of the Boone and Crockett Club, the first private hunting and conservation organization in North America. The two also went on to collaborate on numerous books about hunting, conservation, exploration, and adventure. Since its early days, B&C has had a strong tie with publishing and furthering hunting and conservation.

In 2012, we launched our B&C Classics series of hunting and adventure books, including works from TR and Grinnell, as well as William T. Hornaday, Charles Sheldon, Frederick C. Selous and other adventurers from the late 1800s through the early 1900s. Each title in the B&C Classics series is selected by a committee of vintage hunting literature experts and is authored by a Boone and Crockett Club member.

Unlike other reprints of these hunting and adventure books, the B&C Classics series has been meticulously converted resulting in high-quality, digitally remastered eBooks and paperback editions. Many are complete with vintage photos and drawings not found in other editions. This attention to detail helps transport readers back to a time when hunting trips didn't happen over a weekend, but were adventures that spanned weeks, months, or even years.

We hope you enjoy the books we've selected for this series. They will give you a strong sense of our hunting heritage and provide hours of entertainment for anyone who loves adventure and the outdoors.

JULIE L. TRIPP
B&C Director of Publications
MISSOULA, MONTANA

TO

EDWARD W. NELSON

One of the world's foremost field naturalists, who for thirty years conducted natural history explorations in the wilder areas of our continent from Arctic Alaska to Tropical America; who first revealed to science the White Sheep of our Far North, and collected the types of the Wild Sheep of the desert ranges of Southern California and Mexico. His love of the wilderness, his studies in ethnology, his zest in hunting, exploring, and collecting, his indomitable courage, and his high character and nobility of manhood have been to me an ever-present inspiration.

PREFACE

THIS BOOK IS A RECORD OF MY FIELD EXPERIENCES WHILE ENGAGED IN STUDYING THE COLOR VARIATIONS OF THE WILD SHEEP OF YUKON TERRITORY. It is an attempt to give a detailed account strictly from the point of view of a hunter interested in natural history.

Most parts of the Territory which are inhabited by sheep are also the favorite abodes of moose and grizzly bears, and some of them of caribou. The black bear inhabits the forests everywhere below timber-line; the white goat lives exclusively in the humid belt of the Coast ranges. No other game animals exist in the Yukon wilderness. Most of the fur-bearing animals of the Hudsonian zone are abundant on the timbered slopes immediately below the sheep ranges. The number of species of mammals and birds is small.

In the North, wild sheep dwell exclusively on high mountains, above timber-line, usually well back within the ranges. Nearly all of the mountains on which I hunted, with the exception of Plateau Mountain and those near Watson River, were untrodden by the foot of white man or Indian. The wilderness was primeval, the sheep practically undisturbed, the other game animals seldom hunted. It was not possible to find guides, for there were none. It was necessary not only to search out a route to the mountains, but also to find the ranges occupied by sheep. I have, therefore, adopted the subtitle, "A Hunter's Explorations for Wild Sheep in Sub-Arctic Mountains."

Having made my trips under such conditions, I have tried to record my experiences when travelling by steamboat, canoe, with pack-horses, and on foot; my efforts to find game and the details of hunting it; and a faithful account of the actions of all animals observed. To this I have added descriptions of the country traversed, my impressions of the scenery, and notes on the weather; so that the book might present a picture of the wilderness of Yukon Territory.

All of my actual hunting has been done alone, without guide or companion. For the purpose of keeping a record, each day's experiences and observations were written in my journal before retiring to sleep. The exceptions to this practice were very rare.

A portion of these journals relates to the habits of animals. In view of subsequent experiences, however, I regard those gained in Yukon Territory merely as a training in observation—a perspective for more correctly interpreting the observed traits and life histories of animals. This was a great help during the two following years (including the whole of one) which were spent in the interior of Alaska, where the same animals were much more abundant. For this reason, I have touched only suggestively on habits, but hope to include a discussion of them in a future publication.

The photographs having legends quoted from the text are accurate illustrations, both in time and place, of that part of the text included in the quotations. With two exceptions, all photographs of dead animals exhibit their attitudes before I touched them, after they had fallen and died.

In his interesting book, *Recent Hunting Trips in British North America*, F. C. Selous has given an account of our trip up the MacMillan River. At the risk of some duplication, I have included my narrative of it, not only because most of my hunting was directed toward the finding of sheep and consequently differed from his, but also to make my record of the wilderness country more complete. Selous has also described his later trip to the South Fork of the MacMillan, where he found the woodland caribou, *Rangifer osborni*, abundant. During my wanderings, I met with these animals but once, and then my observation was limited to a cow and her calf.

None of the annals of "breaking the wilderness" have been enriched by more romance than that of the advance of mining interests in Yukon Territory and Alaska. This has been told in several good books, which also include descriptions of the Lewes and Yukon Rivers. Therefore all allusions to the well-known routes of travel and the settled parts of the Territory have been excluded from my narrative. But I have included a short trip up the Katzehin River, near Skagway—the gateway to Yukon Territory. For those interested in natural history studies, chapter XX, which includes a discussion of the variations of the sheep, and also short remarks on some other animals, has been added to the narrative.

A general map of Yukon Territory, including my hunting camps, is inserted at the beginning of Chapter XX.

Appendices are added, giving: (A) a list of books and other publications relating to Sport, Natural History, Exploration, and the Topography of the Territory; (B) a list of the animals and fishes mentioned in the present volume, with their scientific names; (C) reproductions of the original descriptions of the northern species of sheep (descriptions written when knowledge of the sheep was very limited); (D) measurements of some of the sheep killed; and (E) a record of the time of travelling by canoe down the Pelly River.

I have never received anything but the heartiest goodwill and the most kindly consideration from all people whom I met in Yukon Territory. Without exception, willing assistance was always offered, and given when needed, and I take this opportunity of expressing my thanks.

It would be difficult to adequately express my indebtedness to my friend, A. B. Newell, who at that time was Vice-President of the White Pass Railroad, and managed the river steamers between Whitehorse and Dawson. Not only did he place at my disposal all the facilities of that vast transportation system, but he did what was still more valuable for the accomplishment of my plans— he gave his personal interest.

W.H. Osgood and Carl Rungius have both placed all their photographs at my disposal, and I must especially mention the interest of Mr. Rungius in making some illustrations for this book. No other artist has had the experiences that would make it possible for him to record so accurately the animal life of the Yukon region. Mr. H.Q. French has kindly permitted me to use two of his photographs.

E.W. Nelson and Arthur Colton have both read over that part of the narrative which relates to Coal Creek, and I have received much valuable criticism from them.

With extraordinary patience, Dr. C. Hart Merriam has sacrificed his time and read the whole manuscript. I have accepted his numerous suggestions as to its form, and also his still more numerous corrections of the text. My obligation is so great, that I wish to lay special emphasis on his interest and assistance, and in thanking him, to express my feeling of appreciation.

Nobody except myself, however, is responsible for any of the conclusions in the text.

The pleasantest part of preparing the narrative has been the co-operation of my wife.

A legitimate number of the animals killed were reserved for trophies; the others were collected especially for the U. S. Biological Survey, and are now in the new National Museum at Washington.

The Biological Survey, a bureau of our National Department of Agriculture, is an institution too little known, and since it co-operated with me in all my work in the north, thus adding pleasure not anticipated, I would gladly bring its magnificent work to the attention of a wider public than that of the specialists and others directly interested. It was organized in 1885 for the purpose of studying the food habits of our native birds and mammals in their relations to agriculture, by Dr. C. Hart Merriam, who possesses one of the keenest scientific minds which the country has produced. Dr. Merriam saw that the continent of North America, stretching from the tropics to the Polar Sea, comprising vast areas of tropical, temperate, and arctic lands, and supporting a number of widely different fauna and flora, afforded an unrivalled field for the study of the interrelations of species, and the correlation of the distribution of animal and plant life. He was the first to appreciate and demonstrate the intimate relation between the agricultural possibilities of a region and the distribution of its native forms of life.

In order to learn the facts of distribution it was necessary to collect and determine the species inhabiting all parts of the continent. For this purpose trained naturalists were sent into the field to discover the boundary lines of the various fauna, and to bring back collections for critical study. During the past twenty years, nearly one hundred thousand specimens of mammals, besides many thousand birds, reptiles, and plants have been systematically collected in various parts of North America from the arctic regions to the tropics, and from the eastern to the western borders of the continent. From the data thus secured and from other sources, the areas occupied by a considerable number of species have been mapped. The study of this accumulated information has resulted in definitely outlining the life zones into which North America is divided, and in demonstrating that each life zone, except the most northern, represents a crop zone or climatic belt, to which certain crops are best adapted. This close relation of the life zones to agriculture is shown in maps and bulletins published by the Biological Survey.

Throughout its existence the Survey has made exhaustive studies of the food habits of the species of birds and mammals for the purpose of determining their relations to agriculture, and has conducted experiments for the purpose of devising methods of protection for the beneficial, and methods of destruction for the injurious species. The benefits to our agricultural and grazing interests have already been great, and as our lands become more densely populated the economic results will prove of still greater value. To accomplish these ends Dr. Merriam has gathered about him a corps of trained field naturalists, more efficient for the purpose than any similar body of men in the world.

As a nation we should be proud that the men engaged in this work have been broad enough not to neglect the profound scientific problems involved in it—problems touching the origin and dispersal of species. Darwin was perplexed by what seemed a grave objection to his theory, the apparent absence of transitional forms between species. The collections made by the Biological Survey, both of mammals and birds, are extremely rich in these intermediate or intergrading forms, forms connecting many of the well-marked types which were formerly considered distinct species; and one day, when the time can be spared from more strictly official work,* the subject will be enriched by studies based upon this material—studies likely to form one of the most valuable contributions of this generation to our knowledge of evolution—and we shall look back on the work of the Biological Survey as one of the most valuable achievements, both practical and scientific, that ever had its origin in a governmental department.

In the way of field equipment, I had an open canvas shelter, instead of a tent, with side wings so constructed that, when pegged to the ground, they inclined outward at an angle from the perpendicular, leaving extra space for storing provisions. A detachable strip of canvas, a foot wide, could be tied in front and sloped outward over inclined poles. This prevented the

*Since the above was written Dr. Merriam bas retired from his official position for the purpose of devoting his time exclusively to scientific studies. A large part of the results will appear in a comprehensive work on North American mammals.)

rain from blowing in. No one who loves camp life can prefer a tent to a shelter, except in winter. The log fire which is always made before the shelter, reflects warmth directly inside, so that one can sit at ease and in enjoyment in all but the coldest weather. A shelter is also more convenient to erect than a tent.

For sleeping, I had a coon-skin robe, eight feet square. It weighed fourteen pounds. It keeps me warm enough even in winter weather. A lynx-skin robe is better and warmer, but more expensive. A caribou- or reindeer-skin robe is the best of all. Equally warm, it is very much lighter than either of the others. The wolf-skin robe is more commonly used by trappers and prospectors, but is heavier.

Until the month of November I always wore summer underclothing. A gray flannel shirt, and one pair of gabardine trousers last me for two seasons. Heavy woollen socks and moccasins (leather, or preferably moose-hide when to be had in sufficient quantity) provide the footgear necessary for summer. The rubber shoe with leather uppers, soled and hobnailed, if possible, is best for early fall. I never wore a coat, but instead carried a parkay or seamless cloak, made of the skins of ground-squirrels. I wore this only on the tops of mountains, or when the cold required it. A pair of Zeiss prism field-glasses, eight or ten power, an Eastman Kodak for films, 31-4 x 41-4, were always carried on my belt. Any kind of felt hat answered, but usually I hunted without any hat at all. One of the most important things was my Alpine rucksack, which had been made in Germany. Instead of a coat, I always carried this on my shoulders. In it were the parkay and any extra things needed. Sixty pounds of meat could be packed into it, or a whole bear skin or the head and skin of a ram. One small canvas bag would hold all my equipment for a season, except the small mouse traps, and the steel traps. A common pocket knife of good steel, for skinning, a compass, a barometer and a steel tape were always in my pockets. Usually I bought the provisions commonly used by all prospectors and trappers of the country—flour, rice, sugar, dried fruit, butter in cans, tea, bacon and salt; and a few other things when transportation could be provided. Skins were cured with salt when I could bring it. I always had a .22 rifle to use for shooting grouse and small animals, but for large game my Mannlicher, .256 calibre, is the only rifle I have ever used in the North.

CHARLES SHELDON

CONTENTS

CHAPTER XIII

CHAPTER XIV

CHAPTER XV

CHAPTER XVI

CHAPTER XVII

CHAPTER XVIII

CHAPTER XIX

CHAPTER XX

APPENDIX A

APPENDIX B

APPENDIX C

APPENDIX D

APPENDIX E

LIST OF ILLUSTRATIONS

MAPS

THE OGILVIE ROCKIES

To sit on rocks, to muse o'er flood and fell,
To slowly trace the forest's shady scene,
Where things that own not man's dominion dwell,
And mortal foot hath ne'er or rarely been;
To climb the trackless mountain all unseen,
With the wild flock that never needs a fold;
Alone o'er steeps and foaming falls to lean;
This is not solitude; 'tis but to hold
Converse with Nature's charms, and view her stores unroll'd.

—BYRON.

CHAPTER I

THE TRIP TO THE OGILVIE ROCKIES – 1904

THE MOUNTAIN SHEEP of America are among the noblest of our wild animals. Their pursuit leads the hunter into the most remote and inaccessible parts of the wilderness and calls into play his greatest skill and highest qualities of endurance.

My first experience with sheep was in northern Mexico, where they dwell among the isolated groups of rugged mountains that rise abruptly from the great waterless deserts—deserts beautiful in their wealth of color, weird in the depth of their solitude, impressive in their grim desolation. It was there that I became fascinated by the exhilaration of the sport of hunting the wild sheep, and dominated by the desire of following them in other lands.

I was familiar with what had been written about the white sheep, *Ovis dalli*, of Alaska, and the darkest of the American sheep, *Ovis stonei*, of the Stikine water-shed in northern British Columbia; and when in 1901 still another form of sheep, *Ovis fannini*, was described from the ranges of the Canadian Rockies in Yukon Territory—an animal with a pure white head and gray back—I decided to explore for it if the chance ever offered. Indeed, so little was known about the variation, habits, and distribution of the wild sheep of the far northern wilderness, that my imagination was impressed by the possibilities of the results of studying them in their native land. There was, besides, the chance of penetrating new regions, of adding the exhilaration of exploration to that of hunting, and of bringing back information of value to zoologists and geographers, and of interest to sportsmen and lovers of natural history.

The opportunity came in the summer of 1904. A party was organized composed of the artist, Carl Rungius, who has so faithfully painted our large game animals in their true environment; Wilfred H. Osgood, of the Biological Survey, a trained naturalist of reputation, and myself.

Late in June we sailed from Seattle and proceeded over the well-known route to Dawson, purchasing provisions for the trip in Skagway, and going over the White Pass and Yukon Railway to Whitehorse, where we took one of the large river steamers to Dawson. Learning that the game in those parts of the Ogilvie Rockies east of Dawson, at the head of the Klondike River, had been disturbed by winter hunting to supply meat to the Dawson market, we decided to go to the head of Coal Creek, which has its source in the heart of an unknown part of the Ogilvies, and enters the Yukon about sixty miles below Dawson.

We purchased six horses together with packing equipment, and secured the services of two men, Charles Gage and Ed Spahr, to accompany us as packers. After several days of tedious delay, it was finally announced that the small steamer *Prospector* would start down river at 5 P. M., July 7. In due time, therefore, we loaded our horses and outfit on the boat, put on our hunting clothes, and went aboard just before the *Prospector* pulled out from the wharf on schedule time. We soon passed through picturesque parts of the river where it narrows and runs between high cliffs, and farther down between high

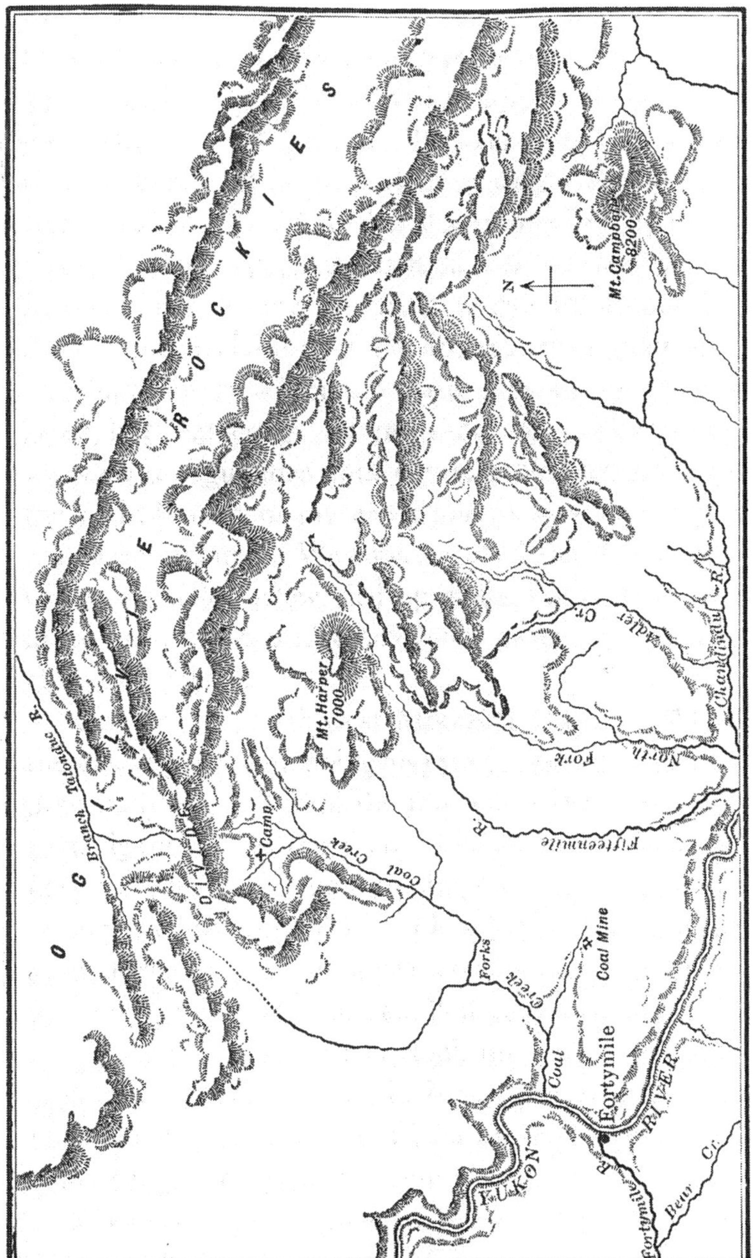

Map of Coal Creek, Showing Author's hunting camp in the Ogilvie Rockies.

rolling ridges on each side, until at 8:30 P.M. we reached Forty Mile. Going ashore, we tried to get information from some of the residents as to the abundance of game and the possibility of travelling up Coal Creek. It was freely given, but conflicting. After a short stop at Forty Mile we left with a vague idea that it would be best to follow up the main branch of the creek and push on till we found the sheep country. We soon reached the mouth of Coal Creek, six miles below, tied up to the bank, unloaded our horses and outfit, and erected our tents on a high bank close to the water.

One of the Northwest Mounted Police was located there, living in a tent, doing his own cooking, and remaining practically inactive until the fall, when the river is closed to navigation. He was there to police the coal mines and keep a check on all people passing down the river who had not reported at Forty Mile. Though this practice stopped soon after, during the first years of the rush into the country, the Northwest Mounted Police, distributed at intervals along the Yukon River, took the names and destinations of all people passing in boats, summoning them to the shore if necessary, and kept a fairly good record of all who were travelling in the country.

Coal had been discovered a few years before, twelve miles up the South Branch of Coal Creek; and two years previous to our arrival, a mine was opened, coal chutes and boarding houses for men were erected at the mouth of the creek, and a narrow-gauge railroad was loosely constructed up to the mine. During the summer a small steamer kept hauling barges of coal to Dawson to accumulate it there for the winter supply of fuel.

At this point the Yukon River bends in a sharp curve and is surrounded on all sides by fairly high mountains, which may be the cause of the constant rain at that exact spot, even when the sky is clear a few miles above and below. Not more than a mile below, a spur of the main interior range rising about

Northwest Mounted Police on Yukon River below mouth of Coal Creek, July 8

PHOTOGRAPH BY CARL RUNGIUS.

Fording Coal Creek.

PHOTOGRAPH BY W.H. OSGOOD. BY PERMISSION OF THE U.S. BIOLOGICAL SURVEY.

three hundred feet above timberline, extends nearly down to the river, and sheep are said sometimes to wander there in winter. I heard that there was a well-defined sheep trail on the top. Game is very scarce everywhere along the Yukon, but occasionally a black bear is seen, and in that particular vicinity I learned that one had shortly before appeared on the opposite side of the river; also that two had been killed a few miles up the railroad. Moose at times are seen along the river, and just below Coal Creek is a canon, extending down between ridges from the mountain spur, where a few days previous the Indians from Forty Mile had killed a cow moose. By invitation I slept in the tent of Mr. Jones, the policeman; but before retiring we had tried to get some information about the interior country from various men employed on the railroad and at the mines, only learning, however, of one point where we should leave the railroad to reach the main branch of Coal Creek.

July 8.— As we were cooking breakfast early the next morning, it commenced to rain and, much to our disgust, continued all day. We could not start with horses that were "green" and too tender to endure the pack with wet backs and, besides, the trail began in a swamp. Hence the day was passed testing our rifles and wandering about with shot-gun and fishing rods. A few graylings were taken, and this first tramping gave us an impression of the difficulty of taking pack-horses through the thick woods. Osgood had a large supply of traps for small mammals, and it was his object to collect as many of the mammals, birds, and plants as possible. Many people visited us in camp that evening, but none could give the coveted information which might assist us to find a good route into the country we wished to reach.

July 9. —In the morning we were up at five and, after breakfasting, packed the horses and made a start, following an old road through a swamp, very muddy and soft, to the railroad tracks half a mile above. The horses, unused to packing, were very excitable and did not go well. They were all large and had been used in the winter stage service between Dawson and Whitehorse until each had become unsound and disqualified; yet they were still serviceable for pack-horses—at least, they were the best we could get. *Caribou*, an old white horse once used for packing over the White Pass trail, proved to be sagacious, very sure on his feet, the best "rustler" of all, and very quickly became the leader when they were turned loose. Old *Mike*, a bay, was steady and gentle, fairly sure-footed, but rather slow. *Danger*, a large bay, had never carried a pack. He was sure-footed, willing, but had an annoying habit of constantly picking feed when being led,' and the conformation of his back was not adjustable to the aparejo, which kept it sore all the time. *Nigger*, a black, had never carried a pack, was clumsy on his feet, and had a tendency to jump at critical places. *Shorty*, a dark bay, was the best pack-horse of all. He followed well without leading, and though constantly lying down at every pause, would get up without shifting his pack. He was the pet, and always kept nosing about for sugar and bits of bread. *Schoolmarm*, a dark bay mare, not accustomed to the pack, carried a Mexican saddle on which were packed trifles and lighter material. Each of us travelled on foot leading a horse, while Shorty was driven ahead of the man in the rear. None of the horses had worked for a long time, and the first day was very trying for them. All kept lying down at every opportunity, thus showing great distress under their packs; it was difficult to lead them, and leading was necessary in that country.

Soon after emerging from the swamp and coming out on the railroad tracks, we reached Coal Creek and first learned the difficulty and danger of fording. The stream was swift and deep, and Rungius, falling in the ford, was nearly carried down. Again we passed through a swamp for two and a half miles, and, coming out on the track, proceeded up the railroad and arrived at some log cabins, called Robinson's Camp, twelve miles from the mouth, about noon. While we lunched, a prospector who was loitering about, volunteered to show us the way to the main branch of the creek, and in the afternoon we again started, reached the creek, forded it, and found a blazed trail on the opposite side which we followed all day as best we could, now and then losing it and going on independently. The woods were dense and most of the ground was covered with soft, dry sphagnum moss through which the horses would sink six inches or more at each step, and which made the travelling tiresome for ourselves. We encountered this soft mossy ground at intervals most of the way. It is common on the sides and even the tops of the mountains until well into the divide ranges. Small spruces always grow in it, and, in places, huckleberries. Fording the creek back and forth, often chopping small trees and thick brush, we kept on until evening, when we found a little grass for the horses and camped by the side of the creek. It was daylight all night, except for three hours about midnight, as the sun went below the horizon, and then, for a short time, there was a fine twilight.

Thus far along the creek were balsam, poplar, white spruce, willow, and alder trees; flowers of various kinds and vetches were abundant. The creek was from sixty to a hundred feet wide; its banks were in some places rough and steep, and in others bordered by long, rocky bars. The mountains, covered with spruces, rose from the level country below, about a mile back from the river on the north side, and nearer to it on the south. The river was swift and deep; the temperature of the water about forty degrees Fahrenheit. During the day we noticed a few very old moose tracks and bird life was scarce. We only saw a pair of solitary sandpipers, a few spotted sandpipers, some Alaska jays, and a rough-legged hawk. After we had pitched the tents and had some tea, I took my rifle and went up the creek, but returned after two hours, having seen no signs of active animal life except a few birds.

July 10.—We packed and started late the next morning, still endeavoring to follow the blazed trail, which we had been told would lead to an abandoned logging camp, sixteen miles up the river. Here and there we could pick it up and follow it for a short distance, but most of the time we travelled independently, following the bars of the river, fording it many times, while the woods on both sides were so thick that Gage was constantly obliged to go ahead and cut a trail so that the horses could get through with their packs. Rungius and myself wore leather moccasins, the worst possible footgear in which to ford these northern rivers, where the current runs from six to ten miles an hour over an extremely rocky bottom on which the smooth moccasins slip almost as if on ice. In many places it would have been dangerous to fall, since a foothold could not be regained and one might become entangled in the driftwood or hurled against rocks while being carried down the continuous rapids. The others wore hobnail shoes, the only thing in which to travel along rocky rivers which have to be forded. Time after time we saved ourselves from falling by holding onto the horses, for they had no difficulty in keeping a solid footing.

Most of the day was perfect, though a light thunder shower fell in the evening. Soon after starting we saw the old track of a black bear; later we killed a porcupine and two Alaska Spruce grouse. We ate the porcupine flesh that night and found it excellent, though rather too rich. The character of the country continued the same, and a few birches began to appear where we lunched. We were somewhat worried because of the scant grass for the horses which, however, had become more accustomed to their packs and were going much better. A small black gnat now appeared, and greatly worried them, attacking their chests, bellies and legs, and causing the blood to run freely. Temporary relief was afforded by rubbing them well with wagon grease, brought for this purpose. One horse had cast a shoe and after replacing it we kept on through mossy, swampy muskeg that lay on both sides of the creek, until camp was made near some low but very rough mountains which came close to the creek. The creek continued to be of about the same width, and as we approached the mountains its abrupt descent made the fording more difficult. We slept at eleven, and did not start until 11:30 in the morning.

July 11.— Getting breakfast, gathering in the horses (which, owing to the scanty grass, had to range some distance for feed), and packing always required two or three hours or more. Having completely lost all signs of the blazes that marked the route, we worked our way up the creek for a mile to a point where rocky bluffs shut in so close that we were obliged to climb around them and proceed along a steep mountain side. While wading the horses around a point in the stream, where it dashed in rapid descent through a rather wide canon, *Danger*, the horse in the lead, went around safely, but *Nigger* lost his footing and fell in the water, so that we were compelled, after getting him out and fixing his pack, to go on with these two along the bank, not caring to risk returning around the point. The other horses were not permitted to attempt it and were taken up the slope on a good game trail. It was necessary soon to take *Danger* and *Nigger* up a very steep ridge where *Nigger* lost his footing and rolled down about fifty feet. The pack was uninjured, but we had to remove it and use *Danger* to take it up the incline. Then, when trying to lead *Nigger* up, he again lost courage and, rearing, fell backward and rolled down some distance, but received no injury other than a bad cut on a hind leg, which later did not seem to trouble him. All this made considerable delay, but finally we again got under way and soon found a good game trail on the slope along which, with some chopping, we passed and descended into a swamp where we picked up the blazed trail. This swamp continued some miles and was extremely difficult to travel through. Fortunately, it had not rained sufficiently to make it impassable and we were able to get through, though not without much exasperating delay, owing to the bogging of the horses and the consequent repacking or constant readjustment of the packs.

Late in the afternoon we emerged at a point where Coal Creek forks; the main branch coming from the north, the other of almost equal volume from the west. A few hundred large spruce trees near here had been cut the preceding winter, and most of the logs had been driven down in the spring to a movable saw-mill, where they were sawed into lumber to be used in the coal mines and docks. At the Forks we saw two king salmon, which were just beginning to run up the creek. Soon two men appeared, who had come more directly across the country from Robinson's Camp the same day, to count the remaining logs piled on the bank near the river. They could give us no information about the country farther up, except to say that five miles ahead there was a canon which would block the progress of pack-horses, and beyond it the mountains were too rough for our method of travel. Here, at last, we found an abundant supply of good grass for the horses, and from there on it was plentiful and of good quality. Mosquitoes were beginning to be bothersome, though not yet a pest. The country was wilder; the mountains, which rose in ridges and formed spurs of the main range, were nearer the creek and were covered with spruces and poplars.

After taking a bite to eat, I started with my rod to try for graylings in front of the cabins, and quickly landed seven of fair size from one pool. Graylings were abundant in all the large pools clear up to the head of the river. I even saw several a half mile below the melting snow, near the extreme source of the creek. Those caught usually averaged from eight ounces to a pound in weight. They are quite shy and generally lie at the foot of the more rapid water of the pools or in the eddies—always where the surface is smooth. They quickly start to take the fly, but with no snap, just rising to the surface to grasp it in a sluggish manner, and once hooked they have no more play than a chub. I have never found them a game fish or worth catching except for food, and then only when other meat is lacking. As a fish for the frying pan they are most inferior, for when cooked they are soft and have not much flavor. It is said that later in the fall they become harder, and perhaps that is so, but on the whole I am convinced that they could never satisfy the taste of one accustomed to trout, bass, or even perch. Still, they do afford a relief from bacon and beans, and when travelling in the north I have always been glad to get them. After catching a mess of grayling, I took my rifle and made a wide circle around a ridge behind the cabins, seeing abundant old moose tracks, two or three olive-backed thrushes, and a few juncos and red squirrels. Returning to camp about 10:30 at night I took the rod again and quickly captured three more graylings from the same pool, even after Rungius had just caught some before me. At 11:30 I rolled under my blanket, beginning to realize that the continual daylight caused irregular hours. It did not, however, interfere with sound sleep.

July 12.—Starting up the creek we found it was becoming narrower and swifter, descending more rapidly. We travelled on bars, fording back and forth, often cutting trails through the woods until we reached the entrance to the canon five miles up. We had passed beyond the signs of man, except now and then the evidence of a trapper or an Indian. Near the canon the mountains were higher, some rising above timberline, where the sides and tops were smooth and mossy, and in some places covered with snow. As we loitered for a few moments on a bar in the creek, I scanned the side of the mountain ahead through my field-glasses and saw a grizzly bear passing along the slope high above timberline. That was my first sight of game in the northern wilderness. The attention of the others was called to it and we watched it for fifteen minutes as it travelled steadily until lost to sight in a canon. We made camp at the foot of the canon, and after supper Rungius, Spahr, and Gage went to locate a route around the canon and, if necessary, to cut out and prepare a trail. I waded the river, passed through the woods to the mountain where I had seen the bear, and ascended to the point where it had disappeared. Moose and old caribou tracks were abundant; the ground, covered with lichens (commonly called caribou-moss), was very soft in places, and high up in the poplars was a grouse. Mounting this slope I realized for the first time the seriousness of the mosquito pest of the far North. They swarmed and buzzed and completely covered my clothes so that large spaces of my coat and trousers quickly became black with them. I covered my neck with a handkerchief and smeared my face and hands with gun grease, but this afforded no relief.

I saw no sign of the bear and, unable to find its trail on the hard ground, I came at last to the peak of the mountain. From there the main ranges in the distance were revealed, all snow-capped and striped with irregular bands of snow, extending east and west as far as the eye could see, thrilling me with eager anticipation to be among them. I descended, fighting the mosquitoes, which followed me nearly to the river, and reached camp at 10 P. M. The others had returned and reported that by lightening the packs and making a double trip we could pass on the slopes above the cañon which was not two miles long.

Just after going under my blanket, short, thrush-like notes pealed out in the sleeping woods, sweet and very beautiful. They came from the varied thrush—the first and last time I heard it—but the music lingered with me all through the summer.

July 13.—We went to sleep with the elated feeling that we were on the edge of the game country. The next morning we found that the horses had crossed the river, and some time was required to find and bring them back. Each night two were hobbled and bells were attached to two others. They seldom wandered far from camp. They were now more hardened to the work and very gentle, easy to catch, and, on the whole, a fairly satisfactory lot for this kind of trip. We put half-packs on the horses and led them around the steep slopes above the cañon without difficulties worth mentioning, and finally descended abruptly to its head, where we made camp. After eating, Spahr and Gage returned with the horses to bring up the remainder of the outfit; Rungius set out to climb a mountain; Osgood stayed in camp to prepare specimens of small mammals that he had taken in his traps; and I started up river to look over the country ahead and find the best route for the next day. Old moose tracks were now abundant on the bars, and those of the black bear were common. The travelling had improved, and from the head of the cañon to the source of the river, except for the constant fording, continued excellent, so we could proceed more rapidly and with fewer delays for adjusting the packs.

We were camped on a bar in a beautiful spot among willows and poplars, surrounded by high mountains, on a curve of the creek above the canon through which it rushed with a distant roar. Just before midnight came a thunder shower, followed by silence. Suddenly the olive-backed thrushes began to sing. All thrush songs awaken a deep feeling, a sense of the woods, of the wild, free life, the mysterious depths of the forest

Across from camp the moutains were particularly rough, July 15

PHOTOGRAPH BY CARL RUNGIUS

The mountains...extended high above timberline, July 14.

PHOTOGRAPH BY CARL RUNGIUS.

and the wild animals therein. The traveller in the wilderness feels their enchantment in proportion to the genuine quality of his love for that wild, lonely life. I fell asleep while the woods were still resounding with vibrant tones. The song was not heard again that year.

July 14.—We started by making a difficult and dangerous ford, and then travelled along the bars, following well-beaten moose trails. These were continuous along the banks of the river on both sides, and like all animal trails took every advantage of the ground. It is usually unwise to deviate from them and try to select a better route, since one learns by experience that animals nearly always choose the best and most convenient places for travelling. None of the moose tracks on the bars were fresh, and everywhere were shed horns, showing that moose were there at the period of shedding in December and January. At the time of our visit most of them were in the lower country, nearer the Yukon River, about the lakes and flat lands, though now and then one wandered up in the ranges to the head of a "draw." Snowshoe rabbits had been extremely abundant every day. We saw them jumping about the woods, and in the late afternoon they were skipping and feeding near the bars, where they eat the willow bark and the herbs growing everywhere among the willows. Wherever the willow and dwarf birch grew densely, their tops were trimmed over large areas as if cut off with a knife. This is rabbit-cutting, about four feet from the ground, made when the snow is deep. We saw no lynxes, although their tracks were abundant on the bars. Bird life was very scarce at this time, and we saw but few varieties during the entire trip.

Three miles above the canon a large branch rushing from the mountains on the east joins the creek. There we penetrated the main range and at last were in the Ogilvie Rockies. The mountains, peaked and jagged, piled up in cliffs and pinnacles, blotched with snow, furrowed by canons, extended high above timberline and we realized that we were in the sheep country. The course of the ranges on the east side of the creek is east and west; on the west side the range nearest the creek runs north and south, throwing off spurs, equally lofty, east and west. In a general easterly and westerly direction there is a series of five or six parallel ranges up to the divide, on which one could travel continuously, perhaps, for hundreds of miles south along the northern crest of the Rocky Mountains. The altitude of timberline is about four thousand feet, and that of the summits varies from five to eight thousand feet.

In exceptional places, where the rock has not been exposed, lichens extend clear to the summits. Here and there on the slopes, in the basins, and under the cliffs, the grass was green. Mosquitoes swarmed on the slopes a short distance above the creek. But where the sheep were we failed to see, though again and again we paused to search the country through our field-glasses. It rained hard all day, and for the first time we were soaked. Except for short stretches here and there along the river, where the spring floods had washed out the moose trails, the travelling was good, the ground hard, the trails well beaten. The fords were easier though more frequent. We made camp at six on the bank of the creek, between towering mountains on both sides. Across from camp the mountains were particularly rough, and perpendicular cliffs rose to a great height, forming peaks.

After supper Rungius went out to sketch a bit of landscape, Osgood to climb a mountain, and I to look for game. I followed up the river for four miles, carefully scanning the mountains through field-glasses, but saw no animals. Here and there along the river banks were diggings where a bear had hunted the ground-squirrels, which, as we ascended to the higher country, were now beginning to appear. Osgood had found old sheep dung on the mountain, thus demonstrating the presence of sheep at some time, but both he and Rungius were a little discouraged at seeing no recent sign.

As I returned I heard 'a constant chirping not far above camp and, approaching, saw a hawk-owl sitting in a tree. These owls were quite common everywhere along the river. It was midnight when we fell asleep, listening to the murmur and roar of the river. Thus far the thermometer had been registering between thirty and forty degrees for the lowest temperature during the night.

July 15.—The next day, which was beautiful and clear, the travelling was still better; old moose tracks were even more abundant, and so were mosquitoes. Dwarf birch appeared more densely on the mountain slopes, the woods continued about the same, though the spruces were smaller. It was, for the first time, a positive pleasure to lead the horses. The trails were fine, hard moose trails, winding about between the mountains, and the fords were easy. We decided to stop and make camp early in the afternoon in order that each might climb a mountain to make a reconnaissance for sheep. After catching a few graylings I started to climb the ranges on the west side. Mosquitoes had become more abundant and troublesome as we travelled up the creek, but on the higher slopes they increased to a swarm. At this camp it was necessary, as a protection against them, to wear gloves and a netting falling from our hats to the shoulders. This proved perfectly satisfactory, for while wearing the netting one could look through the field-glasses and even sight well over the rifle. At times, in the sun, it was a little hot and occasionally one or two mosquitoes penetrated inside; but on the whole it neutralized the mosquito evil with little inconvenience, and in the wind, or cold of the early morning, when the mosquitoes

Looking up Coal Creek, July 15

Peak of Ogilvie Rockies, July 15

We travelled on bars, fording back and forth, July 12.

were not active, it could be fastened up around the brim of the hat, ready to drop instantly when needed.

Following caribou and sheep trails I gradually ascended to the top of the mountain and, not seeing fresh signs, seated myself and scanned the whole country about, but not an animal was visible. As all my hopes had been based on finding sheep on the divide ranges, I was not disappointed, and the scene was a compensation. The mountains extended in all directions, range after range, peak after peak, dome after dome. There were whole mountains in red; others of white limestone, relieved in places by streaks of iron-stained red rock, shining in the sun; there were snow cornices glistening under every crest and precipice; bands of snow streaking the slopes, interspersed with bright patches of green—a vast sea of ridges, basins, rock masses, and jagged crests all blending in wonderful harmony above the timbered valley of the curving stream. It was my first view from a summit of the Ogilvie Rockies. During my descent the fresh tracks of a cow and calf moose were seen at the head of a canon, and at eleven I came into camp. The others had seen no sheep signs.

CHAPTER 2

ON THE SHEEP RANGES – 1904

JULY 16. — FROM the mountain top I had traced the course of the creek to a point about four miles above camp, where it was lost behind an obstructing ridge which projected at right angles to the main ranges. There it was close to timber-line and evidently the main divide was not far up the stream. We decided to advance four miles, make a camp, and remain for a few days to investigate the country. Though obliged to ford the creek several times, we travelled mostly on the west bank, on the way shooting some willow ptarmigan beautiful birds even in their inconspicuous summer plumage. Red-squirrels were more abundant as we proceeded, although the spruces became smaller. Three miles from camp a large branch entered the creek, flowing from the east between high mountain ranges. A mile beyond this, where the main stream forked into two creeks of equal volume, was a small meadow, about three hundred feet wide, filled with excellent grass scattered among the clumps of willow and dwarf birch. It was early in the afternoon when we arrived, and some graylings were caught while lunch was being cooked.

At 3:30 we left camp, each taking a different direction to look for signs of game. I followed up the west fork, with the intention of reaching the divide if possible. The creek, fifteen to thirty feet wide, descended so abruptly that the source could not be far off. There were very few moose tracks so far up the creek, but several ptarmigan were flushed, some with young, and red squirrels kept chattering as they skipped about. The tinkling notes of the water-ousel often sounded from the creek, and once the exquisite harlequin duck was seen floating down among the rocks in the foaming torrent. We had seen harlequin ducks all the way along the creek, and I have since come to associate these beautiful birds with wild, dashing, northern streams. The walking was excellent and, two miles up, the stream forked again, one branch coming from a basin to the south-west, the other from the west. Just below this junction was a cañon, two hundred feet long, filled with snow and ice. I walked through it and found myself at the limit of timber, mosquitoes still swarming about me. Farther up the west fork I saw the diggings and fairly fresh dung of a grizzly, and a mile and a half farther on the creek broke out from vast, bare, rolling hills on the south, fed by numerous streams formed from the melting snow above the cañons and deep ravines. Here at last was the divide. From the summit could be seen the waters flowing into the Tatonduk River, or Sheep Creek as it is locally called, where it enters the Yukon River, below Eagle City. Coal Creek has its sources in the numerous small streams flowing together, all formed from melting snow in the surrounding mountains.

The divide at this point was covered with green, rolling pastures, more than a mile wide and two miles long. On the south it was bordered by a high mountain chain, with a continuous jagged crest swelling up into high peaks, from which numerous spurs projected at right angles, enclosing deep and narrow basins, the bottoms of which consisted of rolling meadows of green grass. On the north was a range of mountains,

I saw the bear slowly walking along the upper surface of the basin.

FROM A PAINTING BY CARL RUNGIUS.

more broken by peaks, crags, and cañons, all sloping down to Tatonduk River waters, finally forming a long, smooth, rolling ridge. Heavy banks of snow lined every crest and peak; the cañons and ravines were filled with it and the mountainsides appeared streaked with white. White limestone, dark, almost black, chert, and iron-stained rock, glowing red, all in sharp contrast, characterize these northern ranges. The summit pastures sloped gently toward the west, where another creek, formed between the ridges, flowed on to the Tatonduk River. A mile down, looking through an opening in the timber, I could see the creek, filled with snow and ice, glistening under the sunlight like a bright lake, while beyond it flowed through vast meadows toward the north and again curved west at the foot of the ranges, not far distant, which separated the waters of the Peel River from those of the Yukon. Dwarf birch and willow were scattered about the smooth, green sward, whose surface was soft and broken by tiny rivulets flowing to the creek below.

I seated myself and turned my field-glasses toward the south range. Suddenly within the field, two miles distant, appeared four sheep feeding on the saddle below the peak of a spur connecting with the range. More careful scrutiny proved them to be ewes. My first sight of the northern mountain-sheep! At last we were in the sheep ranges! As we had eaten no good meat except a few grouse and ptarmigan for eight days, and our bacon was being rapidly consumed, I immediately began a stalk, walking as rapidly as possible down the west slope of the divide on soft mossy ground, in some places miry and filled with willows. Now and then I paused to watch the sheep, which kept feeding quietly in the same place. At the northern end of the spur, then opposite me, the slope breaks, forming a cliff several hundred feet high, traversing the end of the mountain east and west. This cliff curves at the eastern extremity, cutting the smooth slope which, at the brink, rises steeply in a succession of benches to the top of the spur-mountain. The spur encloses a beautiful basin of rolling meadows in an amphitheatre of mountains.

I started to climb at the west edge of the cliffs, thereby keeping out of sight of the sheep. After climbing perhaps three hundred feet I looked up under the precipice, and at its base suddenly saw a grizzly bear walking on some snow toward the curving cliff, where it cuts the east slope. Quickly dropping, I almost slid to the foot, where I could conceal myself in the willows along the stream flowing from the basin. As the bear proceeded, I advanced parallel with it for about a hundred yards, until it climbed over a steep snow-bank to the top of the cliff and stood on the edge of the east slope. As it ascended this snow-bank I noticed a small cub playing about it. It was then 10 P. M. The bear stood for a moment on the highest bench at the edge of the cliff, about five hundred yards above me, and began to dig out a ground-squirrel.

Ground-squirrels, *Citellus plesius*, were everywhere. All the pastures and mountain slopes were filled with their holes and one was continually in sight of them, sitting straight up on their hind legs or running for their burrows. The most characteristic sound of the higher parts of the northern wilderness is their shrill chatter when they see a supposed enemy approaching, or when they disappear in their holes.

Through the glasses the bear could be seen digging, making the earth fly in all directions. At times she would sit and dig, again rise and strike the ground in apparent anger, twist around, watch for a moment, and then begin digging again. The squirrels always have several holes, connected by underground channels, and the bear kept digging out one after another, now and then making a jump to the next, evidently knowing that the squirrel was about to run out. Then she would again dig, until, finally, the squirrel was pocketed, and the bear made a great pounce and grabbed it with both forepaws. As her back was turned, the operation of devouring her prey could not be seen. While the bear was digging for the squirrel, the cub raced about, now sitting still a moment, then jumping up and running off playing, quite indifferent to the mother's task.

After spending twenty minutes digging and tearing out the hard earth until she caught the squirrel, the bear stepped to the edge of the cliff, took a long look below, started quartering down the slope, and disappeared. The wind was in my favor, so, after waiting five minutes, I started. The way was very steep, and because of the succession of benches it was impossible to see more than twenty or thirty feet above each one after it was reached. Holding my rifle cocked, expecting to meet the bear close as I came to the top of each bench, I climbed one after another, always very slowly to keep my breath for a steady shot, until I arrived on the last, when I saw the bear slowly walking along the upper surface of the basin close to the mountain-side, about three hundred yards off. She kept an irregular course, often pausing and looking for ground-squirrels. I followed rapidly, trying to gain, but always stopping when she stopped, ready to drop low if she faced in my direction. After gaining hundred yards, I sat down, rested my elbows on my knees, and aiming at her left hind quarter as she paused, fired, and heard the bullet strike her. She jumped, turned, and stood with forelegs extended forward, apparently panting. The cub at once began to run about bawling. The bear dropped to a sitting posture for a moment and then rose. I fired a second shot at her fore shoulder and heard the bullet strike her. She gave a great jump and stood until a third shot was fired, when she fell, kicked once or twice, and was dead.

The cub was still running about crying, and I went slowly toward it, intending if possible to capture it for the New York Zoological Park. When within fifty feet the cub saw me. It ran

Mountains with fantastic pinnacles and rock-turreted slopes surround us.

PHOTOGRAPH BY W.H. OSGOOD. BY PERMISSION OF THE U.S. BIOLOGICAL SURVEY

Perhaps the highest of those in the divide ranges.

PHOTOGRAPH BY W.H. OSGOOD. BY PERMISSION OF THE U.S. BIOLOGICAL SURVEY

around, looking at me with great curiosity, sniffing again and again, approached a few feet, then continued to run back and forth. Finally, as I kept coming closer, it stood on its hind feet, placed its forepaws on the dead mother and began spitting at me. I stooped low and crept within six feet, ready to place a noose, made from my belt and the straps from the Kodak and field-glass, over its head, when suddenly it pushed forward its nose, sniffed at me several times in terror, turned and rushed up the mountain slope. I started to pursue, but it distanced me so rapidly that the chase was soon given up.

No one who reads this experience should miss the significance of the cub's final action. It was a tiny cub, born the preceding winter, and could have received no impressions of human beings from experience. It did not fear the *sight* of man, but the *scent* of man immediately inspired it with terror. Fear of the odor of man was clearly an *instinct*. What was the origin of this instinct? Surely, in that remote part of the country, the cub's ancestors could not have experienced a fear of the scent of man for generations numerous enough to have the trait registered in the nervous organization and fixed, so that it was transmitted by heredity to the young! This would require frequent repetitions of the experience, through too many generations, and it is not reasonable to believe this possible. In my opinion this instinct had its origin in a period so remote in the past that we have no facts at all to explain it, and we can only affirm its existence, as clearly exhibited in this case. The instinct may include the fear of any strange scent as hostile. All bears with which I have had experience before or after, had this same instinct, and I firmly believe that it was as potent in the grizzly bears encountered by Lewis and Clark as in those inhabiting remote regions at the present time. Casual observers have not always discriminated between sight and scent as they affect the action of animals.

It was then 11:30, and the mists had settled about the crest and extended half-way down the slopes. For a long time while I worked in the twilight, getting off the skin, and everything was hushed and still, the wailing cries of the cub sounded from the mountain top—a weird, wild noise in this mysterious solitude. At such an elevation it was very cold, and being lightly clad I soon became chilled and found difficulty in handling the bear alone, so the skin was not off until nearly two in the morning. The head was left in so that Rungius could sketch it. The bear was an old grizzly, fairly large, in excellent pelage for July; its claws were very long, and there was practically no fat on it. The first bullet shattered the hind quarter, penetrated through the vitals, and came out through a large hole in its side. The other two had struck within an inch of each other, both cutting the heart. Tired and cold, I shouldered the heavy skin and struggled back to camp, reaching it at 5:30 in the morning. Rungius and Osgood, neither of whom had seen any game during the day, came out from the tent to see the skin and hear my story.

The fire was started; tea, bacon, and bread refreshed me before the genial warmth. Now our hopes were brightened, and with the knowledge that we had found the game country all was enthusiasm. I soon rolled under my blanket, but for some time could not sleep. The experience of the night had deeply impressed me with the wild enchantment of the wilderness, the finding of the divide, the sublime mountains about it, the first sight of sheep, the unexpected meeting and killing of the bear, my experience with the cub; the charm of the location while skinning the bear high up on the green slope of the mountain in the midnight twilight; the absence of sound save the murmur of the creek below and the wailing of the cub pealing wildly through the mists above; the dim outline of the summits of the mountains to the west, their peaks tipped golden by the sun low behind them; the mystery of all that unknown country; the strange and beautiful lights and shadows playing on the mountains encircling me; what more could a lover of the wilderness and its wild life demand?

July 17.—We decided to move up the west branch to the forks two miles above, and there make a permanent camp at a point I had selected the day before, on a high bank just at the junction, about a hundred feet below timber-line. It was a beautiful spot; clear, open pastures among the spruce trees were about us, numerous dead trees for firewood were near and excellent grass for the horses was everywhere. Mountains, with fantastic pinnacles, peaks, and rock-turreted slopes surrounded us, and the view down the creek was beautiful in the extreme, as we looked along the timber frieze between the high slopes to the massive ranges on the east. Above all, we were close to the divide and in the heart of the best hunting country.

Leaving the men to pitch the tents and make camp, Rungius and I went on to the divide. From there I could see the bear's carcass and, thinking the cub might remain near it, pointed it out to Rungius, who started to find and kill the cub. I went to climb a mountain on the south, to make a short reconnaissance and descend on the other side to camp. The top was a broad, level flat, rather swampy, and full of sheep and caribou tracks. Old caribou tracks covered the ground, and well-worn sheep-trails extended high up on the slopes, ridges, crests, and over or around all the peaks. Several small birds, unknown to me, were about, and the mice, a species known as *Microtus operarius endoecus*, had made their tiny trails all through the grass. Conies, *Ochotona collaris*, were heard and seen among the broken rocks of the slopes. Their short, thin bleat afterward became a familiar sound high up among the large broken rocks which they inhabit, even on the mountain tops. And numerous marmots were whistling their long,

She fell, kicked once or twice and was dead, July 16.

piercing calls. They were abundant everywhere, near broken rock and in the basins.

Passing a little beyond I looked down on the large basin south of our camp, from which the other stream flows to make the junction. The divide creek and this one form the true source of Coal Creek, the volume of which is increased by the two large creeks entering two or three miles below. The area below me really consisted of two basins: one farther to the east, between two precipitous spurs; the other likewise lying in mountains, and much larger. At the bottom of the former were two exquisite clear lakes of several acres each, continually filled by the melting snow above. The latter was in the form of a great irregular square, at least a mile wide. Undulating in gentle hills and wide green pastures, it produced an impression of surpassing beauty, with great mountains encircling it, rising up in rocks and cliffs, culminating in sharp peaks perhaps the highest of those in the divide ranges.

Except on the bare rocks, all the mountains were more or less covered with lichen-moss, which, in turn, was spangled with exquisite small dots of flowers, some bright blue, some pink, and some crimson. Flowers abounded over all the mountain-slopes, basins, and valleys. Dryas was common everywhere, also a species of cranberry, *Vacinnum vitisidoea*, the leaves of which were always slippery to walk on. I sat for some time looking about through my field-glasses, but saw nothing and, descending on the east side of the slope to the creek which runs through a deep gorge, had started toward camp when I met Osgood setting his traps for small mammals.

Together we reached camp at ten, and found Rungius there with the body of the cub. He had seen it walking under the same cliffs and shot it.

That night was clear and cold, the thermometer going to twenty-eight degrees before morning. When we first settled

Our camp in the heart of the hunting country in the Ogilvie Rockies, July 17.

in this camp mosquitoes were at their worst and very troublesome. All of us slept under mosquito netting. The horses suffered the most, and we had to build several smudges and keep them going all day so that the animals could gather around them. If these smudges were not kept up, the horses would come about the tents and almost beg for them. They would stand about them all day, and feed mostly at night when the swarm temporarily retired from the cold. They scarcely ever went far from camp and constantly returned, as if coming back home and it was not necessary to keep them hobbled. In a few days most of the mosquitoes seemed to leave the vicinity of the tents, though enough remained to compel us to take precautions to avoid them.

July 18.—We were ready to start at eight in the morning; and, asking the men to flesh the bearskin, I started for the divide. Rungius had already preceded me, intending to descend the stream on the other side. I can never endure a companion or a "guide" when actually hunting. I want to be alone among the hills and wild mountains, with freedom to observe. In the solitude of the wilderness, the animals, birds, rocks and flowers become companions. I carried my rucksack, which contained a Kodak, a sweater, a tin cup, tea, a little sugar, chocolate, and a cracker. While hunting I never wore a coat, but could put on the sweater when it became cold. My footgear, leather moccasins, was nearly perfect for this country. Lightness and noiselessness were the main objects required, and moccasins were not slippery except on the bearberry or cranberry leaves, and at times on wet slopes. One soon learns how to walk in them, what ground to avoid, and how to descend over rock and grass slopes. My rifle was a Mannlicher, 256 calibre, the same one that I had already used for big game during the three previous years. The cartridges were jacketed with nickel, split at four places, and the lead was exposed at the tip.

Our horses standing in the smoke to keep off mosquitoes.

It was afternoon when I came out on the divide, and made directly for the bear's carcass, intending to climb the spur and ascend along the saddle to the crest of the main range. A few moose tracks were seen on the divide, made undoubtedly when the moose cross over, since feed is so scarce there that they never loiter. Near the carcass a marmot whistled; in many places ptarmigan were flushed, and Alaska jays, *Perisorius canadensis frumifrons*, were abundant everywhere in the timber, and in the willows above. A pair of golden eagles were soaring along the crest, always a beautiful sight and a constant feature of those northern ranges.

The main range here extends parallel with the divide clear to the meadows of the creek on the west, perhaps twelve miles distant, and east to the north and south range on the west side of Coal Creek. The northern slopes, facing the divide, are very steep and broken into precipices and projecting spurs. The south slope, then visible for the first time, inclines somewhat evenly to another divide, broken here and there by gorges, and sends out an occasional spur. The rim of the crest is uneven, now rising into high peaks, now capped by jagged boulders and pinnacles, and again extending evenly for a hundred yards more, to the next peak. In places on the south side, before the incline becomes abrupt, are green pastures, where grass, weeds, and moss were abundant-all excellent feeding for sheep and caribou. The snow is confined to northerly slopes where it occurs in cornices below the crest, under the cliffs, and in the hollows, gorges, and furrows.

I walked along toward the west, carefully scanning the country ahead through my field-glasses. Mosquitoes swarmed as much as ever, even on the peaks. Soon a heavy rain fell and it was cold. I crouched under a rock, and in half an hour it ceased. Again I went forward, now crossing a pasture to examine the slopes below, then returning diagonally to the rim of the crest so that I could see the country on both sides.

A cañon cutting the south slope was reached after three o'clock, and well below, eight hundred yards distant on the other side, I saw twelve fairly large rams feeding in a grassy place on the slope. Immediately dropping low, I looked at them through the field-glasses. At last, before me was the main object of my trip to those northern wilds; beautiful they were, glistening white in the sun notwithstanding a brownish stain, and game in every motion. Most of them carried fair horns, well spread, and all had black tails. They fed nervously and kept constantly on the move, a few often running with alertness, and every moment one or another would throw up its head to look, either up or down. I remained motionless, flat on the ground, among some rocks, watching every movement. How to stalk them was a puzzle. The cañon was deep with almost perpendicular sides and led up to the crest of the mountain before it could be crossed. It was not possible to descend and then stalk up in plain sight from below, and, besides, they were gradually feeding upward. Their movements soon solved the problem, for they were surely working up toward the crest and a little in my direction.

Then they began to ascend faster and did not pause so much to feed. Some would suddenly run a short distance, jump to a stand-still, and look. But I was well concealed and they did not see me. There was little wind and it was in my favor. Before I realized it, they had reached the top, five hundred yards away. All stood on the edge looking at the country below.

Only those who have been high up above the valleys and woods, among the peaks and crags, and there have seen the mountain ram in his element, can appreciate the sight or realize the emotion surging through me as I beheld them. They stood like marble silhouettes, erect, rigid, on the sky-line of that wonderful landscape-the essence of boldness, grace, energy, self-confidence, wildness! For five minutes they were motionless, sweeping the country below with their keen eyes. Unless hidden from sight I do not believe any moving object could have escaped them.

Then one jumped below the rim; the rest quickly followed; there was a slight sound of falling rocks. They had disappeared like phantoms. Not then experienced in the habits of the northern sheep, I thought that my chance had come. They might come back, but it seemed more likely that they were seeking a spot to rest on the other slope, and shortly would reach some point in a place too rough for a stalk. After waiting a few moments, I started upward toward the head of the cañon and had gone a hundred yards, when two small rams suddenly reappeared on the crest. I dropped, but too late; they had seen me. By some note of alarm the others were attracted, all coming up with a spring, their eyes fastened on me as if by magic. The chance for a close shot was lost.

One of the leaders started to run across the mountain-side, followed by the whole band. As they ran, I fired four times, and a smaller one turned and ran down the cañon, the rest keeping on toward a high peak. It was evident that the single one was wounded, for through the glasses blood could be seen about its head and forelegs. Some were just disappearing, when four stopped under the peak and looked back, while the others went over the top. The wounded ram seemed to be walking with difficulty, yet kept slowly on to the bottom of the cañon, and then crossed to another mountain. Descending half-way to the foot of the slope, I stopped, hoping that the ram would lie down; meanwhile, the other four high up near the peak were feeding. The wounded ram travelled some distance along the side of the mountain and lay down on a rock. I began to descend in plain sight (concealment was impossible), but he saw me from a long distance and was up and travelling

Bull caribou on mountain in Ogilvie Rockies.

DRAWING BY CARL RUNGIUS.

at once. He crossed the mountain-side and disappeared high up over the other end. I went down, crossed the basin, and climbed the side of the mountain, but could see no sign of blood or tracks at the point where the ram was last seen, nor could he be seen even with the field-glasses. A short gully separated this mountain from another rough range, where he had probably gone and so escaped me. Back near the high peak I saw the four rams lying down on some high rocks near the top.

I decided to descend to timber-line a couple of miles down the creek to pass the night, and climb for the rams early the next morning. I soon made a fire on the border of the forest, but there was no water near and it was necessary to descend a long distance to the stream for it. Having done this, and while cutting spruce boughs for a bed, the water on the fire was overturned and a second long trip to the creek was necessary. At midnight I had tea with half the chocolate and half the cracker. It was very cold and my short night was broken by intervals of sleeping and waking. As I fell asleep, the head-net would settle against my face and the mosquitoes would soon wake me. My tobacco had been lost, which was a real deprivation. The memory of the rams moving with virile gameness on the rocky slopes kept lingering between my snatches of sleep, until I rose, at five, and went half a mile down to a stream coming from a cañon, which cut the slope I intended to ascend.

The tea was quickly made from the tea-ball used the night before, and half a cracker and a small piece of chocolate provided my only food that day until late at night. After eating I began to work up the cañon, now through deep gorges, now climbing around them, at length coming out at a point where the view was open for half a mile along the stream to the snow cornice, above which the crest continued to rise unevenly to the peak near where the rams had been loitering the evening before. On a steep slope, a hundred feet above the snow which

He dropped, rolled a few yards, and was caught in the broken rock, July 10.

filled the bed of the stream for a long distance below the crest, were two large dark animals. My glasses showed them to be caribou; one very dark with striking horns, the other lighter, with horns more spike-like. The wind was blowing from me to them, and immediately I began to circle up the mountain side for the purpose of approaching with a favorable wind. The stalk was made slowly to a point above them and then directly down toward them, always in plain sight. They kept quietly feeding, keeping their heads close to the ground, without once raising them to look about in the manner of a deer, sheep, or moose. The sun was brightly shining and mosquitoes were so numerous that my head-net could not be removed. With more than necessary caution I advanced to within three hundred yards and took a sitting position, elbows on knees. Singling out the darker, larger-horned animal, I fired, and distinctly heard the bullet strike him. The ball struck his hind quarters, breaking one leg, passing through the stomach and out on the other side. As the animal had kept walking and changing positions, this was the only good exposure presented for a shot. The other at once began trotting uphill, and I am somewhat ashamed to confess that I fired at it twice, and then, having cooled down, did not shoot again, but deliberately allowed it to go, thinking that I had missed. It soon stopped and looked back, then trotted ahead, pausing several times to urinate or look back, until it disappeared over the mountain range. The other was staggering, and in a moment dropped, rolled down the slope, and landed in the bed of the creek, which had cut a channel through the snow and ice.

I had great difficulty in pulling the carcass up on the snow, where I photographed, measured, and gralloched it, pestered by dense clouds of mosquitoes attracted by the blood. I decided to leave the caribou where it was, and bring Rungius back the next day to sketch and study it in the flesh and get the impression of its natural environment. It was a fine large bull, in thick, dark summer-coat, its mane just beginning to turn white; its horns in velvet of a rich, dark, grayish-brown color, well palmated at the ends, with twenty-one points on one side, fourteen on the other, and both brow antlers particularly well developed, giving beauty and proportion to the head. The length of the caribou was seven feet, the height at fore-shoulder four feet. These were the first caribou I had ever seen, except a glimpse I had had of four running through the thick woods of New Brunswick in 1897. The caribou of the Ogilvies were later identified by Osgood as the true barren-ground species—*Rangifer arcticus*.

I continued the ascent on the snow directly up to the crest. Proceeding along the rising rim, I came to the final climb of perhaps five hundred yards, necessary to surmount the peak and command the mountain from above. This was the highest peak on the range bordering the divide. Its north side consisted of cliffs, precipices, and steep slopes falling to a basin below. The top and southern slopes were all broken rock, stained so dark that, from a distance, in contrast to the others of the range, the mountain appeared black. The ascent was not difficult, though caution was required not to make a noise while climbing over the broken rock.

Going slowly to keep my breath, I came near the top, where the surface rose more gradually to form the point of the peak, when suddenly the heads and horns of a ram appeared on the sky-line to the right, not twenty feet away. He looked at me for a moment and disappeared with a spring. Hastening to the point I saw a fine ram running ahead of three smaller ones directly up the peak. He stopped only a few feet below the summit. Seating myself, I aimed quickly and fired. He dropped, rolled a few yards, and was caught in the broken rock. The others disappeared around the slope beyond. Running forward over the loose rock on the steep incline, I caught him by the horns and held him while he was kicking in death struggles, to prevent him from rolling down. The bullet had passed through his fore-shoulders at the base of the neck. He was a very fat ram of seven or eight years, with shapely, spreading horns. His tail was black, his body pure white, though the short new pelage was stained brownish from the ferruginous rock.

My exultation at this first success in accomplishing the purpose of my trip was complete. For some time I sat looking at the wonderful landscape about and below me. On every side stretched the mountain ranges until the vision was lost in a sea of tumbled peaks, all dotted and patched with the glistening snow; below were basins and wild, green valleys clothed with green and bluish timber—a vast, silent, wilderness reaching on the east to the Mackenzie River, on the west to the Yukon.

After photographing the ram as he fell I made a hollow in the rocks a few feet below, dragged him down to it, and began taking off his skin. It soon began to shower and grow cold with gusts of wind. Two ravens circled about almost in frenzy as I worked, and at times a golden eagle sailed along the crest and soared above. Packing the skin and head in the rucksack, I descended the precipitous and rocky east side of the peak to the edge of the north rim, hoping to find some descent to the basin below from which the divide pastures could be gained. Resting every few steps on account of my load, I finally reached the grass slope, which, after the rain, was very slippery and managed to zigzag down to the gorge of a stream at the foot of the mountain. While resting there, what was my disgust to notice that my field-glasses had been left above at the carcass, so it was necessary to return for them. Again descending and picking up my load I tramped two miles up the swampy, brush-covered ground across the next divide, and descended toward camp. Lack of food, long hours of climbing, together with the chill and wetting by showers, had so weakened me that my legs almost gave out and obliged

Caribou, killed July 19.

me to rest every few steps while walking up the soft ground of the divide. Camp was reached at 10:30 at night, and rest before a large fire, food, and my pipe restored my strength.

The day before, Rungius, while climbing the south range of the divide, had seen three rams running up a round, smooth mountain on the north side and followed them. They saw him, ran over on the other side, and disappeared. Arriving at the top he saw a large band of ewes feeding near, and killed four. Both he and Osgood had returned to the same place with Spahr, Gage, and two horses to bring back the meat. The ewes were still loitering about, and Osgood had killed one. The heads, skins, and meat had been brought back to camp and the larder was well stocked.

Some of the ewes killed were pure white; others had many gray hairs on the back, and stripes down the legs, intermediate in color between *Ovis dalli* and *Ovis fannini*, and all had black tails.

July 20.—The next day we all remained in camp, skinning and preparing the specimens. In the morning, after Rungius had made several sketches of my ram's head, I skinned it. Jays now flocked about us in great excitement, feeding on the raw meat and other camp refuse. Red squirrels also were attracted, and mosquitoes were still with us.

We were feasting on meat. To my taste the meat of mountain sheep, killed between July and October, easily excels that of any other game animal on this continent. It is rich, fat mutton with a game flavor. Nor do I tire of it as of venison; for a continuous diet never diminished my eagerness for it. After October, and until late in June, it is not so good, and during the winter and spring months very poor, quite without flavor.

Until we left this camp the days were warm, sometimes hot, and at night the lowest temperatures registered by the thermometer varied from twenty-eight to forty degrees above zero

Fahrenheit. It never rained continuously, but often showered. On the mountain crests it was usually very cold all through the day, especially when the wind blew.

July 21.—After breakfasting Rungius, Gage, and I started to get the caribou head. Spahr was to follow with two horses and wait at the foot of the divide for us to bring it down to him. After we reached the summit and were proceeding down the gentle descent, forty or fifty ewes and lambs were seen feeding on a grassy slope of the rough mountain to the north. This was part of the band Rungius and Osgood had disturbed. On the mountain side, several hundred feet up on a bank of snow, we saw a black spot which Rungius thought was an animal. The field-glasses confirmed this, but we could not make out what it was, because it was lying down. It seemed too small for a moose, and its horns could only be suspected. Rungius started forward to stalk it, and went rapidly down the divide, then climbed the side of the mountain and gradually approached the snow-bank. Watching through the glasses I saw the animal rise, stand a few moments, and walk aimlessly a few feet away from the snow, quite unconscious of danger. Soon we heard a shot, then two more, and it fell. It was a yearling cow caribou, and almost black. We gralloched and left it to be brought to camp later by the horses, where Rungius could sketch it.

We then went through the timber at the lower end of the divide, crossed a ridge and entered a small, deep basin, flushing ptarmigan at short intervals, and climbed a very steep slope opposite the carcass of the caribou, which was on the other side of the crest. In this and the other basins, in the pastures, and on the clear areas, grizzly bear diggings were abundant. More grizzly bears come to such places to dig out squirrels early in the spring than at other seasons, and by June they begin to roam and are not often seen. The bear already killed was the last we saw on that trip. Abundant diggings, however, do not indicate abundance of bears, as one will dig over much country. All the diggings that I saw near the divide could have been made by two or three bears.

We reached the crest and, going toward, looked down a few hundred yards below on the snow where the carcass lay. Not far below it, on a bank of snow close to the creek, was a small ram standing rigidly, with apparent alertness, looking up directly at us. Rungius at once started to circle around the slope and stalk him. The ram at times kept licking the snow, now and then looking up at us, and I could not understand his indifference. We saw Rungius, when he had approached sufficiently near, sit down and fire. The ram jumped as if hit, and walked on the snow out of sight, while Rungius ran and disappeared in the gorge. Gage and I hastened down and saw him sitting near the dead ram. The bullet having passed through its hind quarters, it had been unable to escape. It proved to be the young ram I had wounded and followed three days before. My bullet had struck and shattered his lower jaw and he was unable to eat. The poor creature was already reduced to skin and bones, and had evidently suffered from thirst. He had wandered back to find the band, but was growing too weak to travel and would shortly have died. I felt great pity for him.

Could the sportsman but know the suffering of the animals he wounds but fails to get—a too common experience—would his enthusiasm diminish? The hunter-sportsman is a strange combination, possessed by the fascination of hunting and killing the animals that he loves-for every true hunter-sportsman loves the wild animals. In their wild life they fascinate him; all his interest is aroused in watching them; his pulse is quickened; his feeling for nature becomes deeper, fuller, and more complete. I never knew a true hunter, be he the rough pioneer or the cultured man, who did not have an intense fondness for the wild animals, a strong interest in studying them and protecting them, and also a desire to alleviate and prevent their suffering; yet there still persists his paradoxical love of hunting and killing them.

The Indian finds in the fascination of the hunt a gratification of those inherited instincts produced and implanted in him by centuries of the struggle for existence. His ancestors had to hunt or starve, and in many places on this continent to-day the Indian must hunt or starve. He must seek food, and the excitement of the chase develops a fascination for it, intensified perhaps by inherited instinct. Part of this same instinct is our own heritage. It may be the mainspring which prompts us to set forth and suffer hardship.

Primitive feeling for nature was saturated with the supernatural and easily took the form of a reverence for natural phenomena, which in turn led to the development of mythological conceptions. It persists among most primitive men to-day, but is lost to us—replaced by the aesthetic feeling slowly and gradually evolved from it. In civilized man the hunting instinct has become broadened and transformed. We have learned to love and contemplate nature. We go back to the wilderness, and the more primitive it is, the more strongly we feel its charm. But the wilderness must include the animals. Our active sympathies, developed by civilization, extend also to them. We feel for them along with their wilderness environment. We learn to know and love them. They become inseparable from the mysterious emotions aroused by mountains, valleys, woods, and waters. They also arouse, kindle, and set glowing the primitive instinct to hunt and kill. The pursuit leads us to nature which in turn leads us to the pursuit. We cannot deny that this must react upon our race. Endurance, strength, skill, boldness, independence, manliness, are the qualities produced.

The time may come when most of us will undertake to work, endure, and suffer the hardships of the wilderness, prompted only by love of it for its own sake. But to many of us, in our present stage, hunting prevents the mere contemplative indulgence in the beautiful from producing effeminateness.

We skinned the ram and went up a short distance to the carcass of the caribou. It was photographed several times, and then, after cutting off the head, Rungius and Gage started back over the crest to take it down to the horses and return to camp. It was 6:30 in the evening, but I could not resist remaining to look for more sheep and hoping perhaps to find the remainder of that band of rams. Following a sheep-trail along the crest, after a difficult and dangerous climb, I finally reached the top of a high limestone peak. This was the last high peak on the south range bordering the divide. Toward the west the mountain sloped downward to vast meadows bordering a creek running north-east. The slopes continued in great expanses of hills and rolling meadows, cut here and there by deep cañons; most of the country was green; but all the exposed limestone glowed white in the setting sun. Later in the season this broad area of green pastures, cañons, streams, and rivulets, must be a magnificent range for caribou, as earlier it must be a feeding ground for grizzly bears. This was demonstrated during a subsequent tramp over it by innumerable tracks and signs of both, and also by shed horns of caribou. Sheep trails crossed it, intersecting from all directions, always along the higher ridges and knolls. All trails had worn through the earth to the limestone, thus marking the country with irregular white lines.

For a long time I watched through the field-glass, but nothing appeared. The sun went below the horizon, leaving a brilliantly colored sky glowing over the distant ranges toward the Tatonduk River. It was after ten and, not wishing to lose the beauty of the landscape under the twilight glow, I tramped hour after hour along the crest of the range continuing all the way to the basin south of camp. The ground-squirrels, marmots, conies, birds, and even the mosquitoes were hushed, and a solemn stillness prevailed. A deep calm pervaded the basins, meadows, and wilderness below, causing a weird impression of the solitude. Not a sound of any kind was audible; not a creature visible. Never did I feel more alone. In this northern twilight there was just enough darkness to cause a feeling of awe at the dim and silent grandeur of the surroundings. I slowly walked on all night, from mountain to mountain, and descended to the gorge of the stream in the south basin, proceeded through it with difficulty, and went down the creek toward camp. At three in the morning a heavy frost spread over the country, and a little later, above and below, all glittered and sparkled like diamonds in the rising sun.

July 22.—Arriving in camp at 5:30 A.M. I made a fire, had some tea, a bite to eat, and then slept until two in the afternoon. As rain threatened, the rest of the day was passed in camp. Rungius had the body of the cow caribou suspended by ropes and propped by stakes, so that he could change it to various attitudes and sketch it, and Osgood prepared the small mammals that he had taken in his traps. Wolverines were common in the vicinity, but only one was seen by Osgood. Minks were abundant along the creek near camp. Arctic weasels were there, though none were caught in the traps, and a few martens undoubtedly existed in the timber along the creek. The Dawson red-backed mouse and the Interior vole were the only two species of mice observed near timber-line.

The day before Osgood had climbed a mountain rising from the basin south of camp, and on it had found several ewes and lambs. But where was the remainder of that band of rams, or others? That question was disturbing me; therefore, I determined to go to the lower end of the divide for a day or two and hunt them alone.

CHAPTER III

SEARCHING FOR RAMS – 1904

JULY 23.—THE horses had disappeared, and Spahr and Gage consumed a long time looking for them, and finally found them not far away, standing perfectly still on a side hill. On *Mike* we put my blanket, a narrow piece of mosquito netting, the frying-pan, teapot, and a few provisions. Spahr rode *Shorty* and Gage and I walked to the divide. Arriving on top, four sheep were seen just below the crest of the spur above the place where the bear had been killed. They were two miles off, and appeared like white specks on the mountain; but even at that distance they had seen us and were nervous, bunching immediately and moving about with uncertainty. The glasses showed that they were rams and I quickly planned a stalk.

Going down into the ravine until out of their sight, I climbed to the foot of the cliffs, from where I could ascend the mountain on the west side near the peak and come out above them. In the broken rocks at the foot of the cliffs were numerous marmots which kept continually whistling, and I was fearful that they might alarm the rams. The surface for two hundred yards, reaching to a point not far from the top, consisted of small, loose, broken rock, over which I had to proceed with the greatest caution, as the rams were very near on the other side of the crest. It was a very steep slope and unless I carefully chose my footing, the rock would slide and fall, making much noise. In such places moccasins are superior to all other footgear. I could carefully feel the surface with my big toe, and at the right spot wedge the toes in the uneven spaces in a manner not possible with stiff soles. Besides, the moccasins were noiseless on hard rock. The rock slide was crossed successfully to a grassy space up which I went more rapidly to the peak, paying no attention to the wind, which was blowing directly from me to the rams. Going slightly to the right and descending a little, I looked below, but did not see them. As I was cautiously retreating to look over the other side, the horns of the rams were suddenly seen on the sky-line just below the peak and not fifty feet away.

At the same moment the sheep ran and I fired at one, which came in sight for an instant, but evidently shot over it. Running forward, I saw them rushing across the saddle, a ram of good size behind three smaller ones. Quickly seating myself and aiming at the larger ram as he was running, now two hundred yards away, I fired and he suddenly left the others, continued a few yards down the slope and dropped dead. The others had now crossed the saddle, ascended fifty yards more, and stood looking back for; a few moments before they again ran and disappeared along the broken slopes. All this was within six hundred yards of the spot where I had killed the bear. The ram lay a hundred yards below, stretched out at the head of a snow-bank, down which I pulled him to the bare ground and drew out the entrails, while Gage and Spahr, who had witnessed the whole stalk, were coming up with the horses. We loaded the ram on *Mike*, and Spahr immediately started with him for camp. I was delighted to send a whole ram to Rungius, who could now study and sketch it in the flesh. He was a fine ram with seven rings; his horns were of the spreading type, twenty-five inches from tip to tip.

From this point Gage and I went to timber-line at the lower end of the divide and made camp, after which he returned to the main camp leaving me alone. A piece of mutton was soon cooked and with crackers and tea, made my supper. Two willow sticks were bent in the form of a bow and placed parallel, ten inches apart with the ends thrust in the ground, so that a small piece of mosquito netting could be hung on them to cover my head while sleeping, for the mosquitoes were particularly numerous here, perhaps worse than at any other point near the divide.

But it was a beautiful spot, in an undisturbed wilderness. The sun had gone down and the sky was aglow. The landscape in front was seen between the spruces. How many times in after years I have felt the beauty of beholding mountains and far distant vistas through spruces whose graceful tops, like sharp pointed spires, lined the near horizon. Down through the deep descending valley, clothed with willows and evergreens, bordered on both sides by high mountains, I could see the broad meadow-lands and the dim mountain ranges beyond.

At last, rolling under the blanket and arranging my head under the netting, I was quickly hummed to sleep by the disappointed mosquitoes. But the protection did not last long and all night I kept rearranging the netting unsuccessfully.

July 24.—In the morning it was raining and a late start was made. To the west of my camp the range on its south side was smooth and grassy, covered here and there like all the other slopes, with moss and lichens. Its north side, not visible from the divide, was rough and rocky. The ascent was rather long; the wind was blowing strong, and it soon became very cold. Old bear diggings were common and ptarmigan were plentiful all along the slopes. Perched near some cliffs was a rough-legged hawk, which kept constantly crying, while across the divide, on the opposite range, were two golden eagles, soaring about

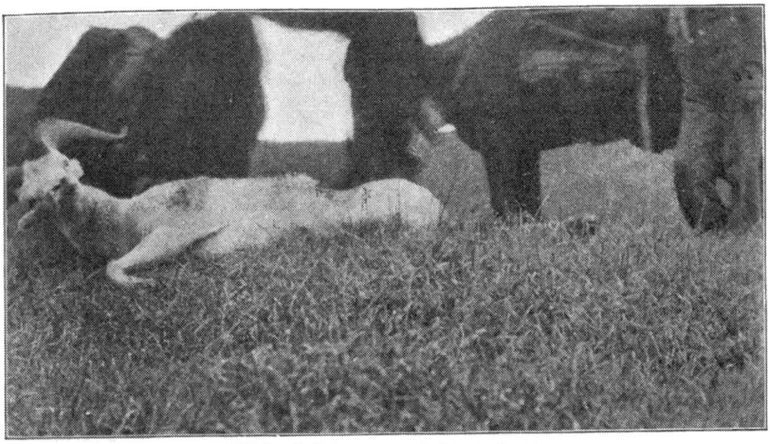

We loaded the ram on Mike, July 23.

1. Point where ram was killed, July 10. 2. Point where ram was killed, July 23.
3. Point where bear was killed, July 16.

PHOTOGRAPH BY CARL RUNGIUS.

the crests and appearing very dark against the sky. When well up, I suddenly saw, a hundred yards ahead, two ewes and two lambs looking at me with apparent curiosity. They ran forward a few jumps, stopped, and looked again. As I kept on they soon began to run, finally disappearing over the top. The wind was blowing directly from me to them.

Reaching the crest and looking over, I saw a startling sight. Cliffs and precipices fell perpendicularly to a small circular basin, surrounded on all sides by walls of rock fifteen hundred feet or more in height. Only one or two routes of descent were possible and these were very dangerous.

The ewes and lambs that had fled over the mountain top now reappeared five hundred yards away on the skyline. My glasses revealed twelve peacefully feeding on the green pasture at the bottom of the basin. With the unaided eye, it was a long time before I could make them out and then only as tiny dots. At times, in the mountains of that locality, the white sheep are most difficult to see, since their stained coats blend so well with the color of their environment. Many times, even when trying to look most carefully, I was surprised at not seeing them, when they were near and in plain sight. These ewes soon began to run as if startled, and through the glasses I saw a small ram, followed by another band, of thirteen ewes and lambs, chasing them two hundred yards behind. From what I learned later of the habits of sheep, they were no doubt merely running across the level in sport after feeding, and had started to go higher up to rest. Thinking the horns of the ram were larger than they proved to be on closer inspection, I circled around the edge of the cliffs to a point near which I thought they would ascend, and, sitting on the edge of a precipice, waited. Looking across the basin, high up near the top of a lofty mountain, I saw nine more ewes and lambs feeding on almost perpendicular cliffs. Clinging with their feet, they jumped about with indifference to their hazardous location, to get the morsels of green weeds and herbs growing among the rocks. The ewes below were slowly feeding upward; now all banded closely together and ascended directly toward me.

It was a fascinating sight to watch the sheep. Those on the cliffs beyond appeared like small white spots, now and then almost sparkling in the sun. At times it was difficult to credit the vision and realize that even sheep could so easily move about on the ides of apparent precipices. Those below kept moving along and were gradually approaching the top. Nearby conies were bleating, marmots were whistling, and twice a golden eagle soared gracefully across the basin. The sheep continued to approach upward, quite unsuspicious of my presence, while the lambs kept frisking about, now leaping on rocks, now running together and butting, now chasing each other and bleating. The ewes seemed indifferent to their gambols, but occasionally one would run about and sport with them. In such cases it was always one of the younger mothers. One of the ewes was particularly dark, even after making allowance for her stained pelage.

Nearer they came, directly toward me, while the small band still continued plainly in sight on the cliffs opposite. The ram was now in the lead and at length stood one hundred and fifty feet directly below me as the ewes came up around him. Pointing my rifle down over the cliff, the barrel was almost perpendicular when I fired at the centre of his shoulders. He dropped to a lying down position, panting and apparently about to roll over. The ewes, not in the least alarmed at the report, looked up, but none saw me, and some even continued feeding. Thinking the ram was dying, I stood up, when seeing me at once, they all ran across the steep side of the basin, where it did not seem possible for even a sheep to find a footing. The lambs easily followed, and in some way all climbed over the crest. I was greatly surprised to see the ram, which saw me as soon as the ewes began to run, jump up and run downward in a diagonal direction. Four shots were fired without hitting him, but when distant about eight hundred yards he stopped and lay down under a large rock. I could see that he was bleeding badly, and thinking that he would soon become stiff, waited quietly, watching the remainder of the band, which had again reappeared on the crest. They descended a few feet below the summit and all lay down, peacefully resting as if nothing had happened. The other band of sheep on the high cliffs opposite had passed over the crest. Once or twice the ram rose, staggered, and dropped again, therefore I felt sure that he would die, and continued waiting for a couple of hours and then stood up to try a descent. The wounded ram immediately rose and slowly, with difficulty, walked downward to the bottom of the basin. Not to alarm him more than necessary, I seated myself and watched him through the glasses. He often paused and stopped as if to lie down again, but kept on. He seemed to limber up as he went along a little faster, often making a jump, and sometimes almost running.

A mile away he crossed the basin and began to walk up the steep slope opposite, then going without difficulty. Higher and higher he went, still farther away, until he lay down under a cliff. The only chance of getting him was to leave him undisturbed so that he might die in the same spot. My bullet must have struck him on the side, too far back to make a quickly fatal wound. Then and there I made up my mind to keep shooting at a wounded animal in the future until assured that it was vitally hit, rather than to take chances, as in this case. A single ewe was lying down on the rocks above the ram. At 9:30 the large band was returning toward the bottom of the basin to feed. They reached it in peace before I started back to camp. This was the remainder of the band that Osgood and

Rungius had disturbed and driven back into the rougher parts of the mountains.

Later I sat by the fire, smoking my pipe, enjoying the solitude, with the same gorgeous sunset sky before me. I again passed the night, sleeping between intervals of fighting the mosquitoes, which were active all night in the timber on that side of the divide.

July 25.—The sun was shining brightly when I rose and climbed the south range. After looking at the untouched carcass of the caribou, I proceeded east along the crest in the hope of finding the rams near the point where they had first been seen. To the south, on the other side of a narrow basin, was a high ridge on the crest of which stood a large bull caribou, making a huge black bulk against the sky. He was motionless in the centre of the snow-bank, with his head held downward—the most common attitude of bull caribou when standing at rest. Having determined not to shoot another caribou while in the velvet, I watched him at times through the glasses, as he stood for two hours without changing his attitude. Later I proceeded, noticing the beds of sheep—small circular hollows which they had pawed out in the broken rock of the slope—and saw that nothing had yet touched the bear's carcass, which was in sight below. About the middle of the afternoon Osgood came along on the crest and I pointed out the caribou, which had then wandered about fifty feet from the snowbank. As he started in that direction, it returned and lay down on the snow. Osgood had seen seven ewes and lambs on a high spur running south from the range, and was approaching to see if any rams were near.

I walked on observing the ewes, which were now feeding on the top of the spur, and while proceeding could soon look down on the basin from which Osgood had ascended. Just beyond the range that I was following was a chain of peaks, the second of which was, to the sight, the highest visible anywhere in the whole region. I determined to climb it. It was rough and steep, and the last hundred yards were difficult to surmount, but finally I reached the top. From this peak I could look down on both sides of the spur and into two pretty crystal lakes lying in a narrow space between it and the next range, which shot up into cliffs, culminating in the high jagged crest of a mountain chain running north and south.

Streams of water could be heard leaping down from the surrounding snow to form the lakes. It was perfectly clear, and I sat down to enjoy the extended mountain panorama. After taking several photographs of the landscape, I left my rucksack and the Kodak where I had been sitting, and descended a short distance along the rim to look over into a cañon beyond. When I had gone a few hundred feet I heard the sound of falling rocks not fifty feet in front, and suddenly seven ewes and lambs jumped up on the crest from the cliff below. They stood for a few moments in alert attitudes, looking at me with curiosity. Oh, for that Kodak, which for the first time was not at hand! As I started back for it the sheep moved around the peak and disappeared. Then on the high range beyond, some small moving objects were silhouetted against the sky-line, and my field-glasses proved them to be ewes and lambs. Moving the glasses, to keep the crest in the field, I could see on every peak and in many places between them small bands of ewes and lambs; some feeding, some lying down, and others travelling along; but not a single ram.

Then I began the descent to the lakes. The slope was exceedingly steep, particularly on the talus; so, suspending my rifle on my back, I zigzagged down, finding great difficulty the last few hundred feet, where the way led among tumbled and confused boulders. There was ice along the shores of the lakes, which were two or three acres in extent, perfectly clear, and fairly deep. As usual, old caribou tracks were everywhere, and the songs of water-ousels were heard as I followed the stream to camp, reached finally at ten in the evening.

This day Rungius had been up the north branch of Coal Creek, below our camp, and had climbed the other side of the range where I had seen the ewes feeding on the cliffs the day before. He reported having seen the same number of ewes-probably the same band.

July 26.—At 2:30 the next morning Osgood returned with the skin of the caribou, having left the head to bring later. He had found it feeding only a few feet from the snow-bank and nearby had seen some caribou cows and calves. Rungius continued sketching the ram that I had killed. By a system of ropes, suspended from a cross-pole, it had been held in a natural position and had been stuffed with grass to give a normal size to the belly. After several pencil drawings Rungius made a color sketch to record the stained color of the pelage.

Soon after noon, I started for the mountain to look for the ram which had been wounded two days before. Reaching the edge of the basin, where I could plainly see the country, no sign of him was visible about the slope where he had been last seen; nor, after reaching the point where he had lain down, could I find any trace of him. I then turned back toward camp, descending to the divide down the bed of a stream which flows through a deep gorge. Just before entering the canon I saw a ewe and lamb standing not far above, looking at me. The ewe was in an alert attitude, with one foreleg raised and curved. At short intervals she would strike her horns to the ground or jump and stamp with her feet and shake her head, tormented by the mosquitoes. Many times I saw sheep act in this way, a sure sign that mosquitoes worried them, particularly about the lips, eyes, and ears. The canon proved to be so precipitous that it became a difficult and dangerous task to descend it. It was necessary to cross and recross the dashing stream, walk down slippery snow-banks, work down bluffs, and often make a detour around the heads of tributary gorges. It is not wise to attempt a descent through unknown gorges, and I determined not to try it again. From one point several ewes and lambs were seen near the peak of the mountain on my left. They had evidently been feeding below and were working upward to rest for the night.

July 27.—The next day was spent in camp. It was the hottest yet experienced and decidedly uncomfortable. With the exceptions noted, the weather had been clear; the days, except high up the mountains, warm, often hot; and the nights cold, the temperature usually falling below freezing point. Numerous jays were now about, and it was amusing to watch them carrying off every piece of meat that they could snatch. I prepared the head of the ram which Rungius had been sketching, and skinned my caribou's feet. Osgood had very kindly prepared the caribou head during my absence.

At 6:30 in the evening Rungius and I filled our rucksacks with provisions, and, taking the mosquito tent, started for my camp at the lower end of the divide. As we were ascending the pastures of the divide, Rungius looked back and saw a fairly large ram, high up the mountain, running down the slope, followed by a smaller one. He immediately started back to gain the foot of the slope, but the sheep passed out of sight, running as if frightened. He began to climb directly toward the point where they disappeared. Then I started down the creek, to intercept them if they should cross to the other range, but it was too late, for I saw them climbing the slope on the opposite side, and watched them for some time until they began to feed near the top and soon passed out of sight over the crest.

At the same time four ewes and lambs were seen up near Rungius, who also saw but did not stalk them. Later we

Carl Rungius sketching the ram.

PHOTOGRAPH BY W.H. OSGOOD.

learned that shortly before this hour Osgood had seen three rams farther along the same range, and wounding the largest he had failed to get it. The two that Rungius and I had seen were evidently the others which were running in fright when we first saw them. Rungius finally joined me and we proceeded over the divide.

Twilight was deepening, and the sky to the west was glowing in colors above the distant peaks, when I saw, silhouetted against the sky-line of the crest directly opposite my old camp, several sheep, probably ewes. They soon lay down and were still visible on the sky-line as the shadows deepened and the sky became crimson. By practice the eye becomes trained to recognize animals in contrast to similar inanimate objects, even when blending in color and at a distance, and often when not moving. My vision was constantly improving in this respect, and I was gradually gaining confidence in my ability to quickly distinguish sheep, inconspicuous as they were in that country. As we approached camp the usual swarm of mosquitoes welcomed us. We soon put up the tent, made a fire, cooked, ate, and went under the blankets. At last, in that spot, I slept, defying the mosquitoes.

July 28.—It was raining when we rose, and after breakfast we waited for clear weather. During my absence the ground-squirrels had gnawed through the waterproof canvas to investigate the few provisions that had been left. It cleared and we started down river, then ascended a steep slope well to the west along the range, for the purpose of examining the lower ranges south of the divide. I particularly wanted to climb the farther peaks above the rolling country. Bear diggings were numerous everywhere, in the basins and on the slopes. We climbed along the broken rock on the west side of the high limestone mountain (which I had ascended after leaving Rungius and Gage several days before), and circled around it to the crest on the other side where the chain continues to the south, and there seated ourselves to look over the country.

While scanning a partly snow-covered range of dark, iron-stained rock, almost black in appearance, there came into the field of my glasses a band of sixteen bull caribou, their manes glistening white in contrast to the black rock of the slope above the snow on which they were standing. Their bodies appeared black in strong relief, although nearly three miles away, and their wide, branching antlers were clearly visible, like small dead tree tops. All stood motionless with heads hanging down, like the single bull I had seen near there a few days before. Here was an opportunity for Rungius to study them in life, and he quickly started. As he passed out of sight below, I watched the caribou. Now and then a few would move off the snow to feed, but they quickly came back, and soon two or three were lying down on it.

Then I went on along the crest of the range and after climbing a peak noticed a dead animal on the snow in the bottom of a ravine and soon found it to be a dead caribou bull. It was the one I had shot at and thought I had missed. It had been shot through the stomach and had lain down on the snow and died. It was fully as large as the one I had killed, but a little lighter in color, and the horns, though as long in beam, had but few points. All the satisfaction I had felt in permitting it to escape without firing at it again now disappeared in a feeling of chagrin. The carcass was badly decomposed, but only ground-squirrels had been feeding on it.

I went on along the uneven crest to the south end of the range, following sheep-trails, among the bleating conies and whistling marmots. From the south mountains I crossed back to camp through the rolling country. A sheep was seen against the sky-line of the mountain three miles to the west and another soon joined it, but at that distance it was impossible to make out the sex, though the absence of lambs might indicate rams. It had showered and hailed during the day and at times was cold on the mountain. During the tramp along the crest I noticed two ravens feeding on the carcass of the first ram I had killed, but they were driven away at intervals by a golden eagle, who claimed a share of the feast. Not finding Rungius, and thinking he had returned to the main camp, I prepared supper, and after smoking my pipe rolled into the blanket at midnight. As I went to sleep the glow of the twilight in the west was still beautiful, while the pastures and mountains behind were covered with dark clouds.

July 29.—Some time later I was aroused by a noise outside and seized my rifle, thinking it was a bear after the provisions stored near by under a tree. It was Rungius returning with a caribou head and skin. When nearing the caribou, he found that they had moved to a snow-bank higher up the slope, and not distinguishing the leader of the band he killed two of the smaller bulls. After he had fired, the leader, followed by the whole band, came trotting up to him in curiosity. Just beyond the bulls he had seen a band of five cows and calves.

Soon after Rungius came in it began to rain very hard and continued until after mid-day, when he started back for the main camp. I intended to remain a few more days to search for rams, and asked him to have one of the men bring me more provisions. Since the mountains and ridges became enveloped in a heavy mist, it was necessary to remain about camp. Alaska jays were now numerous, and two Northern shrikes were there, stealing any morsel that they could find. Although the shrikes would snatch everything and fly off, they would only eat meat. They were extremely quarrelsome and always drove off the jays until they could help themselves. Ground-squirrels had become bold and would come to the frying-pan as I held it, to eat the bacon grease. All these provided interesting company until evening, when Spahr appeared with two horses, bringing a supply of provisions. I sent him back with Rungius's caribou skin. It rained all night.

July 30.—After breakfast, on the range to the south, I saw a ewe and two lambs feeding low. The lambs were sporting about. Through the glasses the dark stripes on the ewe's legs and the gray on the back were distinctly visible. As the mountains were covered with mist, I waited and watched the sheep feeding until they moved upward and disappeared over the crest. Looking back on the spur where I had killed my last ram, I saw a smaller ram walking across the slope. It reached the edge of the cliff, leaped down to a jutting rock below, and lay down. It was still resting at noon when I began to climb the ridge. From the top seven ewes and lambs could be seen back across the valley and laying down on the crest of the mountain I had climbed a few days before. Two hours later they were still resting in the same place. The sun was brightly shining as I continued the long tramp along the ridges, fascinated by the interest of looking down in the basins between the numerous spurs, always hoping to see a bear feeding, or perhaps rams resting. I kept carefully examining the country ahead until the last mountain was climbed, but not an animal was anywhere in sight. Here for the first time I saw the white-tailed ptarmigan, very tame, high up among the rocks.

I could look down on the edge of the vast meadows, extending many miles north and south, bristling here and ere with black spruces, and see well-defined moose and caribou trails, crossing through the long grass. The meadows were about three miles wide and through the middle flowed a large stream coming from a mountain to the south-west, and which was lost to view where it flowed through the mountain ranges fifteen miles to the north-east. On the other side of the meadows, parallel with them, were high mountain chains, similar in appearance to those of the divide. The river is a branch of the Tatonduk or Sheep Creek. Sheep trails extended in all directions from the ridge-tops near me, except toward the meadows. It is probably a feeding-place in spring or late fall.

It had showered at intervals during the day and when I reached camp it was raining hard. While I was cooking supper, my eyes were attracted by an unfamiliar object appearing like a small stump in the centre of a little knoll about a hundred and fifty yards off across the brook. Watching it carefully I saw a movement and knew that it was a wolf, in an attitude almost perfect for self-protection. Its hind quarters were turned directly toward me. Its head, pointing in my direction, was held close to the body in a straight line in such manner that the only parts of the body visible, without close scrutiny, were the narrow hind quarters, the color of which blended perfectly with the grass. My rifle was against a tree. Quickly creeping to it I aimed through the dusk and fired. The wolf jumped and ran zigzagging down stream, but did not present another shot and was soon lost to sight in the timber. As it ran one hind leg was swinging, evidently broken by the bullet. It was too dark to follow then, but I determined to try for it in the morning.

July 31.—The sunset that night and the tinting of the clouds were particularly beautiful, as the faint light glowed through the spruces while heavy clouds hung on the mountain sides, and to the east all was dark. Few mosquitoes were about, the rains of the last few days together with the colder nights having probably destroyed them. The rain kept pouring down, beating through the thin mosquito tent all night, and continued until afternoon the next day. When it slackened it was necessary to search for a spot to safely cross the brook, now swollen and dashing by in heavy volume. Careful search was made for the wolf, but all signs had been obliterated by the rain, which, later in the afternoon, increased so much that hunting for that day was given up.

While I was sheltered by the tent, a ground-squirrel greatly amused me. It began to approach, stopping, after each slight advance, to rise on its hind legs and look at me, until it came to the tent and cautiously pried about, eating grease in the frying-pan and picking up stray bits of meat. The shrikes also were about, flying from tree to tree, fighting over pieces of meat. Then the jays came for their share, and even a red squirrel was attracted to the feast.

At five o'clock in the afternoon it stopped raining and nine ewes and lambs were seen feeding on the opposite mountain, evidently a part of those which had been observed across the basin, now coming back to their original pastures. Then a ewe and two lambs were seen feeding on the conical mountain near where Rungius had killed the cow caribou. The lambs, on reaching a long bank of snow, began a game of butting, backing apart and rushing together again and again. Soon all disappeared over the top. It was then eight o'clock and growing colder.

August 1.—The first day of August was bright, clear, and windy, with scattered clouds hovering here and there over the mountains. I decided to again climb the ridge behind our main camp, and walk east along the crest, thus repeating my trip of a few days before, in the hope that some of the rams had returned. During the ascent the field-glasses revealed a good-sized ram, with several ewes and lambs just under the peak of the conical mountains. After feeding awhile they lay down close to the peak, and I started to walk along the crest, with the intention of stalking them when they began to feed later in the afternoon.

When I reached the top of the spur and looked beyond, Rungius was seen coming on a stalk directly over the peak, well within range, but not in sight of the ram. The ewes below, apparently having seen him, had risen and were quite uneasy; they suddenly jumped and ran around the peak before he could get a shot. Osgood then appeared, standing farther along the crest, and after Rungius motioned to him, both soon disappeared over the top. I kept on to the top of the mountain, noticed that the caribou carcass had not been disturbed and also that the carcass of the first ram I had killed was still untouched except by ravens and eagles.

Later I saw Rungius approaching along the crest and, hailing him, we soon met. He told me that soon after I had seen him, he and Osgood had observed five rams lying under a cliff, but the rams had seen them before they could shoot, and were running when they fired at a distance of four hundred yards, both emptying their magazines without result. Osgood had gone after them, and Rungius and I started back to the main camp, but were overtaken by a very heavy rainstorm and thoroughly soaked.

On the way we looked over some cliffs and could see lying on the talus below seven ewes and lambs, which we left undisturbed. Rungius soon afterward separated from me to kill a ewe from a small band which he had seen in the morning nearer camp, in order to replenish our stock of meat. I kept on, descending to the south basin, where a marmot was sitting up like a woodchuck near its burrow. There were many marmot burrows in the bottom of this basin among coarse, broken rocks.

I reached camp at 9 P.M. and Rungius came in soon after, having failed to find the ewes. Later, Osgood returned, bringing the head and scalp of a three-year old ram. He had persistently followed them all day and finally made a successful stalk. He had shot as one was running, and thought that he had only wounded it as it disappeared in a hollow; and when one appeared on the other side he killed it. The next day, when he returned with Gage for the meat, he found the other ram dead in the hollow, a three-year-old, the one that he had fired at first. His persistent stalk on difficult ground deserves much credit. Apparently those rams were from the band which I had first seen.

For several days I had tramped many miles and had climbed high mountains in search of rams, and was somewhat doubtful of finding other big rams before we must depart; hence, the next day, I decided to hunt the ranges east of Coal Creek, below the forks.

CHAPTER IV

THE FINAL STALK - 1904

AUGUST 2.—WE rose late, to find the sun brightly shining. Rungius soon started to look at his caribou carcass; Osgood and Gage went to get the meat of Osgood's ram. I stood near the fire for a few moments after they had left, and was gazing at the high mountains three miles or more distant, east of the north branch of Coal Creek, where I intended to hunt, when I saw up near the top what appeared to be sheep—whitish spots against the dark background of the slope. My glasses showed six sheep, not clearly visible, but looking like rams.

It was a little after mid-day, and in five minutes I had started down the creek flushing ptarmigan and disturbing ground-squirrels on the way, while red spruce squirrels scampered and frisked about. After passing rapidly along the well-beaten moose trail until near the forks, I again looked through the glasses. Yes, they were rams, nine in all, apparently, with fair horns, and the horns of one, which was feeding to the right a short distance from the others, seemed to be particularly large.

They were on the west face of a high, rugged mountain, about a mile broad, with very steep, green slopes extending from the creek directly up to near the crest, ending against shagged precipices, pinnacled above by high peaks of limestone and iron-stained rock which, under the sunlight, displayed a wonderful harmony of colors—red, black, and white. The slope was furrowed by three ravines, and through the bottom of each fell brooks, dashing and leaping over the rocks of the sharp decline. From a distance these ravines looked like deep concave depressions, giving a wavy appearance to the broad mountain face.

Three of the rams, including the one with big horns, were feeding in the middle ravine; the other six were standing on the edge of the next one, which was so precipitous that it was more like a deep cañon on the mountain side. In studying an approach, it appeared to be quite possible to climb out of sight in the ravine to the right, but should the rams in the meanwhile feed in that direction, they would surely see me. Though it required more time, I decided to pass clear around the mountain, and by winding up the south-east side come in sight above them, thus avoiding any possibility of their seeing me unless they should go back over the crest, which for the next few hours was unlikely.

I waded the creek, circled, and began the ascent through the timber, where were rabbits and spruce grouse, not observed nearer to the divide. Coming out on the south side and circling upward, I not only found it very steep, but it was extremely difficult to force my way through the dense growth of dwarf birch which covered the lower slopes of the south exposure. But gradually winding upward I reached a point high above the sheep, where the ground was so rough and steep that it was difficult to work among the crags and rocks to the part of the crest that I had marked from below as directly above the sheep. The slope now became so dangerous that it was necessary to sling my rifle on my back, so that I could use both hands. At length, I stood at the marked point, just below the crest, and paused awhile to rest and recover my breath after the exertion of the climb.

After a few moments I slowly crawled forward and looked over. A hundred and fifty yards below me was the large ram, lying down near the edge of the second ravine, and a little to the left below it the heads of two smaller ones were just visible. The wind was fresh and fairly strong, blowing directly from me to them. As no other sheep were in sight I concluded that the rest were below in the ravine. The ram was peacefully looking down on that wondrous landscape, without suspicion of danger from above. Sitting with elbows squarely on my knees, I fired at the centre of its body. I heard the bullet strike him before he rose with a jump and stepped forward, quickly passing out of sight over the edge of the ravine. The two smaller rams sprang to a standing position, and looked sideways and down, apparently not much alarmed. None of the others appeared while I remained stretched at full length, motionless, for ten minutes. The big ram then suddenly staggered in sight again on the edge of the ravine and I aimed, fired, and the bullet struck him in such a way that I was confident he had been killed as he dropped back into the cañon. The two small rams slowly followed him.

Then as quickly and as noiselessly as possible, I walked two hundred yards to the right, just below and parallel with the crest, to a point where I could look down in the cañon. Seventy-five yards away on the opposite side and a little below were eight rams closely bunched, all nervously looking down. They had heard the noise of the old ram falling and were

Osgood and Rungius.

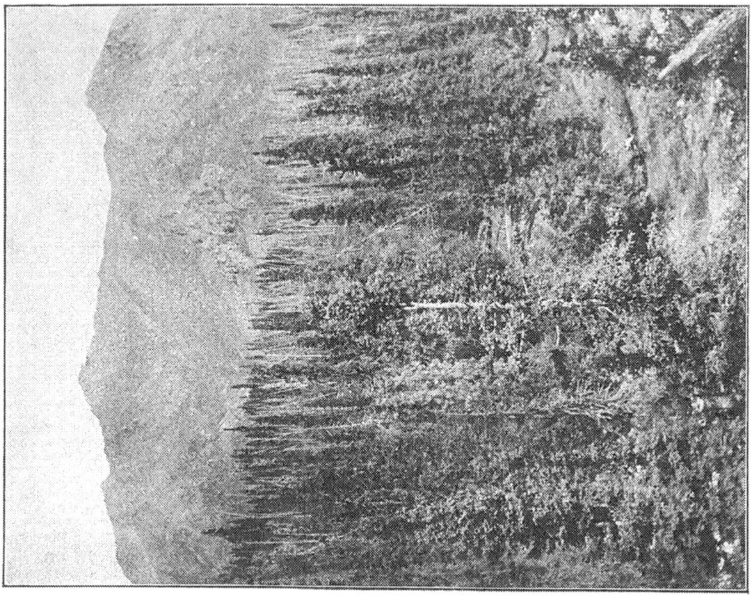

They were on the west face of a high rugged mountain, August 2.

looking in that direction. They had not determined the direction of the danger. I quickly selected the one with the largest horns and off-hand shot him through the heart. The rest jumped and ran a hundred yards downward, and rushed up the broken surface to the edge of the cañon directly below me, where all stopped and looked about in excitement, not yet having seen me.

Selecting the one with the next largest horns I sent a bullet through his heart, and he dropped in his tracks. The others scattered, ran about a little, and stood again, still not having seen me. Selecting the grayest I shot him through the middle of the body. He ran down the cañon slope near the second dead ram, and stood a moment until another shot killed him. The rest, three of which had good horns, bunched, ran a few yards, and again stood and looked up, for the first time seeing me. In alert attitudes they gazed at me for several seconds until I moved, then all dashed across the slope and disappeared through the ravine, again coming in sight for a moment before they rushed around to the other side of the mountain. I went quickly down to the third ram on the edge of the cañon and sat down to smoke my pipe.

After the excitement of the hunt the vast panorama of mountains about me never seemed so beautiful. Directly below were the bare, steep slopes extending to the timber which bordered the creek. Beyond, lay the valley of the west fork, fringed green by the spruces, while the waters of the creek were shining and glistening in the rays of the setting sun, which tinted with gold the heavy clouds on the horizon. The lofty mountain behind camp stood out boldly, its high-turreted rocks and rough peaks forming fantastic shapes against the skyline, and at its base our camp fire burned brightly. Behind, stretching far away, were the bewildering masses of the main Ogilvie ranges, the varied rocks blending their colors and fading like a wavy

He dropped in his tracks. August 2.

Selecting the grayest, I shot him through the middle of the body. August 2.

I quickly selected the one with the largest horns and offhand shot him through the heart. August 2.

A fine old veteran of the crags and peaks. August 2.

ocean merging into the soft, dull blue of the sky beyond. A large ram lay at my feet; below in the cañon was another; above on opposite sides of the leaping stream two more, my final success. Still with me is the vivid memory of those wild sheep rushing across the rocky slope in that wonderful landscape.

After photographing the dead ram near me I began to take off the skin of his head and neck. The clouds gathered fast and it soon began to rain. After cutting off the head I carried it with the skin down into the cañon and then went up to the third ram killed which was very gray, and was selected to represent the "Fannin" type for the collection of the Biological Survey. After photographing him I gralloched him and left him for Osgood to preserve. Then crossing the stream to the second ram killed, which had fallen on an exceedingly steep slope, I photographed him also and removed his skin and head. Both were carried to the ram below, the first one killed. Up to this time I had not been near him and the climax of the day came as I saw lying before me an enormous ram of grayish color, grizzled with age, his large, perfect horns sweeping upward in spirals extending well above the eyes, a finer trophy than I had ever anticipated, an old veteran of the crags and peaks. It was raining heavily, the mountain crests were covered with clouds, and a dense fog was settling all around me. I tried several exposures for photographs, and measured the ram whose length was fifty-nine inches. In the rain and cold I finished skinning him at 10:30 P. M. The head was cut off and left in the skin.

Thoroughly soaked, I rested for awhile and ate a couple of crackers. Far below in the distance the campfires could be seen glimmering through the fog, which soon became so dense that the darkness increased. The nights were now perceptibly darker, so much so that in this heavy fog I could not clearly see the ground. Tying the larger head and skin in my rucksack,

Breaking the hunting camp.

Photograph by W. H. Osgood. By Permission of the U.S. Biological Survey.

Travelling down Coal Creek.

Photograph by Carl Rungius.

also putting another on my back, and taking the third in my hand, I began the descent. The first hundred feet proved the impossibility of going on without lightening the load; so the smaller head and skin were left on a rock at the bottom of the cañon. Then another start was made with the remaining pack rearranged and with the rifle slung on my back. The descent was so steep and the cañon so dark that it was necessary to climb to the slope above and zigzag slowly downward. I was unable to see the surface of the ground and advanced slowly, feeling each step, falling several times, continually stopping to rest and rearrange the pack and the head. Gradually I worked down to timber-line where, though it was darker, the footing was smoother, and finally I reached the creek. It had required two and a half hours to make a descent of less than two miles.

Fording and refording, now resting, now fixing the pack, I kept on in the rain. As daylight returned it became easier to travel and I reached camp at 4 A. M. A fire was soon started; some food and tea taken; then repose, and my pipe; after which strength returned and I slept.

We had succeeded in the main object of the trip, which was to obtain good specimens of the sheep of that region. None were so dark as the so-called Fannin sheep, but some were good representatives of the white Dall sheep, except the color of the tails, which in all of them was black. Probably half the sheep in this locality faintly displayed the pattern of the Fannin sheep, but all were nearer the color of the other. (* See appendix for descriptions of the types; also see plate in Chapter XX.) It is worth recording that all the sheep seen in the first band of rams had the widely spread type of horns; all in this second band had the narrow type.

August 3-6.—The next three days were spent in camp, except that short trips were made by Rungius and Osgood to bring back the meat and remaining skins, to gather the traps and make local sketches. Rungius sketched the heads of my sheep in the flesh, after which I prepared them and spent the time arranging and drying them. The fourth day I went down the creek and up the branch that enters below the forks, on the chance of finding a bear, but saw nothing, and returned after an interesting tramp among the mountains.

August 7 was spent in breaking camp, shoeing the horses, and making up the packs. Osgood had collected one hundred and ten specimens of small mammals and birds, besides the larger game. We slept for the last time in that delightful camp, and the next morning packed and started. The return was rapid as compared with the trip up river. It was all down grade; we knew the route; the trail had been cut; the loads were lighter, only that of the caribou horns being bulky and awkward. There were numerous salmon in the river; bear tracks, those of the black bear only, were more plentiful, and a few fresh moose tracks were seen. On the afternoon of August 11 we reached the Yukon River.

Long before leaving Coal Creek a steamer whistle reminded us of civilization. Our exact travelling time from camp at the head of Coal Creek to the Yukon River, deducting all stops of over five minutes, was twenty-one hours and four minutes. We forded Coal Creek fifty-eight times. While in the hunting country it had rained eight days, but only twice did fog and rain prevent reasonable hunting. Twenty-seven days were clear, and at no time was there a very strong wind.

A steamer was being loaded with coal at the chutes, but owing to their faulty construction three days were required to load a barge; therefore we were obliged to endure the delay. We boarded the steamer August 14, and the following afternoon arrived in Dawson, where everything was packed and sent to Washington.

THE MACMILLAN RIVER

Stood motionless on the crest, gazing at the country below.

Drawing by Carl Rungius.

CHAPTER V

THE TRIP TO THE FORKS OF THE MACMILLAN RIVER – 1904

BEFORE LEAVING DAWSON for Coal Creek we had arranged to join a party which had matured a plan to rent a small steamer to take us up to the head-waters of navigation on the MacMillan River. It was composed of D. A. Cameron, manager of the Dawson branch of the Canadian Bank of Commerce; Judge Dugas, of Dawson; J.A. Patterson, a fine fellow, who, having crossed the Rockies by the Edmonton trail in 1898, had subsequently gained much experience in that northern wilderness, and F. C. Selous, of England. Selous had arrived a short time previously and had taken a short trip in the Ogilvie ranges to the north-east of Dawson to employ his time in hunting caribou during the ten days that he might otherwise have been idling about Dawson. He had engaged an experienced half-breed hunter, Louis Cardinal, as assistant for the MacMillan trip, and the others had two experienced French-Canadians, also Bob Henderson, one of the original explorers for gold in the vicinity of the Klondike River. I had re-engaged Gage and had arranged to get another man at Selkirk. Two hunters, Dougherty and Horn, had taken a passage for the MacMillan where they could kill a supply of moose meat and bring it back to Dawson for sale.

August 21.—The necessary canoes were loaded on board, and shortly after noon, August 22, the little steamer, *Emma Knot,* started and was propelled slowly against the swift current, stopping at intervals to take on wood, until it was tied up to the bank at 10 P.M. It could not be navigated during the hours of darkness—then between 9:30 P. M. and 3 A. M. Before going into our canvas bunks, especially constructed one above the other, under a shelter of canvas on the stern deck, we witnessed a fine display of the Aurora. The weather was clear and continued like Indian summer as long as we remained on the steamer.

August 22.—For the next two days the boat steamed against the current, tying up during the dark hours of the night, until shortly after noon on August 24th we reached Selkirk. There the other man whom I had engaged—Coghlan, by name—met us. A few provisions were purchased, our travelling clothes were left at the Police Post in Selkirk, and late in the afternoon we were all glad to leave the Yukon and enter the Pelly—a river rarely navigated by steamboats—where the boat could make better headway because of the slower current. The current of the Yukon at that season runs four and five miles an hour; that of the Pelly about three or less. We stopped seven miles up the river at the Pelly Road House—large inn owned by the White Pass and Yukon Railway, at a division terminal on the winter stage route—and there took on two canoes kindly loaned us by A. B. Newell, vice-president of the railway.

Four miles farther up, the boat, striking the rocky bed of the river, had a hole punched in its bottom, small, but bad enough to cause us to tie up for repairs. We remained there during the dark hours of the night. We had been assured that not more than five days would be required to reach the head of navigation on the MacMillan River, but were beginning to realize that it would take longer.

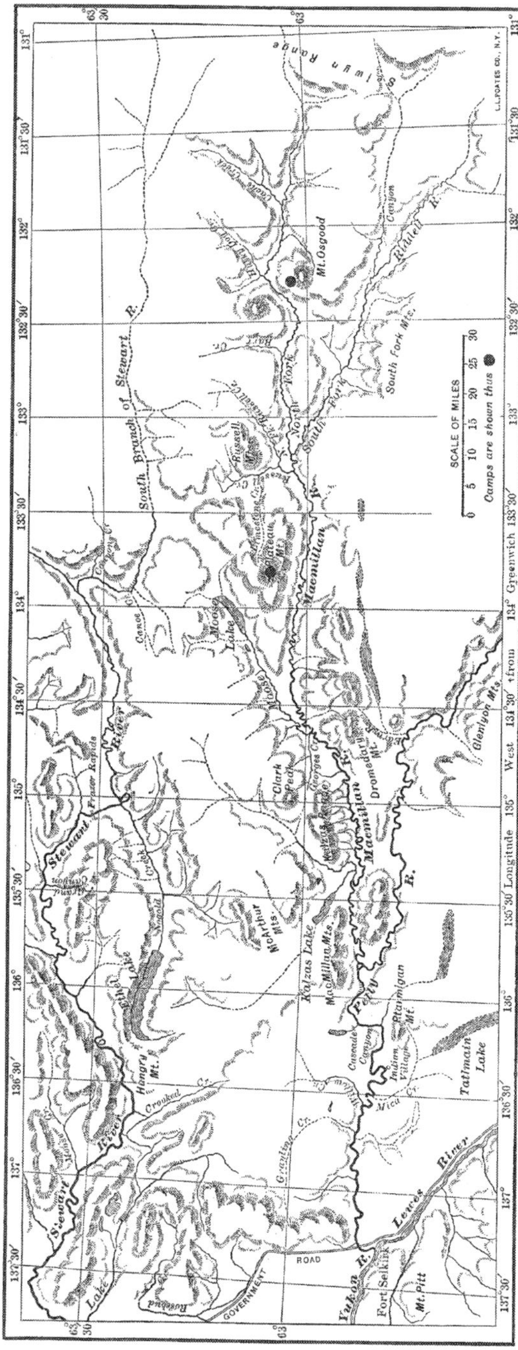

Map of MacMillan River, showing author's hunting camps.

August 25.—Starting the next morning and forcing our way against the current, we glided between high terraces which often shut out a sight of the rolling hills and low ridges farther back from the river. From its mouth to the MacMillan River, the Pelly, tortuous in its course, is from four hundred to eight hundred feet wide, and flows through a low country. It is closely bordered by low hills and ridges, and often flows between terraces, some of which rise far back from the river to heights of one hundred and fifty to two hundred feet. These, often lightly wooded, mostly with poplars, and clothed with grass, particularly on the southern exposures, present a very attractive appearance. Bluffs or high escarped banks are usually on one side or the other, and opposite them are wide gravel bars, fairly smooth, so that it is quite easy to tow a canoe up the river. The distance to the mouth of the MacMillan along the river is seventy-four miles and the current runs at the rate of two and one-half to three miles an hour. Here and there wide flats intervene between the river and the terraced hills.

Now and then we frightened a flock of mergansers, and twice saw a graceful duck-hawk sailing by. The landscape was warmed by the poplars, then showing a tinge of fall color. Numerous old game trails came to the river. These trails often extend along the banks and are used by Indians both in summer and fall. Several men were aboard, to be put off at a wood camp to cut fuel and assemble it into a raft which the boat on returning could tow to Dawson. Late in the afternoon we reached the camp and went ashore to wander about, eating luscious red cranberries and feeling the exhilaration of exercise in the warm cheery sunshine. At intervals along the river were groves of dry spruces close to the bank. Such groves provide the fuel for steamboats on all the northern rivers which are not navigated often enough by steam to encourage woodchoppers to locate wood camps along the banks to sell wood to passing steamers. Our men at once began to fell trees, and all of us assisted in loading them on the boat. From then on we were delayed from two to four hours each day thus to cut and load wood.

After starting again some of us noticed an indifference on the part of the captain about continuing, and I must say a word about this Swedish captain, who was responsible for most of our troubles during the remainder of the time we were on the steamboat. He proved to be nothing but a deep-water sailor, who had somehow drifted into Dawson and become a conspicuous member of the Salvation Army, which for some time had been active there. He was bigoted, lacked every kind of courage and nerve, and, still worse, knew nothing about river navigation, as we soon afterward learned. He was already beginning to doubt the possibility of navigating much farther up the Pelly, giving as a reason "low water."

August 26.—Fog prevented the boat from starting until 6:30 the next morning and we reached the lower end of Granite Canon at nine. This canon, four miles long, is bordered with steep, rocky scarped banks, and cliffs from two hundred to two hundred and fifty feet in height. The river through the canon is fairly wide and deep, though at low water there are several shallow rapids and numerous isolated rocks which it needs skilful steering to avoid. The captain uncertainly attempted to manage the boat, and just before entering the canon put her into the sand-bank of a little island in midstream. Then backing her, while nobody knew what he was trying to do, he took her to the bank and tied her up, saying that if he attempted to go through he would lose her. It was evident that a stiff rapid just ahead had frightened him.

Fortunately, our man Coghlan was an experienced river navigator, and, after going along the bank and looking at the water, he told us that it would not be difficult or dangerous to "rope" up through a part of the rapid to a point where the boat could steam against it. After two hours of discussion and persuasion, the captain was induced to make the attempt. All available ropes were then spliced to a length of over three hundred feet; we all gave a hand, pulled the line along the shore, and fastened it to a tree on the bank. After being pushed from shore, the boat was given a course, and, assisted by the steam-propelled revolutions of the winch, started steaming against the dancing current. The slack of the rope was not even taken up, its own weight adding enough pull to make up for the slight lack of power in the paddle-wheel, which did not have quite enough to propel the boat against the rapids. After two hundred feet the doubtful part was passed, the rope loosened, and we went through the rest of the canon without difficulty.

Soon we saw in the distance the MacMillan range of mountains—the first imposing mountains seen since we had entered the Pelly—and at about five o'clock we steamed into the MacMillan River. The landscape changed and we realized with satisfaction that more than half of our journey had been completed.

The MacMillan River was discovered in 1843 by Robert Campbell—a resolute pioneer of the Hudson Bay Company, to whom we owe the first exploration of that section of the northern wilderness. He named it in honor of Chief Factor MacMillan of the Hudson Bay Company. When Dr. George M. Dawson made his famous trip down the Pelly, in 1887, little was known about the river, only a few prospectors having ascended it for a short distance, without finding good prospects. The Klondike rush of 1897 and 1898 sent a large overflow of prospectors up the Pelly and MacMillan, and soon trappers established their trapping lines over the entire country of both rivers almost to their sources.

MacMillan Mountains from the MacMillan River.

PHOTOGRAPH BY W.H. OSGOOD. BY PERMISSION OF THE U.S. BIOLOGICAL SURVEY.

The peaks and ridges of Dromedary Mountain were visible in the distance.

PHOTOGRAPH BY W.H. OSGOOD. BY PERMISSION OF THE U.S. BIOLOGICAL SURVEY.

But it was not until the summer of 1902 that it was explored and mapped, fortunately by those able and energetic men of the Canadian Geological Survey—R. G. McConnell and Joseph Keele. Its total length is about two hundred and eighty-five miles. A hundred and fifty miles up it forks into two well-defined branches. Its width is from three hundred to five hundred feet; its current sluggish, not exceeding three miles an hour in the lower reaches and usually less than that of the Pelly, while above it is more accelerated-from three to five miles in places. Its volume is not quite equal to that of the Pelly River, and its water is much more turgid. Up to the Forks it traverses a timbered valley from one to six miles wide, interspersed with swamps and meadows, and containing numerous small lakes. High clay banks are common along its course, and wide gravel bars occur in a manner similar to those along the Pelly.

The character of the country is mountainous. The MacMillan ranges come close to the river on the north side, the peaks varying from three thousand to five thousand eight hundred feet above sea level. Continuing on the same side is the Kalzas range with Kalzas Peak six thousand one hundred feet high, close to the river. Farther up the river is Plateau Mountain, which continues in high ranges beyond the Forks to the western edge of the main Rockies, designated by McConnell as the Selwyn range. Opposite the MacMillan range, on the south side, are plateau-shaped masses nearly three thousand feet high, broken by wide valleys as far as Dromedary Mountain, where big, massive mountains continue irregularly up the South Fork to the Selwyn range. The river winds back and forth from one side of the valley to the other in a succession of curves.

Surrounded by impressive mountain scenery, progressing with accelerated speed against a slower current, we steamed up the river for two hours, until the boat was tied to the bank for the purpose of cutting and loading wood. The night came on, clear and cold, while the stars glittered through the trees. It was dark at nine o'clock. A large campfire was made, which spread warmth and geniality to all of us sitting about it. That night the thermometer went down to twenty degrees Fahrenheit.

August 27.—An hour after starting, the captain, failing to "read the water," ran the bow into the mud well outside the channel. We pottered about in disgust for two hours before getting her off, as the usual tackle for such purposes had not been brought. The day was clear and calm. As we passed along the MacMillan range, the peaks and ridges of Dromedary Mountain were visible in the distance, and on the north the Kalzas range appeared, its highest summits close to the river. The scenery all day was like the Canadian wilderness with the added grandeur of imposing mountain ranges on both sides. In rounding the numerous curves, we reduced to half speed, so that the average distance was not gained on the day's trip. A flock of geese was seen, and often, on the bars, tracks of moose and bears.

It had become clear to all that the captain was not able to handle the boat. He kept failing to see the channel, even when it was perfectly clear to inexperienced eyes like my own, and, after running on another bar, he exclaimed that it was suicidal to attempt to navigate the river; and at Kalzas Creek, only thirty miles up from the Pelly, announced that we must load our canoes and proceed as best we could. Before reaching there the boat had been tied to the bank to repair an auxiliary rudder, bent because of his bungling, and we were told to unload. Our destination was a hundred and eighty miles beyond, and to proceed that distance in canoes meant nothing less than the failure of the trip. Consternation rapidly developed into indignation. Two hours were lost in discussion, and finally the boat proceeded. Navigation was better until we tied up near the foot of Kalzas Mountain.

August 28.—After an early start we proceeded all day without much trouble, notwithstanding the captain's constant assertions as to the impossibility of advancing. Perhaps we covered a distance of fifty miles. While winding about between the high mountain ranges on both sides, we noticed much "beaver cutting," and also numerous beaver houses, always situated at the edge of the banks of the river, in an eddy outside the current. Only three beavers, however, were seen during the day.

From that part of the river up as far as I went on the North Fork, "beaver cutting" was plentiful wherever large balsam poplars grew on the banks. The beavers had felled many of these trees by gnawing around the butt until it assumed the shape of an hour-glass. It is a common notion that the beaver is so intelligent that it deliberately cuts the tree in such a way as to cause it to fall away from the bank. Many of the trees, however, had fallen in the direction of the river, and some over the bank. We cannot, therefore, graft on the marvelous instinct of the beaver an intelligence which enables it to reason out a method of felling trees which shall determine the direction of their fall. The size of the trees thus felled varied from one to fifteen inches in diameter. The purpose of felling them is to gnaw off the branches and bring them to the houses for a supply of winter food. All winter they subsist on the bark. Houses of a circular shape, usually constructed against the bank near the fallen trees, consist of an irregular ass of sticks of different sizes, with sometimes a few small logs, and the whole chinked with earth. The green branches are packed about the houses and, undoubtedly, the beaver finds a way of reaching them in the winter.

In suitable tributaries and small channels, where the river has cut a course around the land, the beavers make dams, which

Beaver cutting on the bank of the MacMillan River.

PHOTOGRAPH BY W.H. OSGOOD. BY PERMISSION OF THE U.S. BIOLOGICAL SURVEY.

Beaver house in eddy of MacMillan River.

PHOTOGRAPH BY W.H. OSGOOD. BY PERMISSION OF THE U.S. BIOLOGICAL SURVEY.

back up the water to form lakes, and there construct larger houses. When we were on the MacMillan the beavers existed there in a practically undisturbed state, like that of beavers in early times in other parts of North America. Martens and lynxes were so abundant, and the fur of the former was so much more valuable that the trappers had not yet attempted the more difficult task of trapping the beavers. Fortunately but few Indians hunt on the MacMillan River. The lower part of the river is included in the hunting territory of the tribe at Lake Tatlaman. They are reduced to a few families. Beyond, as far as the Forks, the territory belongs to the Indians living at the mouth of the Little Salmon River, but they never come to the MacMillan except in winter, and then they seldom trap beavers.

Indians prefer the easier work of shooting them when the water is open. They are very fond of their flesh and destroy them indifferently in summer and fall. Two years later beaver trapping had begun, and when Selous went up there he found the beavers diminished. In 1908 I saw MacMillan River trappers in Dawson who told me that all had been trapped, which means that not enough were left to make it pay to trap them.

Everywhere in the upper reaches of the river we constantly saw beavers, both swimming in the water and on the banks. As a warning that certain actions of animals must not be interpreted too quickly, Selous has mentioned the resounding slap of the tail which the beaver makes when it dives. This has often been called a warning signal. He mentions two cases of beavers sitting on the bank, which were not alarmed by the slap of the tails of others, even when sounded close by. On the North Fork I myself twice saw beavers dive when I was concealed in the alders near the bank, so that they were wholly unsuspicious. In both cases their tails slapped the water. Some other interpretation of the habit must be attempted—perhaps it is caused by a muscular contraction to assist in sudden diving.

Besides the beavers no animals except red squirrels—always abundant in the woods—had been seen since leaving Dawson. The variety of birds observed on the whole trip was small. Only the delightful weather, the wild aspect of the country, the rugged mountain scenery, and the approach to the hunting country, offset the tediousness of being cooped up on a small steamer day after day, while our patience was tested by doubts as to the ability and disposition of the captain to take the boat up to within a reasonable distance of the Forks.

August 29.—We were awakened by the boat striking hard on a bar, and I heard the captain exclaim that he would not go on. After two hours, we worked it off and proceeded all day until we tied up opposite Plateau Mountain. While gazing at the crest through my field-glasses I saw seven or eight caribou feeding near the top and gradually moving over to the other side.

August 30.—In the morning, just before starting, I saw a single caribou walking along the crest of Plateau Mountain, and we watched it for some time until it was lost to view. This sight of game had encouraged us, as all day we steamed on, making slow progress against more frequent riffles and around sharper curves, until seven o'clock, when the captain ran the boat hard on a bar and it was decided to remain there until morning. Driftwood was abundant and a huge fire was made, so that by its light we could see well enough to cut wood and carry it on the boat.

August 31.—After pulling the boat off the bar she again went hard aground, a hundred yards farther on, owing to the usual stupidity of the captain, whose complaints were becoming so intolerable that we were almost ready to take to our canoes. After working three hours to make it free, we steamed on again, stopping to pick up a beaver which the half-breed, Louis, had killed the night before. Its tail—considered by many, especially Indians, as a great delicacy—was cooked and served, but it proved too rich and oily for our palates. At noon we came to a bend where a log in a drift jam projected out part way in the channel, and although we sent out men who quickly cut it, the captain positively refused to go on; nor were we loath to leave the boat. We unloaded canoes and supplies in the rain, made a rough camp, when Selous, Rungius, and Osgood started off, each tramping in different directions, and returned later without having seen any game or even signs of any.

Thus ended a steamboat trip up one of the sub-arctic rivers of the north-west—a typical trip on the small boats of that country, irresponsibly manned, as they usually are when attempting to navigate new rivers. What a relief later, after a repast of biscuit, tea, and bacon, to sit before a large camp-fire and feel the freedom and liberty of the wilderness! The party was too large to successfully hunt from one camp, so Selous and I planned to go up the North Fork, taking Louis and Coghlan; Rungius and Osgood decided to go with Gage up Russell Creek to the Russell Mountains, while the others were attracted by the country up the South Fork.

September 1.—The next morning all canoes were loaded and we started. Poling, towing, paddling back and forth across the river, we slowly worked up against the current, and at noon reached Russell Creek, where Rungius and Osgood remained to go twelve miles farther up it to the mountain ranges.

Two years before, gold had been discovered on Russell Creek and a concession was obtained and sold to an English company. A young Englishman named Armstrong had been up there all summer with a force of men for the purpose of prospecting it. We met the whole party at the mouth of the creek, where they were constructing boats to take them down river. It was most fortunate for me, since I was able to secure from them a supply of sugar, which by some oversight I had failed to bring. Wishing luck to Rungius and Osgood, the rest of us soon started and late in the afternoon reached the Forks. There Selous and I separated from the others and started up North Fork. Taking canoes up this Fork, especially when the water is low, is a harrowing journey of persistent, hard work.

CHAPTER VI

UP THE NORTH FORK TO THE SELWYN ROCKIES – 1904

THE NORTH FORK of the MacMillan varies in width from seventy-five to two hundred feet. The current races in numerous rapids around sharp curves, from five to eight miles an hour, often along wide bars, and the banks are full of driftwood, piled high in many places, causing great difficulty in taking canoes around it. This Fork resembles a mountain torrent more than the ordinary river of the territory. We were obliged to tow the canoes as far as we went, making use of paddles only for crossing, and poles only to go around driftwood. The country on the right—between the Forks—consists of low, rolling ridges; on the left it rises gradually to the Russell Mountains, which were then white with snow that had fallen the night before. That snow did not melt again before the following spring.

After going three miles we made camp in the spruce woods, where red squirrels were very abundant, chattering on all sides. Selous took his rifle and wandered for a short distance up the river while I went back in the woods. We returned later, and sat before the fire, rejoicing to be separated from a crowd, so that we could realize a more genuine wilderness charm as we watched the sparks of the fire shooting up through the spruce trees, and heard the splashing of the river as it raced around the banks and glided over its rocky bottom.

September 2.—The next day we towed the boats, each of us doing a share of work indifferently with our men, until noon, when we stopped to make tea and eat lunch. With ropes over our shoulders, we took turns at the heavy pulling, walking on the bars, wading in the icy cold water, toiling around driftwood, crossing from one side of the river to the other, and continually straining to drag the boats up the riffles. It was very hard work and progress was slow. The river ran between ridges which were mostly covered with black spruce and poplars, though here and there white birches appeared. The poplars and birches, tinted with fall colors, brightened the wildness of the landscape. On the bars, numerous tracks of bears attested their annual feasting on salmon, an of which had died before our arrival. Moose tracks, most of them old, were also abundant.

Not long after we had lunched, as Selous and I were hauling the canoes, Louis saw a cow moose and her calf well ahead on the other side of the river, and about to cross. Selous, who was ahead, quickly took his rifle from the canoe and crept forward, while we crouched to the ground. As they waded the river, he circled around some driftwood, waded a slough, and shot the cow just as she was about to enter the woods. She staggered back toward the river and fell dead in a slough. As he signalled that she had fallen, I ran forward to follow him. The calf, trotting about in perplexity, suddenly saw him and coming directly toward him stopped to look at him, the hair on its fore-shoulders erect and bristling. Running back, I took my Kodak from the boat and returned in time to take a photograph, including both Selous and the calf, which was by that time trotting toward the woods. The wind was blowing directly from him to the calf.

The others then came forward, and the moose was dragged up on the bank and dressed. Here was meat for the first time in several days, and we camped there to enjoy the feast. Selous taught me a new delicacy, the udder, which was cut out and boiled for several hours until soft and tender. The next morning it was sliced, rolled in flour, and fried. It proved to be delicious, the choicest morsel of the animal. The same is true, as I learned later, of the udders of sheep, caribou, and deer.

While dressing the moose a small black gnat, slightly larger than the midge of Eastern Canada, swarmed about us and its bite was particularly annoying. The small gnats begin to be troublesome all over the northern country about the middle of August, after most of the mosquitoes are gone, and continue until well into September. They usually are found close to running water, but are seldom seen above timber-line.

We took our rifles and went out for the remainder of the day, Selous going up the bars, while I went back on the ridges between the Forks. I followed a brook through dense spruces, swamps, and deep sphagnum moss, to the top of a ridge. High up on these ridges I found well-beaten moose trails, usually running parallel with the river; in some places they were worn three or four feet through the moss and soft ground to the roots of the spruce trees. These trails are well-defined routes of moose travel, and though intersected by others which are less deeply worn, they parallel all the rivers and often the smaller streams. The country was completely covered with timber and very broken, the slopes of the ridges often very steep; and numerous brooks rising from springs or small lakes farther back fell through small canons. There was little sign of game outside of the moose trails; birds were very scarce, but rabbits and red squirrels abundant. Such is the character of the country between the forks until well up the river near the mountain ranges.

Selous and the calf moose, September 2.

Returning I found a cheerful camp-fire, and after gorging with meat, we chatted awhile before sleeping. Suddenly, a short wailing cry sounded from the dark woods not far distant. It was made by the calf, and we both felt glad that it was old enough to take care of itself, after the loss of its mother. We did not hear it again, and slept in the cold, crisp air under the shining stars.

September 3.—The next day was one of continuous towing in shallow water against a swifter current; the driftwood increasing; the river curving more frequently. At one point, near a high escarped bank, where the river bends sharply to the south, we found a large beaver dam, constructed across the mouth of a creek-channel, made by the escape of a small volume of water around a bar some distance above. Behind it were acres of water flooding willows, alders, and poplars, and not far back a family of beavers occupied a large house in three or four feet of water, surrounded by high poplars and willows. Selous and I waded to it and after examining it with interest I took some photographs of it.

We made camp late in the afternoon near a flat swamp covered with willows, alders, dwarf birch, and strewn with burnt timber. After tramping about in it, Selous returned and reported more fresh moose signs than we had seen at any point along the river. Here we first had a glimpse of the Selwyn range of mountains, rising ahead in majestic peaks and offering encouragement for a better game country.

As we were sitting about the fire fifty feet away from the bank, in a dense thicket of woods, Louis suddenly heard a bull moose walking on a bar on the opposite side of the river. It was several degrees below frost and Selous, though without trousers or shoes, took his rifle and followed by Louis and myself picked his way in the dark through the thick, tangled woods to the bank of the river. But the moose had entered the poplars and Louis in vain tried to entice it out by calling with a birch-bark horn.

September 4.—In the morning a cold stiff head-wind chilled us and continued all day, as we plodded on under conditions constantly becoming more difficult; and we were disappointed not to see the mountains ahead, which were covered with clouds. We finally arrived at Barr Creek, where two trappers, Jack Barr and Crosby, had been trapping the previous winter. We had seen a flock of mergansers that day—the first ducks observed on the North branch. Few birds of any kind had been noticed, except an occasional hawk floating through the air or sitting on a dead tree.

We pitched camp in a delightful spot in heavy spruce woods, and Selous, as usual, went up the river to prospect for game. I had each day set out traps for small mammals, but without success. In front of camp, across the river, were wide bars covered with willows, poplars, and alders, all glowing with a rich fall color. The river, swift and deep, fairly roared as it swirled around a huge pile of driftwood and beat against the banks.

September 5.—It was snowing when we started; the wind continued, and it was freezing in the afternoon, but the travelling was a little better because of more bars and less driftwood. It was gloomy work; all the hills and ridges covered with thick clouds so we could see nothing of the country ahead. At three in the afternoon, when I came around a curve while Selous was a few hundred yards ahead, I saw a large black bear, feeding high on the slope of a ridge which extended parallel with the river. Attracting Selous's attention I hastened forward and urged him to go after it since he had never before seen a wild bear in the wilderness. Coghlan, Louis, and I tied the canoes to the bank, and watched the stalk, all of which could be plainly seen from where we stood on the bank of the river. On the slopes of the ridge were many clear areas, which had been given a reddish appearance by dwarf birch and huckleberry bushes, then colored by the frost. It was in one of these clear spaces that the bear was feeding. At intervals, between them, strips of dense timber and undergrowth, several hundred feet wide, extended down to the river. Selous started upward in a circle, and soon we saw him climbing the ridge in one of the clearings, where there was but one strip of timber between him and the bear, which continued to feed, gradually approaching the timber. Having marked well the spot where he had last seen the bear, he arrived at a point exactly opposite it and started directly toward the timber. His approach was then against the wind and he cautiously and slowly went forward. Through my glasses, I could plainly see the bear as it approached the woods, directly in line with Selous's advance, its glossy black coat reflecting the sunlight, which at times caused it to appear very large. Both Selous and the bear entered the timber at the same time, apparently approaching directly toward each other, and momentarily I expected to hear a shot. Soon we saw Selous emerge a little above where the bear had entered, and proceed with caution, carefully looking about. We knew that he had not seen the bear. Afterward, I learned that the timber was filled with small spruces, alders, and dwarf birch, so he could see only a few feet in any direction. But he must have gone through noiselessly and with skill, passing the bear within a hundred feet or so, for shortly after he appeared, the bear came out a little below the point where Selous had entered the timber, and continued travelling in the opposite direction, still feeding, and wholly unconscious of its lucky escape. It fed along indifferently until it reached the trail which Selous had made when ascending. Then it suddenly threw up its head, gave a great jump, and running with speed down the ridge disappeared in the timber. Once before, in Mexico, I had seen a similar action on the part of a grizzly bear when it crossed the fresh trail of a man, and it was extremely interesting thus to witness a second case. Selous, still looking for the bear, had passed out of sight along the ridge. When the bear began to run, I immediately crossed the river, and, in my efforts to hurry in the direction it had taken, almost bogged myself in a slough. I could not find a trace of it and returned. Selous came in later, after we had made camp, thoroughly perplexed at not having seen the bear at all. Though an excellent stalk was frustrated by such bad luck, the sight of game was stimulating and made us eager to advance, particularly since our goal was then not very far ahead.

September 6.—We had undertaken to go up the North Branch without any knowledge of the country, so it was necessary for us to explore for a good place to find game. The next day was the most trying one of our trip up the North Branch It was cold, cloudy, windy, and wintry. The river was narrower and more tortuous; its banks were continually lined with driftwood and bordered by ice; the current was swifter, and often the water was so shallow that we had difficulty in towing the canoes without unloading them. Until late in the afternoon we worked while hands, legs, and feet were numb with cold. At a point where the river bends to the north and finds its course between high mountain ranges, not far below Husky Dog Creek, we decided to stop and make a reconnaissance with a view to locating a camp at timber-line, high on the ranges to the south. It was so misty that we could not see the mountains, and soon snow began to fall and continued more or less all night. It was dark at 7:30.

September 7.—In the morning three or four inches of snow covered the ground, and snow continued to fall at intervals all day. Selous soon started to investigate moose signs on the flats, while I directed my course toward the mountains, hoping to find a good place near timber-line to make a camp, and also a good route up the slopes, since we were obliged to carry our equipment and provisions on our backs.

South of the river, a hundred feet from the bank, is a terrace thirty or forty feet high which extends north, parallel with the river for many miles. The country behind it, both flat and rolling, extends two miles to the foot of the mountains. This broad, level country, all burnt over, was covered with moss, brush, huckleberry bushes, and cranberries, and strewn with tangled logs. Swampy in places, it is dotted with small lakes, and the standing burnt trees scattered through it give an aspect of grim desolation. Old moose tracks were everywhere, and well-cut trails parallel with the river were frequent. While passing through it I saw several flocks of migrating robins, a grouse, some hawk owls, and many Alaska jays and red squirrels. But no other animals were observed during the rest of the day, and the fresh snow disclosed no tracks of any kind, except those of red squirrels.

I climbed the lower ridges, ascended the mountains to timber-line, and followed along the side of a deep ravine, through which a fair-sized brook, cutting in some places deep canons, came down from a rather broad valley, between high, rough mountains. This valley, gently rising, was enclosed in an amphitheater of rugged mountains, rising abruptly to high peaks and jagged crests glistening in the snow. All through the northern country such places are called *draws*, signifying, I think, a suitable conformation of the land to "draw" the water from the adjacent mountain slopes. At the heads of each of these draws above timber, there is usually an area, level or gently sloping, covered with dwarf birch, willow, and alder, all extending well up the adjacent slopes. The ground is boggy, and the abundant willow growth provides the favorite food of the moose in fall and winter. Everywhere at the head of a draw

Selous towing the canoe, September 6.

old moose tracks were so abundant that the place looked like a cow pasture, and as many tracks were observed among the willows of the higher slopes as in the area below. A well-defined moose trail always runs on each side of the creeks which flow from the draws, and the trail often leads over low saddles between the ranges to the head of another draw.

I chose a place for a camp close to the brook, near the end of timber, in a location suitable for climbing the mountains on either side. The mountains were then so covered with mist that I could not use my field-glasses to find likely places for sheep. On returning I learned that Selous had seen no fresh signs of any kind. Our limited time, the difficulty of climbing the mountains covered with light snow, our ignorance of the country, and the lack of game seen up to that time, did not look encouraging; and since the snow continued to fall, we felt some anxiety as to the ultimate success of our trip.

September 8.—Snow was falling when we rose, but it was a wet snow and not likely to continue all day; we therefore decided to start. A cache was made by suspending some poles about ten feet up between trees, and on it were placed the provisions and materials we could not carry. These caches are always necessary, as otherwise provisions might be taken by bears, wolverines, or wolves. Packs were made up and, putting them on our backs, we started about noon, crossed the flat, and while climbing the ridges were soaked to the skin from the wet snow suspended on the brush. This caused us to become chilled as we toiled upward with aching backs through deep snow and thick undergrowth. The mountains, covered with mist, could not be seen. Late in the afternoon, as we were walking on the slope near the upper flat of the draw, Louis, who was ahead, saw a bull moose feeding in the willow brush some seven or eight hundred yards below, near the brook. Selous, who was following Louis, immediately started to find an approach to it, and concealed as we were behind some low spruces, we had the pleasure of watching the whole stalk.

For a few moments I watched the moose as he was standing and feeding, but as I turned my head to note Selous's course, the bull apparently disappeared, and Louis whispered that he had lain down. I looked carefully through my field-glasses, but he blended so perfectly with the willows and alders that he was not visible. Finally, as he moved his head, I could make out the tops of his horns, then hardly distinguishable from the brush because of the strips of velvet still hanging on them. We waited with keen interest for Selous to come in sight. He had started in a circular course to approach the moose against the wind, which was blowing up the brook. He finally appeared and began to approach with the utmost caution, advancing in a straight line toward the exact spot where the moose was resting. Selous was too experienced to have neglected to mark a tall tree near which the moose was standing when he started, so that he could find the place after circling through the woods. Finally, coming nearer, he advanced step by step to within thirty feet and stood looking. Louis whispered: "Now you see moose jump and run!" But I saw Selous approach a few steps, bend forward, put up his rifle and fire. He immediately shouted, and knowing the moose was dead we hurried to the spot. Selous had suspected that the moose was lying down, and at last had seen the tips of its horns. A step or two nearer brought the head and neck of the unsuspecting bull in sight, and the bullet was delivered at the base of the brain. It was a large old bull, with broad, flat horns, well palmated, spreading fifty-seven inches—an unusually fine trophy.

That was our introduction to a camp soon made near the carcass. We had brought only a large piece of canvas, and when poles had been cut and inclined against a cross-pole, it was thrown over them. Spruce bows were strewn beneath it and the shelter was complete. A big fire was started; the packs were opened; their contents arranged in order under the shelter, and after feasting on fresh meat we sat in front of the fire that night feeling more cheerful than at any time since leaving Dawson. We were at last camped high up among the mountains, a fine trophy was in our possession, and we slept soundly after enjoying the dim picture of the rugged mountain in front, its peak, viewed through the spark-spangled smoke of the fire, towering high above like a huge white spectre. The mercury responded to the higher elevation by descending to sixteen degrees Fahrenheit above zero, the lowest recorded up to that time.

September 9.—It was snowing the next morning, but cleared soon after I started to climb the ridge north of camp and ascend the high mountains beyond. Selous remained in camp to prepare his trophy. The snow on the low spruces and dwarf birches gave a true wintry aspect to the landscape. Up to that time I had not convinced myself that leather moccasins were a failure for walking in the snow, but during the ascent of a steep slope, covered with five inches of snow, I soon realized it. Slipping and often falling, it was next to impossible to climb, but finally I reached the top. The sky was perfectly clear and for the first time I beheld the landscape of the Selwyn ranges.

They are entirely different from the Ogilvie Rockies. Instead of a series of parallel ranges, the Selwyns consist of irregular groups of mountains, often isolated by wide valleys, the summits from six to eight thousand feet above sea level. The sculpturing of the granite is bold, rugged, and massive, the shattered pinnacled crests forming an imposing sky-line. Timberline is between three and four thousand feet above sea level.

Looking below over the vast area of burnt ground, wild and desolate, I could see the river continually curving in its course. Beyond it were two high mountain ranges which did not obstruct a view of the sharp peaks and broken crests of

Selous's bull, shot September 8.

We endured it sitting under the shelter. September 14.

the Russell Mountains. Toward the south-west were the lower ridges and timbered country, including the area between the Forks; and directly south were valleys and woods, extending several miles to a lofty plateau-shaped mountain, its broad dome deceiving the eye as to its altitude. Looking up the river, the vision was lost in a horizon of mountains and peaks, some misty and dim, others glittering in the paths of sunlight where ever it broke through the clouds. The valley above camp was characteristic—a broad area surrounded by an amphitheatre of the highest peaks, rising above shaggy crests and often above vast precipices. Below the highest peak, almost suspended at the foot of a great cliff high on the mountain-side, the protruding slope held a beautiful little lake covered with clear, silvery ice, which reflected the crags and peaks above it. A little farther on, along the same range, but still higher up, was another lake set in almost perpendicular walls of granite, which surrounded it on three sides. The whole country was covered with snow and seemed bleak and inhospitable.

As I looked over the small lake a golden eagle was soaring along the cliffs, rising now and then to the crest, and, after circling over the peaks, again descended until it floated across the valley to the higher summits beyond. Here and there I heard the whistling chatter of a ground squirrel still defying the snow and cold before retiring into its hole to sleep. I wandered about the mountain top and along the crest, hopelessly unable to make much progress because of my slippery moccasins, without seeing tracks or signs of sheep, and at times, when the sun shone through the clouds and mist, almost blinded by the glare of the fresh snow. I returned to camp at dark, somewhat discouraged by the difficulty of ranging over mountains covered with light snow which was not deep enough to provide a foothold. Besides, many of the slopes were so icy that in any case much distance could not be covered in the short hours of daylight.

CHAPTER VII

SEARCHING FOR SHEEP – 1904

SEPTEMBER 10.—THE thermometer again went to sixteen degrees during the night, and the next day was cloudy, with an occasional patch of blue sky, but there was a strong wind all the afternoon. Selous went to the mountains on the south; the men to the river to bring back some provisions; and I over the north ridges to investigate the mountains beyond. I wore shoes of rubber with leather uppers, similar to those used by lumbermen in the forests of the North. In wet snow the uppers would soak through and the feet would soon become wet, but though far from good foot-gear for climbing, they were not so slippery as the moccasins.

Soon after going over the ridge I saw bear-tracks leading down into the timber, and followed them for some distance until convinced they had been made several hours before. Then, abandoning the trail, I climbed the face of the mountain and proceeded along the slope. The tracks of a cow and calf moose soon appeared, showing that they had travelled a short distance outside of the timber to feed on the willows. Crossing a small draw, I climbed to the top of a high smooth mountain, on the left of which was the head of a magnificent elevated draw extending some two or three miles in level, swampy meadows dotted with miniature lakes.

The tracks of a ewe and lamb appeared on the top of the mountain and I followed them along the crest. While walking I flushed a large flock of ptarmigan already pure white. The trail led down a slope so precipitous that I could not descend. Several more flocks of ptarmigan were seen flying about the rocks near the crests; a few ground-squirrels were running about, and an eagle was soaring back and forth against the background of snow on the range immediately to the east. Below, about a hundred yards above timber, I saw the tracks of a band of ten or twelve sheep which had come from the north. All along the trail they had scattered to browse among the willows, and numerous bare spots indicated that they had pawed away the snow to get at grass and weeds.

After searching, a difficult descent was found, and accomplishing it, I followed the trail until too late to proceed further. Returning to camp, which was reached shortly after dark, I heard the cheering news that Selous had killed two caribou, one a large bull with fine antlers, and had seen a cow near them. But what was still more interesting, he had seen a small band of ewe sheep which appeared very wild, and among them had observed two ewes, as white as those of the Ogilvie Rockies, each having two lambs, three of which were white, the *fourth as dark as Ovis stonei*! The men had returned and reported having seen a small brown bear—undoubtedly the brown phase of the black bear.

September 11.—The night was warmer and the next day was fairly clear. Selous went with the men to get his heads, and I returned to the sheep tracks of the day before, about four miles distant from camp. They finally crossed the draw into the timber and through my glasses could see the spoor leading up the ridges beyond, too far to hunt for them and return to camp that day. I then climbed a mountain to the east, and walked through the snow-drifts along the crest, among scattering flocks of ptarmigan, until noon, when seated myself to take a bit of lunch and also to scan through my field-glasses the new country toward the north. Within an hour, when looking through the glasses across a small basin to some ridges beyond, a white ewe appeared, accompanied by a *black lamb*. By white I mean that its appearance was as white as that of the sheep of the Kenai Peninsula, though an inspection of its skin would have revealed dark hairs scattered through it. The lamb appeared black, but the color was nearly that of *Ovis stonei*. They descended with the greatest caution, stopping every few feet to look about, and particularly to gaze into the basin below.

A very steep slope in front of me fell to a low ridge, and though in plain sight, I carefully slid by degrees to the foot of the slope, stopping motionless every time the ewe looked up, for she had reached the basin and while browsing among the willows, kept watching above as well as in other directions. Proceeding along the ridge to the edge of the basin I hid behind a willow bush about five hundred feet above the ewe, and watched them for a long time. They soon fed toward me and came within a hundred yards, when I carefully noted the colors. I have never ceased regretting that I did not kill and preserve them (or science. In half an hour, stones were heard falling from the slope above and two more ewes appeared, descending, both of a whitish appearance like the darker ones near Coal Creek. All continued to browse on willows and scratch away the snow to reach feed on the ground. Among the willows and bare patches of ground, their color blended so perfectly with their surroundings, that often, after glancing away from them for a moment, it was difficult to see them again. After awhile they began to return slowly up the slope, continuing to feed until finally I noticed the two single ewes standing motionless for a long time, directing a steady gaze to the north.

Looking in that direction, I saw, about half a mile distant, a cow moose and her calf, feeding among the willows on a ridge the other side of a small draw; they were gradually advancing in my direction. There in the snow fields, under towering peaks and rugged mountains, while sheep were feeding close by on the broken slopes, I had my first sight of moose above timber-line in the northern wilderness. The cow, between pauses to browse on willows, continued walking without looking up or showing the least suspicion of enemies, presenting a significant contrast to the alert, watchful sheep. When the moose had passed out of sight near the foot of the ridge, I began to walk slowly toward that part of the slope where they were apt to ascend. When I was within one hundred feet of the edge, they appeared, and, instantly seeing me, stopped to gaze at me.

My Kodak was ready, and after a snapshot was taken I began slowly to approach them. The wind was blowing at right angles and evidently carried my scent past them. As I came to within forty or fifty feet, the cow appeared to resent my nearer approach, inclined her ears back, made a slight motion of the lips, and stood in such an attitude of warning that I thought she might possibly charge me. The calf, assuming an attitude of readiness for instant flight, was standing nearer the edge of the slope, its head turned away from me. After taking a nearer snapshot, I determined to walk slowly in a circle for the purpose of testing the effect of coming in the wind, which would give them my scent. Gradually I circled around to the right, and suddenly, as a breeze caught me in the right position, the cow jumped as if receiving an electric shock, and, followed by the calf, went trotting down the slope, to disappear in the timber below. Never was the comparative effect of sight and scent better tested on a cow moose, and in a locality which human beings seldom frequent.

The cow appeared to resent my nearer approach, September 11.

While retracing my steps, I noticed that the sheep were not in sight, but when climbing the mountain I had descended, the ewe and black lamb suddenly appeared on the crest above, glanced down at me for a moment and then ran off. It was very cold and blowing hard before I reached camp, some time after dark, to learn that Selous had followed tracks of both sheep and caribou without seeing the animals. His sympathy was comforting in our common annoyance because of the snow, which, though it glistened in the sun and spread a sparkling white mantle over the country, adding beauty to the landscape, made the mountain hunting most difficult and discouraging.

September 12.—Again I was in quest of rams, and started early for the mountains at the head of the draw. A heavy snow blizzard soon developed and continued at intervals all day. For three miles I tramped through the timber, then to the head, above which, in all directions, numerous marmots were whistling among the broken rocks. I climbed on the crest and after a brief glimpse of the top, the snow beat down so hard that I could see but a few yards, and was obliged to return, reaching camp at dark. I had seen old bear tracks in the timber, and had noticed old moose tracks everywhere on the mountain slopes as high as the willows grew, which in some places on the south exposures was nearly to the crest. Selous had occupied his day by following for several hours the tracks of a bull moose and two cows. The tracks had led in a circle to his own trail made in the morning. As the moose crossed it, he read on the snow that they had broken into a trot, consequently he knew it was useless to continue following.

September 13.—It rained and stormed all night and was warmer the next morning. I climbed the ridges back of camp, proceeded along the mountain slope, crossed the meadows and followed a well-worn sheep-trail to the top of the ridges beyond. Following the ridge against a strong wind, while it continued to snow and rain alternately, I found a bull moose's trail made the night before and leading to the timber on the other side. Continuing, I reached the next mountain, and ascended its peak after working my way upward among boulders and coarse, broken rock, the spaces between them filled with snow which caused many falls and bruises. Later, the snow ceased and the clouds began to rise so that I could look over on the slopes of a high, massive mountain still farther to the west, and separated from me by a deep valley. There, well up near the crest, I saw through my field-glasses, nine sheep, apparently ewes and lambs. The rain again began to fall, so, returning along the ridge and reaching the foot at dark, I struggled for three miles back to camp. Ptarmigan were very abundant on the mountains south of the meadows, and a flock of migrating robins had passed over me.

Selous had been out all day without seeing any game, and since we had exhausted the country within available walking distance from camp, we decided to move the next day near the meadows I had crossed in the morning. Rain fell all night and still more all the next day. We endured it, sitting under the shelter. It grew colder the next night and the following day broke clear.

September 15.—We made up our packs, climbed the ridge, and proceeded along the mountain-slope to the meadows. After crossing them, a camping site was found a hundred yards up a slope, in the timber near the sheep-trail which I had followed two days before. It rained at intervals as we were "packing" over to the new camping place, and it was snowing as we made it, but the snow soon ceased falling.

Selous went to make a reconnaissance of the ridges opposite the north end of the meadows, while I again took to the sheep-trail, intending to go over to the big mountain where I had seen sheep two days before. Three well defined sheep-trails crossed the meadows and passed up through the timber on both sides of the draw. In the timber and for a considerable distance above, was a dense growth of dwarf birch mixed with willow and ,alder. The fact that these trails, seldom used by the sheep, were so well beaten that all the underbrush had been carefully cleaned from them, is evidence of their having been trodden for numerous generations. The dense growth of underbrush made walking through the timber most difficult and tiresome when off the sheep-trails.

Passing north along the ridge and ascending the next mountain, I saw on top of a high ridge to the north-west two small lakes surrounded by narrow meadows, which from my position seemed almost suspended in the air. Through my field-glasses, a cow moose followed by two calves was seen feeding on the shore. I watched them for awhile as they browsed on the willows, when suddenly a mist was blown on the mountains, rain began to fall, and it became so dark that I could see only a few feet below. The weather had again thwarted me, so turning back in mist, rain, and snow, I descended through the woods in the dark, fighting every step against the thick growth of spruce and underbrush, until camp was finally reached. Selous had seen a band of nine ewes on the mountain which I had approached, but not wishing to disturb my ground he had tramped all the afternoon without seeing anything more.

September 16.—It snowed about half an hour early the next morning as I was heading through the meadows directly for the north mountain, but all the rest of the day a strong wind blew from the north. Just before I arrived at the foot, I saw a single ewe and lamb, both white in appearance, following a sheep-trail high on the slope. This trail was so well beaten that it was clearly defined in the broken rock and visible at a long distance. They soon passed out of sight around the slope, and with very slow progress, zigzagging up through snow

The summits of the Selwyn Rockies, September 16.

Selwyn Rockies, September 18.

and over slippery rock, I gained the top of the mountain—a great dome, shaped snow-field glittering in the sun and almost blinding me.

This mountain was the first one rising above the valley of the river where it bends to an easterly course and a new landscape stretched before me. For the first time there was an unobstructed view to the north. Below, bordering the river, was the same desolate flat country all covered with timber, and with lakes and meadow glades scattered about, some of them high on the slopes of the ridges; while rising from the dark-timbered area, as far as the eye could reach, extending beyond the Stewart River on the north, and toward the Mackenzie divide on the east, were parallel chains of majestic, snow-covered mountains—a vast, austere wilderness, all the mighty summits shining under the dazzling rays of the sun. These were the Selwyn Rockies.

Chilled by the strong, cold wind, I went along the crest, constantly pausing to scan the steep slopes below, now advancing to the edge of a vast precipice, now rounding a ledge to seek a view of places where sheep might remain sheltered from the wind. There was not a sound but that from the gusts of wind whirling the snow in clouds about me, and the occasional croaks of ravens flying by. Several large flocks of ptarmigan passed close to the crest, and when flying across the sun their wings reflected an exquisite tint of pink in contrast with the white plumage of their bodies.

After traversing the crest to the north end, I started to descend the steep, dangerous slope in order to return along its foot where I would be less exposed to the piercing wind. When half way down I seated myself to take a look through my field-glasses, and saw seven ewes and lambs lying down a hundred yards above the timber directly below me. They were all alertly watching, and one ewe seemed to be looking directly at me. Quickly sliding into a hollow which led down the slope, I worked my way to a ledge about three hundred yards above them, and, creeping to the edge, looked over. They were still lying down, all looking up the mountain except one, which kept watching below. They had not seen me, and were peacefully resting, but keeping their heads erect in alert, nervous attitudes. My disappointment at not finding rams on such a high, rough mountain was keen, and fearing that other sheep from this district might not be obtained, I determined to kill two of them. Taking a seat at the edge of the ledge for the purpose of studying a method of descent, I found that it was impossible without coming in plain sight of the sheep, and in the hope that they might feed upward toward me was obliged to wait patiently until they should rise. It would have been trying to the patience to have waited, as I did for three hours on that bleak slope, had not the wilderness given up to my eyes one of those rare sights which ever after haunts the memory.

Directly below the vast timbered area, cut with canons and dotted with small lakes, extended in rolling ridges to and beyond, the river. The deep valley of Husky Dog Creek was plainly in view, winding upward to a large lake a thousand feet above the river's dancing riffles which as the current raced over its stony bottom, shimmered in the sunlight. On the north, not far from Husky Dog Creek, a large yellow meadow-land containing a small lake made a bright patch in the dark timber. A look through my field-glasses revealed a large bulky animal walking across it. The animal, now standing still, now feeding, finally remained motionless in the centre for an hour, and then continued to feed again, still keeping in sight in the meadow-land. It was a big solitary bull moose, its horns not distinguishable enough in the distance to show their size.

Shortly after seeing him, when looking over the country on the other side of a deep cañon below me, I saw another small glade containing a tiny lake, its ice sparkling in the sun—a mysterious little opening buried in the wild spruce forest. There I beheld another large bull moose, his huge antlers shining apparently pure white under the sun, and near him a cow and a calf. Silently, alone, unseen, while the wonderful panorama of landscape was spread out before me, I watched that picture of wild life. I was unsuspected by all living creatures except the ravens which occasionally circled above me uttering their hoarse croaks.

For three hours, as I shivered and kept low behind a large rock, the sheep and the moose remained in sight. The bull with the cow seemed to feed about the meadow, its head close to the ground as if cropping the grass off the small hummocks; while the cow, quite indifferent to him, kept browsing on the willows along the edge of the woods, its calf sometimes near, at other times disappearing altogether in the spruces. After an hour, the bull lay down in the centre of the meadow near the lake, while the cow continued feeding. The bull had evidently sequestered the cow for awhile in that hidden spot, to enjoy his short family life-not always, perhaps, so easily obtained. It would not have been a difficult matter to stalk with a chance of success, for I could lay out a good course against the wind to a knoll above and near the meadow which was little more than half a mile distant from me. But having resolved not to go for moose until I had secured sufficient specimens of sheep, I did not want to lose an opportunity when sheep were practically within shot below me.

Finally, the ewes rose and began feeding along the slope in a direction away from me. There was no alternative, and I put up the three-hundred-yard sight. At the first shot a ewe fell dead, and another at the third—both struck in the neck. The others dashed diagonally up the slope, not impeded in the least by the ice, snow, and slippery rocks.

Immediately after firing, I looked through my field-glasses at the nearer bull moose. He had evidently heard the shot, for he was standing and looking up the mountain in my direction, in which attitude he remained until I hurried down the slope to a point where the glade was lost to view. All the ewes, which I had examined carefully through my field-glasses, were of the same color as the darker ones killed on Coal Creek. I gralloched both and skinned the back of one and relieved it of its saddles, which I shouldered as I began the tramp of five miles across the rough country back to camp. It was my intention to come back and get the skins and skulls. Before dark I had struggled across the side of the mountain, and during the last hour stumbled in the darkness through bog, hummocks, and brush, until I thought I was opposite camp and went up in the timber. Not finding it, a shout brought back a welcome response from Selous. I had passed the spot by a hundred yards. The men had gone down to the river, where they were passing the night, and were to return the next day with more provisions. Some tenderloin mutton was soon cooking over the fire, and Selous related his experience of the day, which had resulted in a long, hard tramp without seeing anything but caribou tracks.

CHAPTER VIII

LOOKING FOR RAMS – 1904

SEPTEMBER 17.—THE next day I hunted the ridges and mountains behind camp, and, after a careful search, was obliged to return without having seen anything except some new sheep tracks which indicated the presence of a band somewhere in that locality, and warned me that the country had better be avoided for a day or two. The ground-squirrels had all retired for the winter, but red squirrels were abundant in the woods. Several large flocks of ravens were seen; possibly they were migrating to another locality. Selous had climbed over the mountains on the north-east and found a magnificent draw at the head of Clearwater Creek. There he had killed a bull moose with very small horns, although they appeared large when he shot it. The moon was nearly full and judging by the new tracks of bulls, then occurring everywhere even on the tops of the ridges, the rut was in full swing and the bulls were travelling widely.

September 18.—The temperature was falling fast when we went to sleep, and in the morning the thermometer recorded six degrees above zero. Selous took Louis to accompany him to the; Clearwater draw, and I started to climb the mountain in front of camp. It was clear all day and a cold wind swept the snow in great clouds about the crests. Passing through the timber, I saw the fresh us trail of a grizzly bear going north along the foot of the slope. I began to ascend, but it became steeper and steeper, and as it had been so cold the night before, an inch of snow which covered it was very dry and slippery, and parts of the slope where it had blown away were almost ice. The ascent became more difficult and I had to stretch out my hands and fairly crawl until reaching a point where I could not retrace my steps without slipping. It was so precipitous that it was very dangerous to continue. I had to use the butt of my rifle as a staff and jam it into the frozen ground at each step until, to my relief, the crest was gained. I crossed the rolling fields of snow extending to the main range beyond, and climbing a mountain proceeded along the crest, scanning the country on the other side. No sheep were seen, nor any tracks, and I descended, took up the bear's trail, and followed it until necessary to turn back if camp was to be reached by dark. I had observed through my field-glasses a band of sheep on the mountains north-east of camp and thought that I could distinguish two dark rams. I noticed that the night before a wolverine had followed the back track of Selous's trail to a point opposite camp, where it had crossed the meadows and entered the woods some distance away from the shelter.

After supper, Coghlan and I were sitting about the fire, having concluded that Selous and Louis were passing the night near the Clearwater draw, when we heard them coming up through the woods. As Selous approached the fire, there was an elasticity in his step that did not signify an arduous day's tramp without success, and it was pleasant to learn that he had killed two moose. One had small horns, the other a magnificent pair, sixty-seven inches in spread, with very large burrs and broad blades, one of which was slightly deformed. It was altogether the wildest and most impressive moose-head that I have ever seen. It alone made his long trip from England to those northern wilds a success, and none but those who have suffered discomfort and discouragement of continuous bad weather and tiresome and difficult tramping over rough country can appreciate how richly his hard, persistent work had deserved this reward.

September 19.—That night was still colder, and in the morning the thermometer recorded one above zero, but the day was calm, without a cloud in the sky, and with a light breeze blowing. I ascended the sheep-trail, hoping to find the band of sheep known to be somewhere on the range behind camp. After reaching the top, a flock of robins, the last observed, went by; a wolverine's tracks wandered all over the ridge; and a little further along, the tracks of a black bear and cub crossed over to the timber on the west.

Looking through my field-glasses at the mountain toward the north, I saw thirteen sheep descending in single file on a sheep-trail, all coming in my direction. Quickly advancing several hundred yards, as they disappeared in a saddle between the uneven slopes, I stretched flat on my stomach in the trail, and thus concealed by the formation of the surface, waited. After a while they came in sight, still in the trail and not more than a quarter of a mile away. Two of them were dark, almost like *Ovis stonie*, two slightly lighter; the remaining nine were white, like the sheep of the Ogilvie Rockies. Two of the darker ones were three-year-old rams. Lightly and quickly they stepped along, now running a few jumps, now separating in disorder, and after standing rigidly to scrutinize the surrounding country, they again advanced in single file. Before I could realize it, they were within a hundred yards, on a level with me. Aiming at a ram, my rifle misfired twice, but the third pull of the trigger sent a bullet which killed him. A second shot killed the other ram, and the third, a dark ewe, as the band was running in a circle. Twice I fired at the remaining dark ewe and missed, but at the next shot the bullet struck her and she began to totter in such a way that I knew the wound was serious. The band stopped for a moment and began to walk toward the other side of the ridge while I was taking my Kodak from my rucksack. The wounded one staggered along and I followed quickly. The band stopped to look at me, and being near I took several photographs of it. All the time while I was following, a breeze blew directly from me to them, and my scent did not frighten them. Soon they walked away, and finally broke into a run as they circled around the top and disappeared. It was about noon.

Walking ahead I saw the wounded ewe fifty yards below, lying down on the slope, and a final shot killed it. Here at last was success. Although the rams were small, I had secured a fine series of the sheep of this district, and that was the main object of my trip. Under a blue sky, in the cold, crisp air, warmed by the shining sun, I worked until dark to take the skins off. I then put two of the heads in my rucksack, threw the four skins over my shoulders, and slowly staggered down the slope and through the woods, which were then dimly lighted by moonlight.

Alas for the remainder of that band! Without suspicion of danger they had circled around and descended by the same trail on which I had come up in the morning. Selous, who had remained in camp all day to prepare his moose scalp, had gone for a moment to the water hole back of the shelter, when he saw them standing near on the trail. Not knowing that I had killed any sheep, and in order that we might not miss the chance to get mutton so close to camp, he permitted Louis to take the rifle and kill two.

I had not even paused to eat lunch, and after refreshing myself .with tea and food, we sat about the crackling fire, which radiated its genial warmth through the freezing dry air. After going under my sleeping robe, for a long time I remained awake, inspired by the infinite glory of a wonderful aurora flashing in an arc from mountain to mountain. The woods, the snowy meadows, and the rugged mountains before us were bathed in the soft moonlight under that magnificent, brilliantly lighted circle of flashing light.

September 20.—In the morning the thermometer recorded three degrees below zero, and just after waking, as I was looking along the bleak crest of the mountain opposite, my eye caught a large, dark object on the skyline. Quickly taking my field-glasses, a sight was revealed that will never be forgotten. A large bull moose, the monarch of the vast northern forest, stood motionless on the crest, gazing at the country below. His antlers appeared large and white under the sunlight, as the outline of his huge form stood out boldly against the background of cliffs and snowy peaks behind. What a pleasure it was to have Selous there to enjoy with me that wonderful picture. The moose soon turned back out of sight, and, after a bite of breakfast, I went well toward the lower end of the meadows to a point where the wind was favorable, and gradually climbed to the crest, hoping that he might still remain above the timber. His trail indicated that he had descended to a strip of forest extending up a small draw, and emerging on the other side he had continued to the main area of woods beyond. For a long distance the blood sprinkled on the snow along his trail revealed the romance of the annual rut-rivalry and strife. His battle must have been unsuccessfully fought some distance away, for there were no other tracks near. I followed the trail for an hour to a point where the woods were dense and filled with brush, and then concluded to return to camp. Selous and Louis had gone over to the Clearwater draw, the former intending to pass the night, and Coghlan had gone down in the timber to get

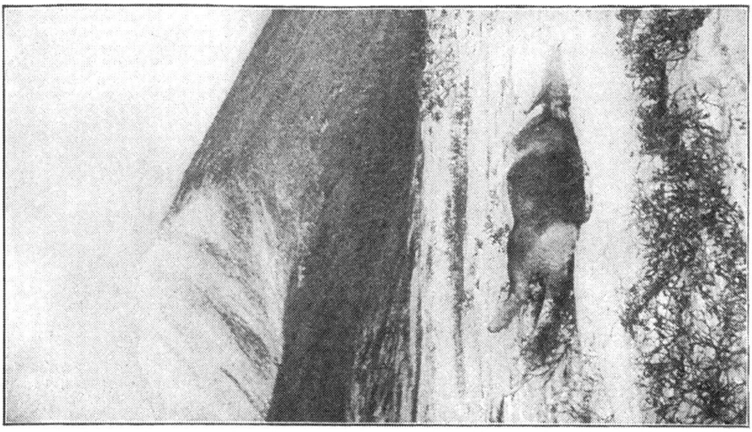

First ram killed, September 19.

Second ram killed, September 19.

Ewe killed, September 19.

some birch bark for the making of a horn to call moose. The remainder of the morning and a good part of the afternoon were spent in preparing the sheep skins until Coghlan returned, when a horn was quickly made. I then went to the north end of the meadows and gave several calls and waited until dark, but there was no response and I returned to camp.

September 21.—Louis had returned with the big moose head and the next morning both he and Coghlan, bringing all the trophies they could carry, started for the river. It was still below zero and another perfect day. Going to the north end of the meadows I climbed to the saddle between the two mountains, observing that several moose had recently travelled over it, and descended to the timber on the other side. Shortly I came upon the tracks of a large grizzly and followed them along the slope of the north mountain, until the trail went into the timber. Climbing high and circling about, I examined the west face of the mountain for sheep, but observed no signs. Descending, I went through the timber to the two lakes where, on September 15th, the cow moose had been seen with two calves. I reached them late in the afternoon. Fresh moose tracks were all about, and, excited by my presence, the jays and red squirrels made so much noise that it seemed almost like a natural warning to any moose that might be near.

The lakes were surrounded with timber; a light wind was blowing, and it was impossible to find a good place to call. I went up on the slope of a bare hill near one of the lakes and gave a call. Immediately to the right, on the other side of the lake, sounded the grunt of a bull, and, in a moment, I heard another bull coming from the left. In front of me was a clear space by the lake, and both bulls were moving about in the timber not more than two hundred yards away, but they would not come out. I waited in silence. Soon the grunting of one continued still more to the right and I knew he was circling.

I took several photographs, September 19.

The other had ceased for some time when I heard him around the hill behind me to the left. After a while both ceased, and I knew that they had received my wind.

It was then dark at six, and after passing through a fringe of timber, I slowly and carefully climbed the steep slope of the mountain in the light of a brilliant full moon. Reaching the top, I walked for three miles through the snow-fields on the edge of the crest. Below were white meadows dotted with frozen ponds and little lakes, their ice sheets dimly reflecting the bold, rugged mountains, which appeared sombre white above the deep shadows on the slopes, while the lofty outlines of the sharp peaks behind stood out like huge sentinels in the pale, clear sky. All the snow-fields sparkled golden under the mellow rays, while the dark timber area below on the other side, filled with glittering lakes, made a mysterious contrast to the peaks across the river—peaks softly glowing and almost yellow in the strange effect of distant moonlight. There was not a sound to break the weird, gentle beauty of the scene. It was a crowning effect of that stern, sublime wilderness, then so calm and peaceful, overspread by the radiance of the moon. I walked slowly, and descended on the sheep-trail to camp, where the fire was breathing its sparks up into the cold, clear air. Selous had not seen a moose, but at the last moment had observed a small band of ewes on the mountains near Clearwater draw and had killed an old ewe of the whitest color of the sheep in that locality. With great generosity he later gave the skin and skull to the Biological Survey, where it could be compared with their numerous specimens.

September 22.—Our men had reported ice running in the river. This made an immediate departure necessary, since continued cold might increase it to such an extent that it would block and freeze, thus closing navigation. The next day-the last one in camp-was slightly warmer. Selous remained there all day.

We had hunted all the available ranges except a small one on the extreme northeast side of the draw, and, after tramping to its foot, I began to climb. The tracks of a ewe and lamb passed along the crest, and several fresh moose-trails crossed it. I went to the north end where it almost overhung the river. There I took some photographs and placed my compass on a rock for the purpose of studying the topography of the river. When I started back I forgot it, and I hope it is still there, pointing thirty-five degrees east of north toward the most beautiful and impressive range of white-capped domes, peaks, and crests, in all that locality.

Descending to the draw, I called for moose, but there was no response and I returned, walking through woods and meadows by moonlight. That night tramp was made sadly and regretfully, knowing it was my last in those high mountains, endeared to me in spite of rain, storms, snow, and disappointments. Love of the wilderness persists and drowns all feelings resulting from bad luck. Large rams had not been found. At that time they were feeding on the ranges nearer the South Fork, as I learned the following year from one who had hunted there and found the band.

The men had again been down to the river with an other load. The thermometer went up during the night to ten degrees above, as we slept for the last time in that little shelter-camp, nestled in the woods and facing the broad meadows and bold ranges beyond.

September 23.—The next morning our packs were made up, and we staggered down the steep side of a ridge to the flats below and crossed directly to the river, reaching it by the middle of the afternoon. While descending, we had seen signs of black bears, where they had been feeding on dwarf juniper berries. After lunch, the men went three miles down river to the cache for the purpose of bringing up a canoe, and I went about two miles up river and called for a while, but no moose appeared. Returning, I found Selous cooking at the fire, and shortly after our men returned, poling the canoe. After all our material was moved into a heavy spruce wood nearby, a large fire was started, the light of which danced about the trees and caused the red squirrels to chatter.

September 24.—By morning the thermometer had gone up to thirty-two degrees. It was raining and, except for a few moments in the afternoon, continued to rain all day. I started down river, intending to go to two fairly large lakes some distance below the cache, to call for moose. Soon I reached a beautiful beaver dam five feet high, which lifted the waters of a small stream into a lake of several acres, surrounded by spruce woods. Shortly after crossing it, I came to a trapper's cabin, made by Bob Riddell, who intended to trap for martens in that locality the coming winter. Trappers had been all along the lower MacMillan River for two years and besides Riddell, there was one still farther up at Cache Creek. Riddell's main cabin was at Husky Dog Creek, and he had then gone over on the South Fork to hunt with Mr. Cameron and the others.

Proceeding along his blazed trail I struck off across the flats and reached the lake about five in the afternoon. Scarcely any fresh moose tracks were observed in the lower country, and none about the lakes. I called until dark and then went directly to the river, striking it, unfortunately, three miles below the cache. There was a driving rain and it was a discouraging tramp through the dark woods, pushing my way through alders, swamps, and tangled underbrush. The smouldering camp-fire was a welcome sight, and after a change of clothing and some needed food, I slept while the rain dripped through the shelter.

CHAPTER IX

DOWN THE NORTH FORK. PLATEAU MOUNTAIN. 1904

SEPTEMBER 25.—As it required some time to gather all our effects and load the canoes, we did not start until 2:30 in the afternoon. It was then warm and clear. The river had fallen since we had come up; many of the riffles were doubtful of passage, and the canoes, as they were swept along in the current, kept scraping the bottom. But all the hard work of towing them up was more than compensated for by the pleasure of going down. Assisted by the paddles, guiding the canoes through dancing riffles, we went swiftly careering through the wild timbered valleys, the mountain panorama unfolding itself at every curve. Shortly before dark we reached the place where we had camped September third, and immediately after landing I took the birch horn and, going about three hundred yards from the bank, gave a few calls. I was in a swampy thicket of willows, alders, and dwarf birch, sparingly dotted with spruces and broken by open spaces of a few square yards. In a short time, after hearing the chopping and the whistling and talking of the men, while dense clouds of smoke from the newly made fire were floating down the valley, I concluded that no moose would dare to approach within a mile of the place, and returned to camp. Louis was on the bank repairing Selous' canoe—an old one which had kept leaking all the afternoon—when he ran to the shelter, saying that he heard a bull moose approaching. Taking a horn and beckoning to me to follow, he quickly walked along the bar, with Selous and myself trailing close behind him. We stepped into the thick brush and paused to listen. Yes, the well-known grunt of a bull moose was clearly audible not more than three or four hundred yards away, and sounding an approach in our direction. We crept forward as silently as possible, stopping as the bull, pausing to listen, ceased grunting, and going forward again when he resumed.

Intercepting the line of the bull's approach, and reaching a spot where the brush ahead was less dense, we stooped close behind a log, and Louis, after giving a low call, rubbed the horn up and down on the willow brush, thus producing a noise similar to that made by a moose rubbing his horns. Directly toward us came the eager grunting, ceasing now and then as the bull stopped to listen, until at last it sounded very close. Not a stick cracked, nor was there the slightest noise from horns striking the trees and brush, or from footsteps. It was almost dark, and except for some faint light in the small open space in front, the thicket appeared perfectly black. How was it possible for that large, bulky animal to continue his mysterious approach so swiftly and silently on swampy ground, through a dense thicket of tangled brush and fallen logs, without making an audible sound except that of grunting? As it sounded almost upon us, we saw a large bull suddenly appear, looming out of the darkness like a giant spectre, not more than seventy-five feet away, his antlers looking big, broad, and very white against the dark background. With rifle pointed, I rose and could just see the ivory sight which was held in a line with the centre of the hull's chest when I pulled the trigger. Click! A miss-fire, and almost simultaneously Selous' smothered expression of disappointment! The bull had stopped as I rose, and when the trigger fell, he jumped to one side and disappeared in the brush. I sent three shots after him, but could only guess the direction as he was not in sight. After the first jump there was a crashing in the willows—and then not another sound was heard. The grunting ceased; he had glided off more mysteriously and silently than he had come. Thus was lost my only opportunity to get a bull moose, and one with horns which seemed larger, perhaps, than they really were, though they still grow in the memory-image of that short glimpse. Later, I learned that the caps in some of my cartridges, then four years old, had deteriorated and were apt, especially in cold weather, to miss fire.

The night was clear and fairly cold, the thermometer registering twenty-three degrees above zero, and we soon went to sleep. I was suddenly aroused by a trembling hand on my shoulder as Coghlan whispered that a moose had crossed the river and was heading directly toward the camp. Taking my rifle, with nothing on but underclothes, I quickly followed Louis through the woods as Selous had done on the night of September 3d. We reached the bank just after the moose had recrossed to the other side and gone in the woods. Louis tried to coax the bull in sight with the horn, but in vain. It appeared that about an hour and a half before that time, when Selous and I were sleeping, Louis had stepped out to the river bank and had given a few calls for amusement before he retired. The bull had evidently heard the sound from a long distance and had gradually approached and crossed the river. His tracks on the bar, which were seen the next morning, showed that he had come to within fifty feet of our camp.

September 26.—Before daylight I went out and called again, but without result. We did not start until an hour before noon, and reached the Forks early in the afternoon. I had carefully deducted all time for stops, and found that the actual time consumed in running down river from the cache to the

Forks was six hours. It had required six days with interruptions to drag the canoes up the same distance. Not long before arriving at the Forks, we met Jack Barr and Crosby, trappers who had passed the preceding winter trapping in that locality. They were on their way to Barr Creek with the purpose of bringing provisions to their cabin. They had spent some time with Rungius and Osgood in the Russell Mountains, where they had a "line " cabin. Both were fine types of the woodsmen who trap in the northern country, and though efficient in killing moose for a supply of meat they were not much interested in game. They had trapped at the foot of the mountains which we had hunted, but did not even know that sheep lived on them; in fact, they had told Rungius and Osgood that we would not find sheep.

Mr. Cameron and the others who had gone up the South Fork had returned a few days before and left a note, informing us that they had found caribou in abundance and killed ten good bulls; two bears, a lynx, and three small sheep—the only ones seen. Judge Dugas had killed a small moose shortly after starting up the South Fork. Later, we learned that he had also killed a bull caribou farther down on the bank of the MacMillan River.

We went on down to Russell Creek, where a note from Rungius and Osgood advised us that they had gone down river. We kept on until later when a slough was entered and camp was made in a pouring rain. Selous had remained behind with Louis to call, and I went up to the end of the slough and called until dark without result. I was greatly interested to see a beaver swimming near me with a large stick held by one end in its mouth. Reaching its house, the stick was skillfully worked into it under the water. All along we had seen beavers, sometimes swimming, sometimes sitting on logs, and twice I saw them sliding down the bank into the water.

Jack Barr and his dogs.

PHOTOGRAPH BY CARL RUNGIUS.

Carl Rungius and his big moose.

PHOTOGRAPH BY GAGE.

Just after dark when Selous, who had failed to lure a bull, had returned, Dougherty, one of the men who had been on the *Emma Nott* and had landed near this place, came into camp and said that he and Horn had their camp half a mile down river. During the time they had been there, a small bull moose and two cows had been killed, but very few had been seen. They could not hunt far from the river because they had to kill game near enough to bring it to a raft which they had constructed for the purpose of holding the meat and floating it to Dawson.

September 27.—Early in the morning, while it still continued to rain, I went out to call before breakfast, but unsuccessfully. The rain continued all day. After the swift current of the North Fork, that of the main river seemed very tame, but to float with it was fascinating just the same. The canoes glided along easily, as we continually watched ahead eagerly, anticipating a sight of game when rounding the curves, each of which brought a new stretch of the river into view. In the middle of the afternoon, Coghlan saw a calf moose trotting on a bar and called our attention to it. I landed shortly after it went into the woods, and going around in a circle to get a favorable wind, advanced in its direction. Selous entered the woods a short distance below. Before going far I heard sticks cracking and sounds that indicated the mother and calf were trotting away, hence I returned to the canoe and proceeded down river. Louis, who was alone, went into the woods, as he told me afterwards, and saw the bull running about the cow and playing with her, while the calf stood at one side. Selous was in another direction, and the animals had run off before he returned. Had I known better the habits of the moose at that season, the bull might have been killed.

Shortly after, as we were gliding around a sharp curve, looking back, I saw a black bear emerge from the alders and walk toward the bank of the river. The boat was quickly turned toward shore, but it was too late, the strong current having swept us around the curve into an unfavorable wind, and before I could step out of the canoe, the bear threw up its head, sniffed once or twice, then turned and ran into the woods.

About dark, I arrived at an abandoned trapper's cabin on the river bank opposite Plateau Mountain, and found Rungius and Osgood installed in it. Selous came soon after, and that evening, while the rain beat down outside, there was a delightful reunion. They had hunted in the Russell Mountains, and Rungius had killed a bull moose with fine antlers, two cow caribou, a small female grizzly, a black bear, and a wolverine. The last three had been shot while feeding on the carcasses of his moose and caribou. Osgood had devoted his time mostly to trapping small mammals (which were very scarce) and in trying to find sheep. They had not found sheep, and very few of their tracks had been seen in the Russell Mountains. Osgood had killed both a bull and a cow moose near the bank of the river a short distance above that cabin. While floating down the river, they had seen four bears, and the day before two had appeared on the bar opposite the cabin, but had run off in the woods before Osgood could get a shot. Both had hunted on Plateau Mountain, where Rungius had killed an old bull caribou with fine horns, and Osgood a smaller bull. Since they thought that other caribou were about there, Selous and I decided to go up and hunt for them.

September 28.—It rained so hard the next day that all of us stayed about the cabin in the morning. In the afternoon I crossed the river in a canoe and tramped about the timbered ridges. Nothing but old moose tracks were seen; and a few grouse, hawks, and rabbits. The latter were then beginning to turn white. The bird migration had mostly passed.

September 29.—We passed another congenial evening in the cabin, and the following morning it was colder and raining, while snow was falling on the mountains above. My recording thermometer had been broken the night before and I was unable to record any more temperatures during the rest of the trip. Osgood and Rungius started down river for the purpose of establishing a camp near the Kalzas Mountains, while Selous and I made up our packs and started to climb the mountain. It was very steep in places and the walking was heart-breaking, particularly on the lower slopes where large areas, burnt over and storm-swept, were full of fallen spruce trees in tangled masses, surrounded by a dense growth of dwarf birch. Rabbits were very abundant, and a yellow-haired porcupine was seen—the only one noticed on our trip. Red squirrels were everywhere, and the jays joined them in giving sounds of life.

At 4 P.M., after a tedious climb, we reached a good place to camp, about half a mile below timber-line, on the slope of a narrow draw through which a swollen creek rushed, leaping in cataracts as it descended through icy gorges to the river below. Everything was covered with fresh snow, which still continued to fall as we erected the shelter and started the fire.

September 30.—The temperature fell at least to zero and the morning dawned bright and clear, but a strong wind blew from the north-west. Selous and Louis climbed Plateau Mountain, and I started to climb the ranges to the north-west. The adjoining mountains, separated from Plateau Mountain by draws, extend in vast rolling plateaus north-east to the Russell Mountains. They are about six thousand feet high and covered with dwarf birch and moss. Two or three miles across the rolling summits the west slopes descend abruptly in broken rocks, cliffs, and precipices.

When I reached the top, the wind was so strong that it was not easy to face it and hence quite impossible to use my

Plateau Mountain in August.

PHOTOGRAPH BY W.H. OSGOOD. BY PERMISSION OF THE U.S. GEOLOGICAL SURVEY.

MacMillan River and Dromedary Mountain from the slope of Kalzas Mountain.

PHOTOGRAPH BY CARL RUNGIUS.

Running through the ice in MacMillan River.

PHOTOGRAPH BY CARL RUNGIUS.

field-glasses. There was a magnificent view of the MacMillan River below, which appeared like a huge reptile winding back and forth between the ridges; and on the other side of it, Dromedary Mountain stood forth boldly in snowy outlines, a strong contrast to the sombre timbered area below.

The tracks of a bull moose, which had crossed the summit, and descended to the timber early that same morning, were before me, and a short distance farther on, the fresh tracks of a cow moose and calf, joined by those of the bull, which had circled back again to meet them, showed that all of them had been feeding on scrub willow. Going toward the west, I came upon the tracks of five mountain sheep and followed them toward the north for two hours, until, having found a sheltered spot behind a rock where I could use my field-glasses, I saw that the trail was visible on the snow for two or three miles ahead, leading toward the Russell Mountains. Turning west again, I found fresh tracks of a cow caribou and a calf and followed them until the trail descended into a basin, when, looking across it, they were observed feeding on the opposite slopes near the summit. The calf fed quite independently of its mother, who neither looked up from her feeding nor appeared suspicious of danger, or paid the least attention to the calf when it strayed to a distance from her. After circling, I took up the sheep tracks and again followed them north to a point where the trail turned to the west. Following it, I crossed gullies, rocky slopes, basins, and ridges, until I could see the trail on the snow, two miles ahead. Then I knew that it was necessary to turn back or I would be caught on the summit in the dark, a long distance from camp.

Unfortunately, I had no protection for my ears, which were frozen several times and rubbed soft again. After ascending to the east slopes of the mountain, I found abundant fresh moose tracks, all leading to a depression near the top which was the apex of several willow-filled ravines. Below was a large draw extending down between two mountains to the timber. The mountain-slopes on both sides were covered with willows, and moose tracks were numerous everywhere among them. There was a fine view of Moose Lake—a fairly large sheet of water. It was not frozen and appeared to glisten all over, shining out of the vast deep forest about it. Its outlet, Moose Creek, was . visible, flowing in a meandering course through the timber to the MacMillan River. Beyond the wide forest was a series of high, rugged ranges bordering the Stewart River.

Turning to the left, I climbed to the top and went in the direction where the cow caribou and her calf had last been seen earlier in the day. Numerous large flocks of ptarmigan were flying about, and soon the cow and calf were seen feeding on the flat top. As the sun was directly ahead I could not photograph them, even after approaching to within seventy-five yards, before the cow saw me. To have circled would have brought me in an unfavorable wind. The cow looked at me a moment, and, joined by the calf, trotted twenty-five yards in my direction and both stood looking at me. I advanced again and both, moving off a short distance, again stopped and looked. As I came very close, both turned and trotted across the top and disappeared around the slope. It was interesting to observe that the surface where these two caribou had been feeding was completely covered with their tracks in all directions, and if the single trail leading up to the spot had not been clearly visible I should have been deluded into believing that a whole band had been feeding there. I crossed over to the edge of a deep canon which separated the mountain from Plateau Mountain, the precipitous slopes of which were directly opposite, rising six or seven hundred feet higher.

High above, near the top, my eyes caught a large, dark animal moving along the side, and a look through my field-glasses revealed a bull moose with the right antler well developed, the left broken entirely off at the base. An unusual sight it was to see that bull moose slowly walking, often stopping to look about, just below the crest of the massive dome-shaped mountain, usurping the territory of sheep, caribou, and the grizzly bear. He continued to travel until appearing like a black speck in the glittering snow before he disappeared from sight.

Turning my field-glasses toward the slope across the canon, a bull moose suddenly appeared directly opposite me, lying down a hundred feet above the timber. He seemed half-buried in the snow, and his chin was resting on it, while his small horns reached well up above the body. To the naked eye, in his resting attitude, about three hundred yards distant, he looked like a large bush, his horns appearing like the tops of willows and completing the resemblance. He was resting on an incline so steep that it was impossible to approach noiselessly from above, and it would have been equally difficult to approach through the woods from below without alarming him. He had chosen a safe spot for undisturbed rest. Taking my birch horn from my rücksack, I gave a low call, but he neither moved nor pricked up his ears. I sounded several more calls, some of them louder, but not the slightest movement did he make. I waited for an hour, calling at intervals, very much interested in watching him, but not once did he show any suspicion of my presence or pay any attention to the noise made through the horn, nor was he alert and watchful. He seemed to sleep until just before dusk, when slowly rising and pushing his forefeet forward, he almost slid down the slope to the timber and was not seen again.

Some time after dark I reached camp, a few moments before Selous came in. After an arduous tramp all over Plateau Mountain he had not seen fresh tracks of caribou, but just before reaching camp he had seen a small bull moose high on the mountain-side, but had not attempted to kill it. We knew that the caribou, following their restless habits, had abandoned that locality for awhile at least, and therefore we decided to make for the river and go directly to Selkirk without pausing to hunt any more.

October 1.—In the morning we went back to the river and in the afternoon I went two miles below to call, while Selous started in an opposite direction. Both of us were unsuccessful and returned to the cabin. Selous, however, had shot a little brown crane.

October 2.—We paddled down river all the next day until dark, when we made camp. It is worth recording that I saw a ptarmigan on the bank of the river—a most unusual thing even in summer, and especially in fall. I have never before or since seen one so far down in the timber.

October 3.—It was cold, and from that time until we reached Selkirk, the temperature at night must have been at least near zero and at times below. The river was full of slush ice, which somewhat impeded the progress of the canoes, though it was not solid enough to prevent them from easily slipping through. Not long after starting, a wolf was seen running along a bar, but it entered the woods before Selous could get a shot. At the foot of the Kalzas Mountain we found the camp of Rungius and Osgood. They had been calling every day without results. It was clear that the frenzy of the rut had passed and most of the bulls were then feeding up near the heads of the draws. After lunching, Selous and I went on, and the others were to join us below at the cabin near Kalzas Creek. As I was ahead and rounding a curve, I saw a lynx sitting on the bank of the river. My bullet struck it in the centre of the back and it ran into the woods, where I found it a few yards from the bank, lying down. It died in a few moments, and we took its skin and skull and proceeded until it was time to camp.

October 4.—In the morning there was a great deal of hard ice in the river and it impeded our progress. When the cold season approaches, ice formed on the bottom floats to the surface in the morning, and this, together with that discharged by creeks, almost fills the river during the night, and runs very thickly in the morning. During the day much of it packs in the sloughs, lodges on the bars, remains in the still water in favorable places along the bank, and much of it wears out through friction. In the afternoon, therefore, the river does not contain so much ice and navigation is freer. Continued cold causes the floating pieces to freeze together during the night, and sooner or later large fields of it coming down the river, jam in the canons or on the sharp curves, all freezing together. Unless a thaw comes soon after, the whole river may thus freeze and navigation is closed until the following summer.

The ice continued to increase, and in some places we had difficulty in pushing the canoes through without breaking them. As it was, Selous's canoe received a large hole which could be only temporarily patched, and it leaked badly all the rest of the day until we reached the cabin at Kalzas Creek, where we found a trapper, named Lebell, who had arrived shortly before, intending to pass the winter there. Rungius and Osgood appeared later and we passed the night in the cabin. While floating down they had seen two lynxes. Bird life in the MacMillan was then almost absent, a few mergansers, a golden eagle, and the one ptarmigan were all I had seen while coming down the river.

October 5.—The canoes had been well mended, but next morning the ice, frozen together in large cakes, was running so dense that we felt some apprehension about getting down before the river was blocked. In many places we could not push through it, but were obliged to let the canoes drift until an opening could be found where we could reach channels of clear water. A mile down from the cabin, near the top of a hill on the right, a fine black bear was seen feeding on berries, and insisting that Selous should go after it, we backed our canoes in the ice on the opposite side as he went ashore. He soon disappeared in the thick brush on the hillside. But a moment after, the bear, having caught the wind blowing toward it from the boats, threw up its head, sniffed the air, and ran off. It disappeared before Selous could get close enough to shoot. While approaching, he had seen it through the brush several times but could not get an unobstructed line for a shot. Early in the afternoon, shortly before reaching the Pelly, I saw a lynx walking on a bar and undershot it three times before it ran into the woods. After making camp on a bank of the Pelly, Louis heard a bull moose grunting not far off and Selous accompanied him into the woods where he tried to coax it with a horn, but it was not heard again.

For the next two days we paddled down the Pelly and late in the evening of October 7 we reached the Pelly Road House where Rungius, Osgood, and I remained for the night, while Selous went on down to Selkirk. The Pelly was full of ice, particularly above the canon, through which we had to float with it. A herring-gull and a cross fox were the only live objects observed on the Pelly.

We remained at Selkirk until the afternoon of October 9, when the small steamer *La France* picked us up and carried us to Whitehorse, where we arrived early on October 13. Gage had gone back to Dawson; Coghlan remained at Pelly Road House to pass the winter looking after the horses used on the stage route between Whitehorse and Dawson, while Louis had gone up the Lewes River to catch dog salmon, which pass the mouth of the Pelly without entering it, for a supply of food for the dogs at the Selkirk Police Post. All had been excellent men, hard-working, efficient, always interested, and willing. When they left Selkirk, we realized that our MacMillan trip had ended.

CHAPTER X

THE WATSON RIVER COUNTRY – 1904

OCTOBER 13.—MY friend, A. B. Newell, had arranged for me a trip to mountain ranges along the Watson River. C. E. Wynn-Johnson, an Englishman who had lived for several years at Skagway, was in Whitehorse waiting to accompany me, and Newell intended to join us a day later. The day was passed in Whitehorse purchasing provisions, completing preparations, and wandering about the town.

October 14.—We took the train the next morning, having loaded three pack-horses and our provisions on a freight car. A young man, Burwash by name, had been employed as packer, and proved to be a willing and efficient assistant. The train stopped at Robinson, a side track twenty miles from Whitehorse, where the freight car was switched off. It was with sincere regret that I bade adieu to Selous. He had been a charming and unselfish companion, and his considerate manners and gentle courtesy had endeared him to every man with whom he had come in contact. Experienced hunter that he is, perhaps more so than any other man living, his enthusiasm for nature and the wild life in the wilderness is as fresh as ever, while his love of natural history is intense, and his skill as a hunter extraordinary.

Osgood's tireless energy had given me an insight into the character and ability of the men Dr. Merriam had gathered on the staff of the Biological Survey. Not only was Osgood indefatigable in collecting birds and mammals and hunting big game, but he also worked until late hours in the night preparing his specimens.

Carl Rungius, a skilful hunter who has spent many years hunting big game in the Rocky Mountains and Canada, had used every opportunity to study his art. He made numerous color sketches of the game country, besides accurate drawings of the animals. He has since produced many realistic paintings of moose, caribou, bears, and sheep, revealing them in their true environment in Yukon Territory. The train sped on; I saw Rungius and Osgood waving; we unloaded the horses, threw on the packs, and started.

The country through which we tramped was fairly level, but barren, except for scattered clumps of pines and many small ,lakes. There were many holes of the ground-squirrel, tracks of rabbits, and not two miles from the railroad some very old tracks of moose. In the lakes, several species of ducks were abundant, and during the fall migration one of the lakes provided excellent shooting. I was interested to notice that the tops of nearly all the stunted pines had been completely gnawed off by rabbits, exactly like the willows along the bars of the rivers. Eight miles distant from the railroad were some cabins occupied by Bill Schnabel, his wife, and a miner named Foley. There we unloaded, and Burwash started back with an extra horse to bring Newell, who was to join us the next day.

Bill Schnabel proved to be a very interesting man of distinct personality. He had been a cowboy in the States and had come to the Yukon during the early days of the stampede, having been a packer over the White Pass trail. He had been one of the first prospectors of the Atlin district, had travelled along the Yukon River above and below Dawson, and was then working an old prospect which he had located a few years previously, eight miles from his cabin.

October 15.—The next day, pending Newell's arrival, I went out to investigate the country. I was in a vast forested area at the foot of massive mountains, the southeast slopes of which were bare, the tops and opposite slopes covered with snow. Most of the country had been burnt over and was covered with poplar, pines, and spruces, with willows and dwarf birch growing densely. I tramped all day and saw nothing but a few old moose tracks and bear diggings. Returning at dark I found that Newell had arrived, and the following day we packed the horses and started for the sheep mountains, eight miles distant, between the Watson and Wheaton Rivers. Schnabel's prospect was near there and to it he had cut an excellent trail on which the horses travelled easily, through a rolling, timbered country. That all this area had at one time been covered by a glacier was evident from the numerous large, circular depressions on the surface, some of which still contained small lakes. To the east was a high, massive range culminating in Mount Gray and extending more than twenty miles to Lake Bennett. To the west were various mountains and short ranges, separated by draws and wider valleys, not trending in any particular direction.

Newell and Johnson left the trail to make a circuit on a mountain side, and Schnabel and I continued to his cabin. Immediately after arriving, we went some distance below and, climbing some low hills, scanned the mountain-slopes for sheep, but did not see any. The others were there when we returned, but nobody had seen any game. The cabin was situated at timber-line, at the head of a rolling, rocky pasture on the west side of the valley. In front, about a mile below, was a lake three miles long and half a mile wide, from the east shore of which the slopes of Mount Gray inclined upward, well pastured with grass, though steep, rocky, and furrowed with gorges, canons, and ravines. The crest, flanked almost continually with cliffs and high precipices, is serried with peaks and pinnacles, irregular and confused, presenting a long sawtooth sky-line. East of the cabin was a V-shaped draw, separating two high, irregular mountain ranges which lacked trend or continuity in any direction. Some of the mountains are rough and vary in height from five to seven thousand feet, others are dome-shaped and appear like huge, rolling plateaus. To the south, the mountains continue to Lake Bennett; in all directions they are massive and high, but present an appearance of confused groups, rather than well-defined ranges, like the Rockies east of the Yukon River. The inspiring grandeur of majestic mountain landscape is there, but the undefinable wildness seems lacking as compared with that of the Rockies.

October 17.—The morning was warm and pleasant and Newell, having to return to Whitehorse, left early. Johnson and Foley started up the draw behind camp while I climbed the mountain to the south. It was covered with an inch of snow and fox tracks were abundant, also fresh signs of sheep. It is a high mountain, reaching westward along the Wheaton River and the slopes are cut into canons and ravines. From the top I could clearly see Lake Bennett and greatly admired the deep, broad valley of the Wheaton extending in a westerly course between massive domed ranges. The aspect of the timbered country below was singularly strange, quite different from any I have seen elsewhere in the northern country. It appeared like a vast forested plain, terraced irregularly in every direction between great circular, hollow bowls, each of which contained a pond, the surfaces of which reflected the rays of the sun in a manner to cause a shining appearance which spangled the whole lower country. It showed the results of a retreated glacier, the surface being diversified by kettle holes, drumlins, eskers, and kames.

Looking across a canon along the side of the mountain, a transparent whitish spot on a rock caught my eye. My glasses revealed a ewe sheep which was soon joined by another that suddenly jumped up on the same rock. Higher up near a peak, I saw seven ewes and lambs feeding upward between pauses to look and watch. Turning the glasses below, I was almost startled to see sixteen more ewes and lambs feeding on the grass slope just above the timber. Pure white in body, most of them had black tails, though the tails of others were practically white. To be sure of securing meat as well as a specimen of the sheep of the district, I decided to shoot one now that the chance offered and at once planned an approach downward through a cañon which would lead me near and opposite to where they were feeding.

It was a difficult descent, and when nearly opposite the point I climbed the side of the cañon and peeped over. Surprised to find that the sheep were not in sight, I concluded that, having entered another cañon farther over on the slope, they were moving up; consequently I started diagonally upward on the loose, broken rock, hoping to intercept them from above. Suddenly I heard the sound of a big rock falling from high on the mountain opposite me, and, looking back, I saw Schnabel sitting among the loose rocks and signalling to me that the sheep were farther along the slope and higher up. I realized immediately that they had seen him and were off to climb the mountain. Notwithstanding my keen disappointment, I kept on climbing higher, but the sound of rocks and small boulders falling behind, caused me to wait until Schnabel, who was scrambling along, joined me.

The sheep were then badly frightened, and as he came up I saw them running four hundred yards distant high on the mountain, entering among some cliffs on the other side of the cañon. It was our only chance, and we both shot as they ran.

He rushed ahead and kept firing his .30-40 cartridges until his magazine was empty, but he did not hit one. When his last shot was fired an old ewe stopped on the edge of the cliff. I told him to stoop low, and, aiming a little above her, I fired and she fell. Immediately recovering and gaining her feet, she slowly walked downward and disappeared along the slope. Schnabel then went diagonally below while I climbed above, in order that one of us might get near enough to shoot her. After going some distance among canons and boulders, I heard three shots, and looking below, saw the ewe running, but she passed out of sight before I could shoot. Hastening toward her, I soon saw her standing two hundred yards below, and, as I fired, she fell. Schnabel then came around the slope seventy-five yards from her and she rose. He fired three times, missing. We both followed her as she walked down the slope and each fired again, both bullets striking her in the middle of the body. She continued to walk around the slope and passed through some very rough places for two hundred yards before she lay down. As we came up she was in dying convulsions. My first two bullets had passed through her stomach. One of Schnabel's, hitting her in the hind quarters without breaking a leg, had passed through the stomach and emerged, tearing a large hole well forward just behind the lungs. Our last two bullets had torn large holes in the centre of her body and all the entrails that had not already fallen out, were protruding. Yet this animal had kept on walking over a rough surface, crossing canons, descending and climbing for half an hour, and did not even fall at the last two shots.

Such extraordinary vitality is difficult to realize, but it is not peculiar to mountain sheep. It has been my experience that most of our other big game animals have the same vitality as sheep, and exceptional cases like this are not uncommon when the vitals are not immediately reached, or the bones disabled.

The skin was soon taken off and the meat cut up and carried to the foot of the mountain. It was then dark. Schnabel hung part of it on a tree and I shouldered the rest. We then staggered and stumbled four miles through the woods to camp.

Johnson and Foley came in later, after having been obliged to make a dangerous mountain descent in the dark. They had emptied their magazines at a band of fifty sheep running at a distance, and had seen several others which they were unable to stalk. At that date rifle sights could not be seen at 5.30 in the afternoon and not until six in the morning.

October 18.—The next day was windy and it seemed natural to be again on the tramp to find rams. I climbed the mountains to the north-west of camp, and dense dwarf birch rendered the walking very slow and tedious. I noticed a very old moose track and one of caribou. These animals are more abundant to the westward, but very scarce in the district where I was. Conies were abundant high up among the broken rocks and a few marmots were heard. Rabbits were exceedingly abundant and all were then white. No fresh sheep tracks were seen, although I tramped about on the crest and slopes until well into the afternoon. Golden eagles, ravens, and flocks of ptarmigan were as numerous as in the mountains east of the Yukon River.

As I was descending, I saw across the valley two white specks on the north-west slope of Mount Gray, and my glasses revealed two sheep feeding high among the rocks. They soon lay down, and, it being too late to reach them before dark, I crossed the valley to determine their sex, but when I reached the lake there was not enough light to distinguish them.

The shallow water at the head of the lake was covered with a thin sheet of ice. Beavers had damned the mouth of the inlet and the water had backed up to form another small lake, which also was covered with ice. In the middle of the latter they had constructed a large house. As I approached, the ice was cracking and I plainly heard splashing. Creeping silently to the shore, I saw three beavers at work on the house. At intervals each would swim under the ice to the shore and get a stick, which was held at one end in the teeth and taken under the ice. Every few feet the beaver would force its head against the ice, break it, and breathe for a moment. One proceeded in this way to the house, breaking the ice four times, another six times, and another seven. Reaching the house they would drag the stick upon it, and spend ten minutes in working it into the structure. They would then return for another stick. When it was too dark to watch them longer, I silently withdrew and returned to camp. Johnson had tramped all day without seeing a sheep.

October 19.—Early in the morning I looked across the lake, to a spur projecting from Mount Gray, and saw two sheep feeding among scattered clumps of willow not far above timber-line, and opposite our camp. They were rams, the same two that I had seen the day before. One was six or seven years old, with fair horns, the other about three. I reached the lake, intending to cross on a raft that Schnabel had constructed some time earlier in the summer. The day was clear and cold, but a strong wind was blowing, and not being able to manage the raft with a pole, I had to proceed two miles to the upper end, where I took off shoes and socks, cut a pole, and breaking the ice as I waded, finally reached the other side and immediately began to climb.

The west slopes of Mount Gray are exceedingly steep and broken, and besides, an inch of dry snow had made them slippery and very difficult to climb. Finally, I reached the cliffs and snow cornices bordering the crest, and proceeded south in the direction where the sheep had been seen. Crossing two deep, rocky cañons, where conies were bleating, I reached the edge of a deep, wide cañon and looking beyond saw the two rams lying down on the top of a turretted pinnacle, about five hundred yards away. They were facing in my direction and there was no possible approach except on the crest, which was inaccessible from that point because of continuous cliffs. It was very cold, and the wind was so strong that I could barely keep on the slope. I remained motionless for a long time until so thoroughly chilled that it was necessary to retreat and retrace my steps to start my circulation again. Thus I kept watching and walking for most of the afternoon, waiting for the rams to move to a spot where, after crossing the canon, I could approach them. Finally, when it was too late to stalk them, both rose and stood rigid, looking at the country below. No sight of animals in the American wilderness is quite so wonderful and inspiring as the mountain ram standing erect on his beloved crag and gazing at the wild country below him. Soon they began to feed indifferently on the very walls of the pinnacle, and then descended and walked along, picking at weeds and grass until they wandered a few yards upward under some cliffs. Darkness was approaching and I had to act. I purposely aimed four feet above the larger one, in order to strike the cliffs so that he might possibly run toward me, and fired. At the sound of the rifle, both jumped to an alert position and looked downward. Another shot, and the larger ram gave a spring, and, followed by the smaller one, ran fifty yards along the slope and over the crest. My plan had failed and I was disgusted that I had not aimed straight at the ram.

It was dusk when I reached the woods at the lower end of the lake, and about dark as I neared the brook at the inlet. When near the bank, I was startled to see a dark, shadowy object jump into some thick brush not eight feet from me, but instantly recognizing a lynx, I fired at it. Advancing two steps, what did I see but the dim outline of another crouching low on the ground five feet in front of me, too frightened to expose itself and flee. Quickly pointing my rifle at it, without even seeing the sights, I fired and killed it, driving the bullet through the middle of its body. After skinning it, I proceeded, following a terrace almost overhanging the shore of the lake.

It was full moonlight. The wind had stopped, the sky was clear, and the woods were hushed and still. Now and then a duck quacked; more often a muskrat splashed, and everywhere I saw the silvery ripples of the water as they swam about. The border of ice attached to the shores glittered in the soft light, and the crystal waters of the lake mysteriously reflected the massive form of Mount Gray towering among the snow-clad summits, mystic and imposing under the golden light. All about through the silent, desolate woods, the hoots of the great-horned owls sounded; white phantom forms of rabbits continually flitted about as I slowly advanced.

Reaching camp I found that Johnson and Schnabel had seen the same band of ewes again, but had been unable to approach them.

October 20.—While scanning through my glasses the slopes of Mount Gray the next morning, what was my surprise to see a small ram feeding low on the slope two miles to the south! I watched it for an hour as it fed slowly upward, but no other appeared. I was certain that he was the smaller of the two which I had stalked the day before. Without having suspected it, my second shot must have hit the larger one and he was evidently dead. I went to the lower end of the lake, climbed the mountain, found a way over the crest, searched everywhere, but could not find a sign of him, the wind having filled the tracks with snow. It was dark when I returned to camp. Johnson had seen nothing.

October 21.—The next day we left, caught the train, and reached Whitehorse in the evening. A few grizzlies and black bears wander about that section of the Watson River country, but moose and caribou seldom range there. Now, alas! Mining prospects are being worked, and the sheep are practically exterminated. A sight of big game is only to be obtained twenty or thirty miles farther to the west.

October 24.—I sailed from Skagway on the steamer Cottage City, and left that wonderful country where I had passed the summer. The voyage down the coast was delightful, and continually enlivened by the hosts of gulls that followed the steamer. The weather was calm, and apparently as warm as when I had come up in June.

October 29.—I landed at Victoria, and immediately made preparations for a trip after wapiti on the north end of Vancouver Island.

CHAPTER XI

THE KATZEHIN RIVER IN ALASKA – 1905

DURING THE MONTH of May, in the year 1905, I had been hunting the big bears on Montague Island, which stretches across the entrance to Prince William Sound in Alaska. On my return I had reached Skagway June 3, with the intention of leaving immediately for the Upper Pelly River. By previous correspondence I had engaged accommodations for myself, another man, and our equipment, on the little river steamer *Quick* which, by the terms of a contract made with the trading post—Nahanni House—at the mouth of the Ross River, was scheduled to leave Selkirk June 10, for the purpose of conveying a year's supply of provisions and trading goods to the post.

On my arrival in Skagway, I received a letter from the captain, informing me that the date of leaving had been deferred and was uncertain. This led to a correspondence which kept me in uncertainty for more than a month; and, finally, I was obliged to give up waiting for the *Quick* and go to Dawson, to try and make other arrangements for transportation up the Pelly.

In the meanwhile, I remained in the vicinity of Skagway, quite uncertain, not only of the outcome of my continued efforts to get definite information from the captain of the *Quick*, but also of my attempts to arrange elsewhere for transportation.

During that anxious period, I made two short trips for the purpose of fishing for graylings in the lakes and rivers beyond the summit of White Pass, both with indifferent success; and also a third trip up the Katzehin River, to find black bears, which were said to be numerous there, and to see the white goats, which are very abundant in the mountains.

June 14.—My friend C. E. Wynn-Johnson and I started on this trip by going first to Haines Mission in a small steamer, which later brought us to the mouth of the Katzehin, a glacial river entering Lynn Canal sixteen miles below Skagway. About noon we were landed at low tide well out on the sand flats, and immediately began to track our Peterborough canoe up one of the numerous channels of the river.

The Katzehin River flows from the Meade Glacier which lies in ranges fifteen miles from the coast. With a heavy volume of water, it rushes in abrupt descent through a wide glacial valley, the floor of which has been smoothed by the swift waters to a rough bar, over which the river divides into numerous channels, nearly all indistinguishable from the main one.

After working through the flats, which at low tide cover an area of several square miles, and entering the main river where it flows in a single channel for half a mile or more, we were immediately enclosed by high mountains which surround the valley. Above this, several channels were encountered, all flowing to a junction, and each again dividing at intervals in such a way as to form many large creeks running parallel over the entire surface of the wide, continuous bar. Then began as difficult a task of tracking a canoe as I have ever experienced. The water was one continual, swift riffle, and it required all of our combined strength to pull the boat against it. We could not select the right channel and kept hauling on the line until, after having proceeded from two hundred yards to a quarter of a mile, the water became so shallow that it was necessary to retreat and try another channel until the right one was found. In this way we progressed until midnight before camping, and again all the next day, gaining only ten miles to a point where the river bends sharply toward the glacier, then four miles distant. There we made camp on the bank of a clear creek, emerging from a cañon, evidently flowing from a lake high up in the mountains and entering the Katzehin River at the curve. High, rugged mountains with precipitous slopes and sharp, serried crests, broken into spires and pinnacles, reared up very close on both sides of us.

The following morning I started north along the slope of a mountain, while Johnson went in an easterly direction. Two bands of goats, each numbering fifteen or twenty, were feeding in a grassy space near the crest above me, and I watched them more or less all day. Not having a permit to shoot one out of season, I did not attempt to go after them. It would have been quite possible to have stalked them, although that mountain, like all others of the coast ranges near the Katzehin River, was exceedingly difficult to surmount because of its steep slopes. The goats remained near the green pastures all day, alternately feeding and lying down; but now and then one would climb a sheer precipice, apparently for no other reason than sport, and soon return again to the band. In no sense were they alert or watchful, like sheep, and I seldom saw one raise its head to look about.

During the whole day, only one old track of a black bear was seen, and that was in the bottom of a cañon. The woods were exceedingly dense, filled with willow, alder, and devils club. In places, the latter, so thick that it was impenetrable, formed the most serious obstacle to progress everywhere on the slopes below timber-line. In no part of the northern coast country have I seen devils club so dense.

Johnson, after a long tramp, had seen nothing but goats. The next day we started for the Meade Glacier, which loomed up at the head of the valley, seamed, turretted, and spired. It required two and a half hours to cross the several channels of the river, since we were obliged to walk back and forth to find fording places, and the wading through the stiff current was attended with much danger.

Goats were scattered about high on the mountains to the east, both singly and in small bands, many of them feeding on the walls of cliffs, others browsing among the second growth well down on the slopes. Now and then one would appear apparently glued to the perpendicular wall of a peak, which it would slowly climb, and on reaching the top would loom up against the sky-line. Arriving at the glacier, which was practically a mountain of ice, I climbed up at one side, and, crossing deep crevasses bridged here and there by narrow walls of ice, climbing up and down the pinnacles of the irregular surface, travelled two miles back into the ice world, which continues, perhaps, a hundred miles or more behind the coast range. Evidences of life were limited to a few old black bear tracks seen on the bars, and a porcupine observed close to a channel of the river.

We tramped about the next day without seeing anything but goats, and, June 19, placed our canoe in the main channel of the river and raced to the mouth in an hour and a half. The tide was low and we had to wait until afternoon, when the small steamer came to bring us back to Skagway. Soon after starting, I saw a most interesting sight. Bald eagles and gulls were very numerous about the flats, and as we were coasting a mile out from the shore, a gull, hotly pursued by an eagle, flew rapidly by the steamer. Soon a second eagle joined the chase, and then a third. For half an hour we watched the gull trying to escape the death pursuit, until finally it succeeded. One of the eagles would directly chase it, the other two at the same time flying in a parallel course, one on each side, twenty-five yards distant.

The middle eagle with long, sweeping wing-beats, would rapidly gain on the gull until near enough to swoop, with talons extended to seize it. But the gull would suddenly dodge by making a rapid dive or a quick, perpendicular ascent, when the momentum of the eagle would carry it far beyond. Then one of the other eagles would quickly swing around and resume the chase as the first aggressor was returning to a flanking position. Again and again an eagle would gain, swoop, and miss, as the active gull successfully dodged, until at length when all were approaching the shore, the eagles gave up the chase and alighted on trees, while the gull wheeled and disappeared among the other gulls flying over the flats.

THE KATZEHIN RIVER
THE PELLY RIVER

Looking toward the Meade Glacier, June 17.

CHAPTER XII

THE PELLY RIVER – 1905

HAVING STOPPED AT both Whitehorse and Selkirk in the hope of finding a means of transportation up the Pelly, I arrived in Dawson July 12, where good luck at last came to me. It had just been decided to send the steamer *Vidette*, the patrol-boat of the North-west Mounted Police, up the Pelly on an inspection trip, for the purpose of investigating the condition of the Indians and of gathering as much information as possible about the trappers and the country. My friend, Major Zachary Taylor Wood, commander of all the Police in the Yukon Territory, invited me to go on the *Vidette* as a guest, and it was to leave Selkirk July 17. Major Wood, who had been commanding officer in the Territory from the days of the first rush into Dawson, was keenly interested in science and natural history, and had taken special interest in my trips. In every way he assisted me, and it is owing to his courtesy more than anything else, that I was enabled to carry out the plans for that summer, which had long before been decided upon.

The next night I boarded the steamer *Dawson* and reached Selkirk the morning of July 17, to find the *Vidette* already there, under the command of Captain John Taylor, of the North-west Mounted Police, whom Major Wood had detailed to make the Pelly River inspection. Besides the regular captain, pilot, and crew of the *Vidette*, several trappers and prospectors, who had come down the Pelly early in the summer to get provisions, were there waiting for the boat to start, and thoroughly happy at the generosity of Major Wood, who had asked them to join the boat as guests of the government, thus saving the long, hard journey which they would have had if they had been obliged to pole and track their loaded canoes up the river.

Tom Jeffries, a tall, broad-shouldered French Canadian, whom I had engaged to accompany me for the summer, was there waiting for me. He had passed his early life among the lumber camps in Eastern Canada, and following his vocation had gradually drifted westward until the Klondike rush, when he joined that excited crowd of gold-seekers. He, like so many others, had wandered about the Yukon Territory in the hope of locating a good prospect, until, after repeated failures, he had taken to trapping for the purpose of getting a grub-stake in order to again indulge the never-fading hope of finding gold. Though not a hunter, he was a thorough woodsman and was reputed to rank among the best canoemen in the whole country. Also, he had spent one winter on the banks of the Pelly opposite the Glenlyon Mountains, where, later in the fall, I intended to look for sheep. I had obtained a fine Strickland canoe from the White Pass Railroad, and had purchased the old horse *Danger*, one of our pack-horses of the preceding summer. Horse, canoes, and provisions were loaded on the boat, and at 2:30 in the afternoon we started and were soon steaming up the Pelly River.

July 17.—The *Vidette* was a small stern-wheel steamer of light draft and powerful engines; her captain and pilot were experienced river navigators and had long been in the service of the government. Two of the trappers, Van Gorda and Corning,

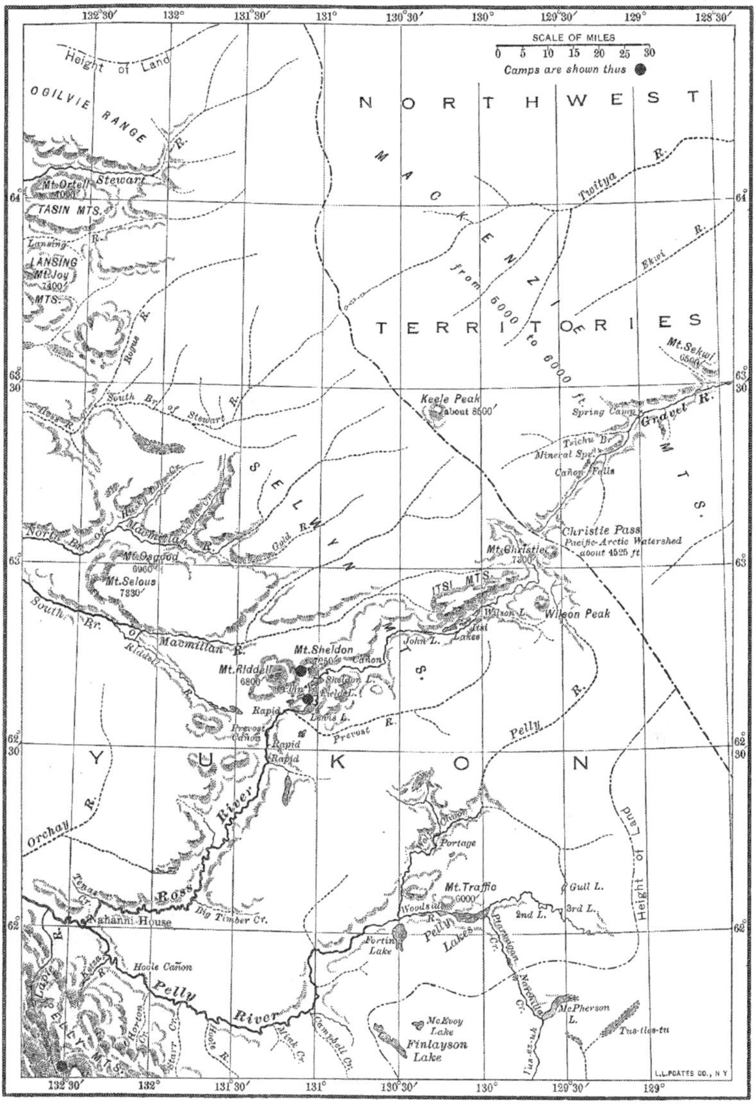

Map of Ross River, showing author's hunting camps, including that in Pelly Mountains.

OTHER HUNTING CAMPS ALONG THE PELLY RIVER ARE INDICATED IN THE MAP OF YUKON TERRITORY.

were returning to their cabins on the upper Pelly above Hoole Cañon. Another, Rose, had a cabin on the Pelly, fifty miles below Ross River; and two other prospectors were about to winter at Hoole Canon to prospect the creeks in that vicinity.

How delightful it was to be again steaming up the Pelly in a comfortable little steamer, under sunny skies, with interesting companions, and with the anticipation of exploring new country and studying the sheep!

Two of the trappers had occupied cabins that I had seen the previous year on the banks of the MacMillan, and I tried to get from all as much information as possible about the country and its animals. But the trappers and even the market hunters of Yukon Territory and Alaska, with rare exceptions, care little about the habits of animals and have not cultivated the power of accurate observation. Though some are good moose hunters, and understand where to find and how to kill these animals, they appear to know little about their life history, and even such observations as they have made are unusually tinctured with erroneous interpretation. Many of them agree on the methods of trapping lynxes, martens, and beavers—the principal animals trapped—but all differ as to their habits. I did not, therefore, get much reliable information about the denizens of the northern wilderness, until, when thirty miles up the river, we picked up a young English trapper, J. F. Hosfall, with his wife and four children, who were tracking a long poling boat loaded with a year's supplies. They had started for Kalzas Creek on the MacMillan River, where they intended to pass the winter and trap in the country about Kalzas Lake. Captain Taylor at once took them aboard and I first made the acquaintance of Mrs. Hosfall, that remarkable woman who so appealed to Selous, when he met her the following year, that he incorporated a short sketch of her, together with some incidents in her life, in his book, *Recent Hunting Trips in British North America*.

Mrs. Hosfall taking in the salmon net.

PHOTOGRAPH BY H.Q. FRENCH.

My acquaintance with her was often renewed in after years, and I have found her the most interesting character I have known in Alaska or Yukon Territory. Her father, a sturdy, upright American, was one of the traders who had settled on the Yukon River in the early days of the advent of the Alaska Commercial Company; and, like nearly all of these men, had taken to himself an Indian woman as companion. Born about twenty-five years before I met her, of a mother in the tribe of Indians occupying hunting territory in the vicinity of the Porcupine River, in early youth she had been taken to the missionary established at Fort McPherson on the Peel River. During the summers she was trained in reading, writing, cooking, and domestic work. Fall, winter, and spring she had joined her mother, and with her had followed the band of Indians, thus leading the wandering life of these aboriginal hunters and trappers. She had even wandered as far as Great Bear Lake, and after marrying Hosfall when she was twenty years of age, she had accompanied him in his trapping life, having been three years near the head of the Chandelar River, and having spent the last two years trapping on the Pelly. As a tribute to her resourcefulness, Selous has related her remarkable experience after the burning of her cabin, which occurred in the spring before I met her. He well remarks that she has inherited the best traits of both races. Her graceful figure was lithe and sinewy; her face was stamped with an exceedingly sweet expression; her manners were modest and refined; her language flowed in a soft, sympathetic tone. These traits gave to her personality an idealistic reality—the only time I have ever seen it among Indian women—which the romantic Indian maidens of fiction have often called forth in the imagination.

In all that pertained to hunting, trapping, woodcraft, and life in the far Northern wilderness, Mrs. Hosfall combined the instincts and knowledge of the Indian with the

The Hosfall Family, 1909.
PHOTOGRAPH BY H.Q. FRENCH.

Nahanni House, July 22.

Indian camp on bank of Pelly, July 20.

capacity of the white man. Supple, strong, and enduring, she could pole or track a boat, handle an axe, build a cabin, shoot a rifle, hunt, put out traps and nets, as well as most experienced white men. In addition she could cook even better than most white women—certainly very much better with the provisions gleaned from the woods, and under the conditions in the wilderness. She was also skilful to a high degree in all the practical work performed by Indian women—dressing animals, and tanning their skins, catching and drying fish, making moccasins, robes and clothes; and in the execution of their artistic products of headwork and porcupine-quill work, she was as efficient and creative in design as the best of them. She spoke English perfectly, and also the Indian language of her race. Her knowledge of animal life, based on interested observation and experience, was so accurate that I have never found reasons to doubt her assertions about it. She was accompanied by four little daughters, the oldest five years, the youngest born the preceding winter—healthy, active, bright-eyed little creatures, very pretty, and with the sweetest of dispositions. They were truly little wild sprites of the wilderness in which they had been born and bred. The two youngest were born on the banks of the Pelly, each in midwinter when the thermometer registered many degrees below zero and when Mrs. Hosfall was in her cabin *entirely alone*—her husband being absent on the trapping line. When one considers the conditions, and realizes that Mrs. Hosfall was obliged, unaided, not only to endure confinement, but also to keep her fire burning and to cook and care for the other children at the same time, the fact that she passed through it all successfully provokes some reflection on the advantages of leading a natural life. The highest tribute to the character of Mrs. Hosfall is the fact that she is not only beloved by all trappers, prospectors, and other white men who have known her, but she is absolutely respected by them.

The boat steamed ahead and the next morning arrived at Granite Canon, where the experienced captain directed her course along the left bank, and soon threw out a rope, which was pulled by half a dozen men just enough to take up the slack. This was sufficient to assist her powerful engine to overcome the resistance and propel the boat over a short, strong rapid. That was the only assistance required to navigate the long rapids of the cañon. What a contrast to my experience on the *Emma Knot*, when we were trying to go through the year before! Later in the morning we reached the mouth of the MacMillan River where the Hosfalls were left to occupy, for a short time, a small cabin constructed on the bank of the Pelly, close to a big eddy, which was an excellent place to set a net and obtain a stock of King salmon, which were then beginning to run up the river. After leaving the mouth of the MacMillan, I entered a region entirely new to me.

The Pelly River, discharging a volume of water slightly less than that of the Lewes, joins it at Selkirk. The Yukon River is formed by their junction. In the summer of 1840, the Hudson Bay Company, having established a post at Fort Halkett on the lower Liard River, commissioned Robert Campbell, one of those doughty Scotch pioneers in its employ, to explore the North Branch of the Liard to its source and cross over the divide of land in search of a river flowing westward. With two Indians, Lapie and Ketza, and an interpreter, Hoole, Campbell successfully crossed the divide and discovered the river, which he named in honor of Sir H. Pelly, a Governor of the Company.

After floating down a few miles on a raft they returned, and, in 1842, the Hudson Bay Company constructed a trading post, Fort Pelly Banks, thirty-one miles above Hoole Canon. In 1843, Campbell, accompanied by Hoole, two French Canadians and three Indians, left that place in a canoe and descended to the Lewes River, which he named after Chief

Factor, John Lee Lewes. In 1848, Campbell established Fort Selkirk at the junction of the Pelly and Lewes.

In 1849, the post at Pelly Banks was accidently burnt and in 1850 was abandoned. In that same year, Campbell descended the main Yukon to the mouth of the Porcupine, and proved that the Lewes, Pelly, and Yukon were identical. In 1852, on the 21st of August, Fort Selkirk was pillaged by the Chilkat Indians, and the post had to be abandoned. Campbell set out in a canoe, ascended the Pelly, crossed to Lake Frances, descended the Liard, and arrived at Fort Simpson the 21st of October. After winter set in, he travelled overland to Crow Wing in Minnesota, arriving there the 13th of March, and reached London the 18th of April. Such a wonderful journey, undertaken for the purpose of persuading Sir George Simpson to re-establish Fort Selkirk, deserved more recognition than it received, for the directors of the company decided to abandon the Selkirk trading post altogether.

As an explorer, Robert Campbell, discoverer of the Pelly and the Lewes, the true sources of the upper Yukon, deserves to rank among those mighty men, Hearne, MacKenzie, Dease, and Simpson. He left no book to exploit his achievements, but fortunately Dr. George M. Dawson established communication with him before his death, and thus preserved a precious account of his career.

In the '80's, wandering prospectors were gradually spreading over the Yukon Territory, and some of them ascended the Pelly to prospect along its bars.

It was not until 1887, however, when the late Dr. George M. Dawson, the eminent Canadian geologist, navigated the river from old Pelly Bank Post to the Lewes, that a survey of the river was made and positive information about it was published.

Dr. Dawson and his party ascended the Stikine, proceeded down the Dease and up the Frances to Frances Lake, crossed the divide, and after descending the Pelly to its confluence with the Lewes, ascended the latter river, and crossing the Chilkoot Pass, arrived at the head of Lynn Canal September 20.

The results of that exploration were published in a report of such excellence and accuracy, that to my mind it is not only a model of what such reports should be, but has not since been equalled by any of the numerous publications of explorations issued by the Geological Surveys of either Canada or the United States.

Not only are the topography, geology, climatic conditions, and natural history, treated as fully as the limited time on such a long journey would permit, but space is also given to the history of the region and a discussion of the Indian tribes inhabiting it. The accompanying maps are complete and accurate.

In 1892, Warburton Pike ascended the Stikine, wintered on the Dease River, and in the spring of 1893 crossed Frances Lake on the ice, and travelled overland by a route farther to the south than that followed by Dr. Dawson. He discovered the Pelly Lakes and observed the main tributary of the Pelly, one hundred and forty miles above the mouth of the Ross, but did not ascend it. Descending the Yukon to Ikogmut, he crossed to the Kuskokwim and reaching its delta, canoed around the coast to Nushagak, where he embarked on a schooner bound for Unalaska. His delightful book, *Through the Subarctic Forest,* in which he narrates his remarkable journey, mentioning too lightly the dangers, difficulties, and hardships, will forever remain one of the classics of north-western travel.

After the rush into the Klondike in 1897, numerous prospectors and trappers ascended the Pelly and its tributaries, but all except a few trappers, and now and then a stray prospector, had abandoned it long before I made my trip.

The mountain regions bordering it, except here and there on the outside ranges, had not been penetrated, and the game animals, particularly the sheep, had practically not been disturbed.

Of all rivers navigable by canoe in Alaska or the Yukon Territory, the Pelly is quite the most enchanting. Its current is swifter than that of the MacMillan. Above its confluence with the latter, it flows in a meandering course back and forth in a wide valley, lined on one side or the other by long, smooth, hard gravel bars, or lofty escarped banks often castellated into turrets and pillars of fantastic shape. Numerous fine groves of tall spruces are scattered along its banks; tall poplars, growing on smooth, hard ground, continually fringe its shores.

The valley, varying from three to ten miles in width, is terraced on both sides, the land rising in a succession of high benches clothed with aspens and scattered spruces, and brightened by openings carpeted with green grass, which give it a happy aspect. Lofty mountain ranges, whose axes parallel the main course of the Pelly, extend far beyond the Ross River, and include the Glenlyons, which almost overhang the right bank of the Pelly.

July 18.—We steamed up this magnificent river while the days were clear and the sun was hot. No obstacles impeded the progress of the skillfully managed boat, which climbed over every riffle and kept strictly to the main channel, only stopping for the purpose of cutting a wood supply or tying to the bank during the dark twilight between midnight and two in the morning.

July 19.—Before me was the map made by Dr. Dawson, a map so accurate that as we progressed I could locate not only every island, but every grove of spruce trees. His description of the country proved to be so correct that I must again call attention to the accuracy of his report, a high tribute to that eminent man in whose death Canada suffered a loss not easily repaired. After passing the Glenlyons, we were close to the mountains of the Tay River on the left, until those of the Pelly range loomed up in the distance.

Bird life at that season was as scarce as usual, and only a few moose tracks were seen on the bars. The beaver cuttings were old—all beavers having long before been trapped. During the steamboat trip we did not see an animal of any kind except red squirrels.

July 20.—The following morning we reached Rose's cabin and left him there. He had told me there were sheep in the mountains behind, and I intended to investigate them on my return in the fall.

In the afternoon, shortly after seeing an old Indian and two boys on the left bank, we came to their camp, where four families were occupying tents. They were catching salmon, and numerous fish were hung to dry on poles. They had an abundant supply of moose meat, and never have I seen Indians in the north of such healthy and vigorous appearance. As I took the horse off the boat, all started to run, and their dogs, which were tied near the tents, became greatly excited and struggled against their chains in efforts to attack him. None of the Indians of the upper Pelly River had ever before seen a horse. Reassured, they soon came back and Captain Taylor distributed some presents including cigars, which the squaws promptly began to smoke, while even the children begged for them.

Soon after leaving the Indian camp, the Pelly ranges were more distinctly visible, high dome-shaped mountains fronting the river, and now and then I could see a snowcapped peak appearing far in the interior. To penetrate the Pelly Mountains and hunt the sheep was the object of my trip. In these ranges Indians had their hunting grounds, principally for moose, since they only kill sheep on the outer range. Except for an occasional prospector who had wandered near the outer range, no white man had hunted in their depths, and practically nothing was known about them. For the purpose of penetrating them I had brought *Danger*, but the question of a feasible route, and the habitat of the sheep, remained to be solved. I hoped to get from the Indians sufficient information to enable us to reach the outer range, from which it would be necessary to find a way into the interior ranges beyond.

The river above was shallow, and once some difficulty was experienced before overcoming a swift rapid, but the boat steamed on until midnight, with glorious mountain vistas on both sides, and starting again after two hours, approached Nahanni House at eight in the morning, the steam whistle blowing and colors flying.

July 21.—As the *Vidette* rounded the curve into Ross River and made fast, I gazed from the deck at the multitude of Indians—men, women, and children—all assembled on the bank and nervously rushing about. That tribe of Indians had been less in contact with white men than any other in the north, and their behavior called to mind the gatherings at the Hudson Bay trading-posts in early days. The sight was one to be long remembered. When the gang-plank was put out I suddenly rode *Danger* to the shore and approached the Indians on a trot, while men, women, and children were fleeing in all directions and shouting in fright. My progress was suddenly checked, however, for at once a dozen or more dogs rushed at the horse, howling and snapping. If the trappers had not quickly beaten them off, the horse surely would have been disabled.

After a short time we decided to make a temporary camp on the other side of the Pelly River, not only for the safety of the horse, but to keep our provisions at a distance from the dogs. The boat brought us across, the provisions and equipments were unloaded, and the *Vidette* departed to ascend the river for the purpose of finding the limit of steamboat navigation. Captain Taylor, a charming gentleman, had been a delightful host, the company had been attractive and interesting, and that steamboat trip up the Pelly was the most fascinating one I have ever taken on the northern rivers.

We soon erected a shelter, cached our provisions, and while *Danger* was feeding in the long grass growing abundantly near the camp, we recrossed the river to the Indian encampment. With the exception of the Indians we had seen below on the river, the whole tribe was there, waiting for the return of Mr. Lewis, owner of Nahanni House. He had gone to Victoria, and was to return on the *Quick* with ammunition, which was entirely lacking at the Post, and the Indians could not depart to hunt until they were supplied with it.

The tribe of Pelly Indians, including ail its members, comprised eighty-nine Indians. There is some doubt as to its exact ethnological status; but none that it should be included in the group of tribes referred to by the Hudson Bay Company's people as Nahanni. It is also closely allied to that branch of the Nahanni group designated as Kaska, which includes two cognate tribes occupying the territory tributary to Dease River east of McDames Creek, and to the upper Liard River. The tribe is called by different names by the adjacent tribes, and Dr. Dawson proposes the name of *Es-pat-o-ti-na*. By comparing numerous words of the Pelly Indians with those in the vocabularies appended to Dr. Dawson's report, I found them to correspond very closely, if not exactly (most of them are the same) with those of the *Ti-tsho-ti-na* tribe—the western branch of the Kaska.

Two years before I arrived there, Tom Smith, a trader, had established the post, which later was purchased by Mr. Lewis, who named it Nahanni House. Before the establishment of that post, the Indians had traded through Indians of

Liard Post on the Liard River, and sometimes with the Indians attached to the trading-post at the mouth of the Big Salmon River on the Lewes. Missionaries had never been among them, and their contact with whites after the Pelly Banks Post was abandoned in 1850, until Nahanni House was established, was only incidental, as when individuals of the tribe had met wandering prospectors.

Owing to these facts more than anything else, they were the healthiest and finest looking Indians I have ever seen in the interior of the northern country. Most of the men were fine specimens, and also the women, who bore children abundantly and reared them in health and vigor. They were all absolutely honest and lived a primitive Indian life, except that after Nahanni House was established, they used tents instead of the old brush shelters. They wore white man's clothing, and utilized the other novelties provided by the store. Up to that time they had not permitted a single one of their women to mingle with a white man; the tribe, therefore, was in that respect the single exception among all the tribes, both coast and interior, in the whole north country.

Their habits are exactly similar to those of other northern Indians. Their country has been partitioned, and sections are allotted to different members of the tribe, who spend the fall, winter, and spring hunting and trapping until the salmon arrive, when they catch and dry enough to last them for a short time, until they again begin to hunt. At that time, they differed from other Indians in not having acquired the lazy habits usually characteristic of life near a trading-post, nor had they been in the least demoralized by whiskey. Neither did they suffer from some of the habits acquired through well-meaning, but short-sighted and misdirected missionary enterprise.

Walking into their camp I soon found one of them who knew a few words of English, and after several had gathered about me, we held a conversation. One had the skin of a sheep, and as he handed it to me his dog snapped at my leg, and immediately several dogs rushed at me, while the squaws came running from the tents and clubbed them away. Indian dogs dislike white men as much as a white man's dog hates an Indian. Had I been alone, those dogs might have killed me, especially if I had fallen.

As a result of the fragmentary information I could get from the Indians, I decided to strike across the country and reach the Lapie River at the point where it emerges from the mountains, and try to penetrate the more distant ranges by following up its course.

Later the *Vidette* returned, having encountered a rapid, four miles above, which she could not force through. After spending the evening on her deck we slept under our shelter until awakened by the whistle announcing her departure.

CHAPTER XIII

THE PELLY MOUNTAINS – 1905

JULY 22.—THE next day was very hot, and after sifting out provisions for the trip and arranging a pack for Danger to carry, we spent the rest of the time about Nahanni House. It consisted of nothing but a small log cabin used for a store; a small log warehouse, and another cabin which Lewis occupied. Jim Grew, who had constructed a small cabin across the river for head-quarters while trapping during the winter, had charge of the post during Lewis's absence. He was over seventy-five years old and had served at different Hudson Bay trading posts all the way from Labrador to the Pacific. Though still active, he was too old for the hard work necessary for successful trapping; nevertheless he could not depart from his old life, and chose to die in the wilderness. His life was a mere existence, and three years later he was found dead in a cabin on the MacMillan. Dan McKinnon, his partner, was occupying Grew's cabin. Van Bibber, a stalwart fellow brought up in the mountains of Kentucky, was there to meet his partner, Van Gorda, and with him was a young Indian boy from Liard Post. These two men had wintered in the vicinity of the Pelly Lakes, and had planned to return there.

July 23.—The whole month of July had been exceedingly dry and very hot. The next day was no exception. Many

Indians had come to our camp for the purpose of seeing the horse, which aroused intense interest among them. That morning three appeared very early and watched us throw the pack on *Danger.* So great was their astonishment to see him walk off with a pack of two hundred pounds, that they followed us for three miles and showed us an Indian trail which led to the Lapie River, six miles above its mouth.

For the first five miles we travelled slowly, in a northward direction, crossing some heavily timbered ridges, often pausing to chop trees and brush, until we descended to a fairly level country sparsely timbered with spruces, poplars, and willows. After crossing seven miles through this, we came out upon a high bench rising directly from the Lapie. Through the valley of the river, which there emerges from a box cañon, I could see the interior Pelly ranges and the snowy peaks of the divide. As we were descending the bench to the river, the familiar chatter of the ground-squirrel greeted us. We slept near the brawling river, under a clear sky, and the noise of the current brought back many reminiscences of my trip up Coal Creek.

The Lapie River, so named by Dr. Dawson after one of the faithful Indian companions of Campbell, who first discovered it on his initial trip down the Pelly, enters the Pelly ten miles below the Ross. Its character is strictly similar to that of Coal Creek, but it carries a much larger volume of water—so large, in fact, that at the stage when I was there in both July and August, there was not a single fording place anywhere within fifty miles from its mouth. Through that distance it descends at the rate of thirty feet to the mile. From its source in the divide ranges, it flows in a north-east direction; its length is between eighty and a hundred miles; its width for the last forty miles, from seventy to a hundred feet, becoming narrower above.

July 24-26.—For the next three days the travelling was exactly like that on the upper reaches of Coal Creek, except that we were obliged to keep on the left bank, for even if a ford could have been found, it would not have been practicable to have taken a horse along the other side, because of continuous ridges sloping precipitously to the river. When we had travelled about twenty miles, the high, rough mountains completely engulfed us. The main divide was not more than twenty or thirty miles farther on in a straight line, and a fine large tributary, flowing from extremely rugged mountains more to the southwest—perfect sheep ranges—entered the Lapie a short distance north of the divide. I decided to ascend this branch to timber-line and make my camp. Timber-line was twelve miles distant, and nine hundred feet above that part of the Lapie. Moose tracks had been abundant along the bars of the river, nearly all going down stream, but their trails were not so well defined as those on Coal Creek. Rabbits, ground-squirrels, and red squirrels were plentiful, bear signs scarce, and bird life almost absent, except for golden eagles, Alaska jays, ravens, and goshawks. The weather was fair, and there were no mosquitoes, a most singular fact, which can only be accounted for by the extreme dryness of the season. I cannot forget the last tramp up the branch between lofty slopes topped by cliffs and jagged crest-lines, the magnificent mountains close by on both sides fairly hanging over us, as we climbed around canons through which the creek dashed in cascades over precipices and roared through deep gorges, until we reached the limit of the timber. There, where two forks join, each flowing from mountain-girdled basins, we made camp in the big spruces near the bank of the chattering stream.

Among all the spots in which I have ever camped, that was one of the most enchanting. The hard, dry ground was cushioned with spruce needles. Some of the spruces with big, gnarled trunks spread their dark-green foliage in canopy-tops, ornamented with thick clusters of hanging cones. Most of

Looking up the Lapie River, July 25.

The glories of the Pellys were spread out before me.

them shot up spires, their pointed tops giving the country that wild desolation so characteristic of the northern wilderness. Many inclined at sharp angles over the creek in graceful contrast, pleasantly breaking the austere straight lines of the forest, and producing a bowery effect above the splashing current as it raced in serpentine course down the valley.

Directly in front was the rolling basin of the South Fork, surrounded by a jumble of high peaks reared above snow-striped slopes, all the blending colors of their rocky surfaces in sharp contrast with the bright green of the upper reaches of the basin below, while numerous water-falls, pierced by the sun's rays, as they dashed down the slopes, gleamed in different tints.

The mountains around the basins of the East Fork, perhaps smoother in outline, were equally high, and even richer in color.

Behind, almost overhanging the camp, reared up a long, high, savage range of limestone and granite; its slopes carved into canons and precipices; its crests serrated in rising and falling outlines, trimmed with radiating buttresses, spired peaks, and bands of snow, richer in contrasting colors than any of the other ranges observed in the Pelly Mountains.

But these inspiring views were near. Beyond, stretched a bewildering sea of summits, the more distant ones fading to the sight and suggesting the mysterious unknown.

The evening light glowed in the sky as we threw the load off the tired horse and made a fire. Luminous banks of burning crimson clouds hung over the summits of the South Fork; the sky in the east was cold and gray, while the light rays of the sun, then sunken below the nearer mountains, failed to reach the valley, then overspread with a deep purple hue, in sombre contrast to the brilliantly lighted mountains beyond. We did not attempt to erect the shelter that night, but slept beneath the spruces.

July 27.—Early in the morning I started off to obtain, if possible, a supply of meat for camp.

No description of the Pelly Mountains has ever been written. When Dr. Dawson spoke of them as dome-shaped granitic masses, smoother to the west, more serrated to the east, covered with a small herbaceous growth, slopes and peaks extremely uniform, shaped by normal processes of denudation, he was necessarily judging from the appearance of the outer range as observed from the Pelly River.

Once inside the outside range, they present an entirely different appearance, and it becomes clear that the denudation has not reached such an advanced stage.

The Pelly Mountains may be somewhat loosely defined as a group extending from the valley of the upper Liard in a north-west trend of crest outlines to the Orchay River, where they swing westward toward the Rose River. A gap of twenty miles of low ridges connects them with the Glenlyons, which may be considered as an interrupted continuation of the Pellys.

The series of parallel ranges extends through a width of from thirty to perhaps fifty miles, the peaks rising above sea-level from five to eight thousand feet.

They were formed by erosion from an uplifted plateau, and although a general trend can be detected, the ranges are so intersected by others, equally high, that it may be more proper to call them a complex, rather than a well-defined series.

In appearance they are more similar to the Ogilvie ranges than any other mountain group I have seen in the north. But in general they are higher, bolder, more irregular, and rougher; the valleys and canons are deeper, the crests hold more snow during the summer, the rivers draining them are larger in volume.

Timber-line, about 4,500 feet, is higher, and willow and dwarf-birch grow so much more densely on the lower slopes that all the mountains are more difficult to climb than those of the Ogilvies. Nature has carved the Pellys in more rugged outlines than those of the Ogilvies, and has given to them the same rich, contrasting colorations. It has carved even more beautiful basins among them, and filled them with the same kind of exquisite crystal lakes fed by melting snow. The same richly colored flora carpets the slopes.

I was about to climb among these wonderful mountains, and keeping close to the creek which headed in the east basin, where numerous graylings lay at the bottom of the pools, I saw, floating down among the riffles, two harlequin ducks, those exquisite creatures which adorn the dancing mountain creeks. The dense willow brush and dwarf-birches so impeded walking that it required an hour to go two and a half miles to the head of the basin. It was hot and sultry and a light haze hung about the crests. Again I was walking over emerald-green pastures in an amphitheatre of mountains, with ground-squirrels running about in all directions, while above me two golden eagles wheeled in flight.

Beginning to climb a mountain on the west side of the basin, I was surprised to see a chipmunk picking up some kind of morsels among the rocks. Soon I was cheered by reaching a sheep-trail leading up the slope, and, following it, I at length reached the top, 6,900 feet altitude, according to my barometer.

For the first time the glories of the Pellys were spread out before me—high, ragged ranges shooting up into the sky in all directions, the vision lost in a sea of peaks. No wind, not even a distant sound disturbed the silence.

The western face of the mountain fell in sheer cliffs for two thousand feet, the whole wall studded with castellated pillars of rock projecting upward from it; while below was an exquisite cliff-bound basin containing a shining lake.

A mile and a half across the basin was the crest of a mountain, below which was a cornice of snow covering about an acre and extending down a steep slope. As I turned my field-glasses along the crest, a grizzly bear standing on the sky-line just above the snow, came into view. The bear, high on the mountain-crest, outlined against the sky, presented a wonderful picture of wild life in a stupendous landscape.

It soon jumped over into the snow, walked back and forth several times, then lay down about thirty feet from the edge and appeared like a small, black spot. Shortly I saw, not a hundred yards distant to the right, in line with the snow, a band of twenty sheep feeding indifferently, though they had often looked toward the snow at the time when the bear had been moving. It was too hazy to clearly distinguish their horns, but I thought they were rams. Since it would have required many hours to descend and make the wide circuit necessary to climb, unseen by them, I did not attempt it, but watched them.

In half an hour they started single file directly for the snow, and to my complete astonishment walked up on it, not twenty feet from the sleeping bear. Eight that were ahead paused in the snow, apparently looking at the bear; then all slowly walked on over the snow and disappeared on the other side of the crest. Stranger still, as the first sheep came upon the snow, I saw the bear's head rise up, until, as they stood still, it went down and the bear remained asleep long after they had gone over the crest.

After eating some lunch, I followed the sheep-trail for some distance along the crest, when I saw on an opposite mountain, separated from the one on which I was walking by a deep, narrow valley, a large band of sheep feeding well up the side. I counted about eighty in all, mostly ewes and lambs, with a few small rams. Descending over the steep, broken rock talus to a ridge, I walked along it until the sheep were not more than five hundred yards distant in a straight line across the valley, and, concealing myself among the rocks, I watched them. Some were feeding, some lying down. About ten three-year-old rams kept together, slightly separated from the rest. A hundred yards above was an old ewe lying on the slope, keeping an alert watch both up and down. In half an hour, when another old ewe walked up to her, she rose and went down to feed among the others, while the ewe above lay down to replace her as the "sentinel" to protect the band.

As the "sentinel"! Never was the posting of guards better illustrated; and what a positive conclusion one could have drawn if not especially aroused to continue watching and observing! Half an hour passed, while the sheep below were feeding, resting, always alert, and on the lookout for danger; the lambs were nursing and frisking. Then the "sentinel" rose, descended, and mingled with the others, leaving none on guard in her place

Thus entirely unprotected they continued feeding, until the lengthening shadows warned them of evening, and they slowly fed upward toward the crest to lie down for the night. During all the time that I watched them, the lambs kept playing, chasing each other, butting, and running back and forth.

I was so dose that through my glasses the colors of all the sheep were clearly discernible, and I carefully made notes in the small note-book which I carried. The majority of them were nearly of the same type as that of some of the Stone sheep killed on the Sheslay River north of Telegraph Creek on the Stikine, the skins of which are in the American Museum of Natural History in New York. From a short distance, the heads appeared perfectly white, the bodies light gray, intermediate in color between typical *Ovis stonei* and the saddle-backed sheep, so-called *Ovis fannini*. None had necks as dark as typical *Ovis stonei*, a few would be classed as *Ovis fannini*. Four were almost as white as the light colored sheep killed on the MacMillan. Several had lambs strictly resembling their mother in color. Four of the darkest ewes had white lambs. Three of the whitest ewes had very dark lambs. One dark ewe had two lambs, one white, one dark. The saddle-backed ewes had lambs, singly and in pairs, varying in all shades of color from whitish to very dark.

I was a long distance from camp and it was not possible to stalk the sheep without descending on the other side to the foot of the mountains, so that I could climb around the other mountain in a course which would keep me hidden from their sight. But since many days might elapse before rams could be found and meat had to be obtained as quickly as possible, I made the descent and began a circling ascent of the mountain. After three hours of slow and tiresome work, I was near the crest and carefully circled for the purpose of establishing the position of the sheep. At length, about to come in view of the place where I hoped to find them, I crawled flat on my stomach, and lifting my head saw all standing, banded closely together, about a hundred and fifty yards opposite me. About to lie down, they were taking one last look below. A large ewe stood a few feet to the right, and not caring to fire into the band, I aimed at her, and, fortunately, hit her in the heart. The whole band, led by a large ewe, at once dashed wildly along the slope and disappeared over the steep, almost vertical walls that flanked the slope slightly beyond. The ewe had no milk, and therefore no lamb. Her head was pure white and the grayish pattern was so subdued that the color could be compared most closely with the darkest specimen I had killed in the Ogilvies.

It was nearly eleven in the night; twilight color had overspread the landscape; the peaks distant to the west were still illumined with rosy light caught from the fading sun. Taking the hind quarters with as much extra meat as could be carried,

I staggered downward to the foot, kindled a small fire, and made tea, which greatly refreshed me. I then shouldered the load and more rapidly went down the sloping pastures of the basin, until I plunged into the dense brush. It was among the dark hours that I toiled through the willows, and broad daylight again when I walked into camp at 3.30 in the morning. But we had a supply of meat; I had once more been high among the mountains; the sight of mountain-sheep and that of a grizzly bear had set glowing my love of the wilderness; I had again heard the chatter of the squirrel and the whistle of the marmot.

The shelter had been erected, and old *Danger* was peacefully lying before it, near the dead fire. Jeffries jumped up, and almost shouted when he saw the fat mutton. The fire was soon blazing and nothing less than as much meat as could be crowded into a big deep frying-pan satisfied his craving for it.

CHAPTER XIV

HUNTING RAMS – 1905

JULY 28.—AFTER a few hours of sleep was awakened by the loud clucking of a ptarmigan close to the shelter, and soon heard the peeping of the scattered chicks, which were hurriedly gathering about her. Several ground-squirrels, whose holes were very near the camp, were running about or sitting up and chattering. Jeffries had started the fire and prepared another great quantity of meat, most of which he consumed with the eagerness of a starving man. During the morning I remained in camp to arrange everything in order.

After lunch I started for the mountain south-east of camp, and in two and a half hours succeeded in reaching the crest. Looking through my field-glasses along the slopes of the rough mountain behind the camp, I could see seven sheep which were too distant to make out the sex. Proceeding along the crest I reached the highest peak, seven thousand five hundred and fifty feet in altitude. A sheep-trail followed the ridge-roof of the crest, and a few old tracks of ewes and lambs were there. I heard one cony, and saw two rock ptarmigan. Mists bringing light showers of rain, all gathering exclusively around the mountain on which I stood, continually floated by and enveloped me, while to the south-west the sky was clear, and I reached the head of the basin just as the sun was sinking.

Massed around the basin were gothic-spired ranges whose peaks fell in vertical cliffs many hundreds of feet to the steeply inclined talus which led to the soft, green pastures below. The serried crests, marbled with snow, burning with red, iron-stained rock, glowing with granites, caught the sunlight and were bathed in a rosy hue, while numerous little rainbows, formed in the spray of the small cataracts that dashed over the precipices, reflected their brilliant colors in contrast to the dark rocks and shadowed area below.

I had gone several miles and had not seen a sheep since my field-glasses had revealed those on the mountain behind camp. Descending to the upper reaches of the basin, which contained several small lakes, I started down the creek toward camp. In forcing my way through the dripping willows which covered a valley a mile or more wide, I found many shed horns of moose. The valleys in the Pelly Mountains are filled with willows, all of which had been cropped by moose, a fact indicating that later in the fall and early winter when they come up from the lowlands to browse in the higher country the whole region is a magnificent moose range.

While passing through these willows, I flushed at least ten broods of ptarmigan, and saw several harlequin ducks floating with the current of the creek. I was thoroughly soaked before reaching camp at midnight, when Jeffries was aroused from sleep and given another chance to eat a large quantity of meat.

July 29.—Early in the morning I climbed a little knoll near-by and through my field-glasses, scanned the range behind. Two miles to the north-west, near the top of the smoother portion of a high spur which projected out from the slope, I saw twelve sheep, and more careful inspection revealed their spiral horns. Rams found so quickly! Hastening a mile down the creek to a point where a good view of the spur could be obtained, I seated myself to make a study of the situation. The spur, a high butte with two cone-shaped peaks rearing up from its grassy surface, was connected with the mountain by a knife-blade ridge rising almost vertically to a group of crags a few feet below the dominating peak—the highest in the vicinity.

Three of the rams were feeding near a fourth, which was lying down in front of the outside peak; three others were lying on the saddle between the peaks, two of them facing in opposite directions; five more feeding near them on the face of the spur, and one was lying down half-way up on the inside peak. There was no method of approach except in plain sight of the rams, and I waited for two or three hours in the hope that they would move to a position favorable for a stalk. Among them I noticed only three rams with large horns. They passed the time indifferently, feeding and resting, and though moving lazily, each kept constantly looking about—never neglecting the habit of alert watchfulness. No sentinel was posted at any time.

While I was waiting, a mile to the right along the slope appeared two rams travelling rapidly, now walking, now running, in the direction of the band. By observing their horns, I judged one to be five years old, the other, two or three. At first I thought they were detached members of the band hurrying back to join it. But reaching the spur they caught sight of the sheep above, approached cautiously to within a hundred yards and stopped, as all the rams jumped up and watched them. Several times they circled about the band without approaching nearer, while the rams in the band appeared to assume a threatening attitude. Finally they passed the band without attempting to enter it, and disappeared around the slope.

Repeated observations of the habits of sheep in later years gives me a clue to the actions of these two rams. They were members of another band of rams living in another part of the ranges, and having been separated by fright, or for some other reason, were probably trying to regain their own band, composed of members with which they had been born and reared. Bands of sheep have a strong tendency to exclude foreign members, and it is only after a single sheep or two have hovered about another band for days, sometimes even for weeks, that its members relax and admit the outsiders on terms of intimacy.

Once a hen ptarmigan came . through the dwarf-birch within three feet of me, while her chicks surrounded me as I sat motionless, until the mother, becoming suspicious, began to cluck, when all the chicks ran to her and she withdrew into the bush. The curiosity of the ground-squirrels was aroused, for several came almost to my feet, and after sitting up and chattering at me, quickly scampered away. Several Alaska jays flew about me and sat in the trees near-by, evidently waiting for some of the spoils that human beings usually provide for them.

At two in the afternoon, all the sheep slowly fed over the top of the spur and were lost to sight. At once I began to follow the plan worked out while waiting, and started to make the ascent of a high promontory protruding from a mountain opposite the spur and separated from it by a deep cañon, the head of which I might be able to climb around, and, if possible, cross the face of the spur and stalk the sheep if they should be feeding on the other side. In an hour I had ascended far enough to see that the ground at the head of the cañon was too precipitous to traverse. The only alternative was to find a way to the bottom of the cañon and ascend the slope of the spur to the two peaks. This involved great risk of frightening the sheep, for if they should be feeding on the other side near the top, now and then, according to their habits, one or another would probably come back to inspect the opposite side, in which case

He stopped long enough to receive a bullet in his heart, July 29.

He remained doubled up and almost suspended, July 29.

I would surely be observed. But knowing that the next day they might be far away, I decided to take the chance, and after much difficulty reached the bottom of the cañon and climbed up a notch in the opposite wall to some willows through which, in half an hour, I had fought my way, reaching a smooth, grassy slope that led steeply upward between the peaks. No sheep had re-appeared above, so I began to ascend slowly and cautiously, knowing that at any moment a ram might suddenly appear on the summit and see me if I was moving. Step by step I advanced, keeping as low as convenient, stopping every few feet and lying flat, always intently watching the crest above. My caution was increased as I came within rifle-shot of the top, and with rifle cocked, ready to fire at any ram that might appear, I finally reached a point within a few feet of the crest. There I rested a few moments to get my breath and steady my nerves. Then, creeping forward over the top, I slowly raised my head and looked over. Not a ram was visible. A succession of rocky walls, broken and rugged, jutting out in a curve from the spur, obstructed the view toward the mountain. Retiring from the skyline, I went a short distance around the outside cone and, creeping forward, again looked over. I could then see the whole area below, but no rams were there. The slope fell to a creek, on the opposite side of which sheer cliffs rose up to the rocky debris covering the side of the mountain. I knew that the rams had ascended and were somewhere near the higher crest above.

But one resource was left, and that was to climb the rim of the spur to the highest peak of the mountain. From there it would not be difficult to clamber along the crest and possibly find ,the rams in a place favorable for stalking.

That ascent of fifteen hundred feet I shall never forget. The connecting roof-ridge was so narrow that for most of the distance it was not more than a foot or two wide. The view

The ram simply stiffened out without rising and died, July 29.

Niche in the side of splintered wall, July 29.

in the direction of the sheep was cut off by projecting crags. On either side sheer precipices or confused vertical masses of sculptured rock fell several hundred feet to the inclined surface below. The knife-edge, however, had been carved by the elements eroded just enough so that small, sharp projections of rock, like an irregular series of teeth, protruded and provided a foothold. Slinging my rifle over my back and holding on the sharp nodules of rock above I toiled upward on this rough ladder-like precipitous path. I had started at four, and it was six P. M. when I reached the base of the pyramidal peak which rose fifty feet above the crest-line. The altitude was seven thousand eight hundred feet—more than five thousand feet above camp.

There I rested for a few moments. Not a sound reached my ears except the tinkling of the rills trickling down from the snow. A stupendous mountain panorama surrounded me. When my breath was regained, and the excitement, owing to the danger of the climb was subdued, I started to creep along the narrow rocky crest which, twenty feet farther on, was so abruptly broken that I could not see beyond. After going ten feet on my knees, I saw a pair of horns perfectly motionless, a hundred and fifty yards ahead and slightly below. Nothing more, but I knew that a ram was below them. Stretching on my stomach, foot by foot I crawled ten feet to the edge of the break, where I was thoroughly concealed by a crag rising three feet above the surface and falling perpendicularly to the crest below. Carefully moving my head to the side of the rock, I looked down. There were the twelve rams a hundred yards away, all lying down without any suspicion of the enemy who now had them at his mercy. All were facing in the same direction, looking down the slope up which they had ascended. Below, at the bottom of the valley, was the winding creek, gleaming through the dark green of the spruces. In front of them were piled precipice upon precipice. They were at the edge of a brink which

In front of them were piled precipice upon precipice.

FROM A PAINTING BY CARL RUNGIUS.

behind them fell fifty feet to a desolate basin of shattered rock filled with boulders and surrounded with turreted cliffs and craggy buttresses.

Their mixed colors were those common to the sheep of the region, the dark ones predominating; their heads, with the exception of three, were white. Each maintained an alert watch both in front and along the crest opposite to me. They kept jerking their heads to fasten their piercing gaze in those directions only; no danger could come from behind without their hearing it; the peak was in my direction, where they evidently felt safe from approach. I was facing the sun and could not take a photograph. Only three of the rams had large horns, the rest varying in age from five to three years.

Lying on my stomach and resting my rifle along my arm on the side of the rock, I fired at the ram which appeared to have the largest horns. At the crack of the rifle all jumped up and for a moment stood in wild confusion. The bullet had apparently gone true, for the ram simply stiffened out without rising and died. But another of the rams with large horns was holding his head in the air, his lower jaw falling loosely and bleeding. He suddenly dashed over the precipice, followed by the third with large horns, and by two small rams. Somehow reaching the foot, they again came in sight and dashed across the broken rock under some cliffs by my right, where they were lost to sight. Not hearing any more sounds of their running and knowing that they were standing, I remained perfectly still. The rest continued to stand and look, jerking their heads in all directions except toward me. None had even suspected the direction of the shot.

I watched the cliff for about three minutes, until a ram with large horns suddenly appeared, running down the slope. When a hundred yards distant, he stopped, long enough to receive a bullet in his heart. Then I heard a clatter of hoofs on the cliff, and saw the ram with the broken jaw leap on the top and stand on the skyline looking in the direction of the last ram I had killed. As I shot, he fell over the wall of the cliff and caught in a rift near the foot, where he remained doubled up and almost suspended. The other three had descended to the band, which, having run for a few hundred yards, had scattered and stood looking, not even then having located the direction of the shots.

Sitting on the rock, I rested and smoked my pipe. Three hard-earned trophies were before me. Under such circumstances, among mountain-crests, when the pulse bounds and the whole being is exhilarated by the intensely vitalizing air, while the senses, stimulated by the vigorous exercise of a dangerous climb and the sustained excitement of the stalk, are attuned to the highest pitch of appreciation of the Alpine panorama, there is no state of exaltation more sublime than that immediately following the climax of a day's successful hunt for the noble mountain ram.

A heavy wind suddenly swept by and dark threatening clouds began to gather directly above me. Hastening down the ledge, I found a niche in the side of a splintered wall which fell sheer a thousand feet to the ragged surface of the slope below. By edging along on a protruding shelf of rock I reached it and comfortably stowed myself under its protection, facing the rough-hewn peaks of the western ranges fading in the far horizon, while the sun, about to sink behind them, appeared like a big, crimson globe.

The clouds above grew black, lightning flashed along the crest, peals of thunder reverberated among the high-walled precipices, and after a heavy rain, great balls of hail half an inch in diameter fell in myriads, rattling and bounding among the rocks, rolling down the precipitous slopes, lodging in crevices and on projecting rocks, and speckling white the broken surface of the mountain. The storm was local and directly overhead. The sky to the west was clear. Through a canopy of darkness could be seen the shadowed valley of the Lapie, in strong contrast with the rugged snow-striped ranges beyond, whose snowy peaks, rising under a clear sky and gilded by the sun, were rosy gold set in delicate, floating clouds of pink. Nature concentrated all her wrath in a short space of time. After the hail, the clouds broke away, leaving a steel-gray sky overhead.

I quickly photographed the first ram, and finding a route down the precipice, photographed the others and then took the entire skin of the second. This was much whiter than the others, whiter than the type of *Ovis fannini*. Both the others were darker and approached more closely the type of *Ovis stonei*. The neck of the light one was pure white, those of the others were so full of dark hairs as to have a more grayish appearance.

Before the skin was off the rain began again. Stowing both the skin and the head in my rucksack and ascending to the crest, I struggled down the slope and reached camp late at night.

July 30.—Early in the morning, while I was preparing the head and fleshing the skin, Jefferies looked back on the mountain-side and saw two sheep. Through my field-glasses, I saw that they were the same two young rams which had passed in the opposite direction the day before. They had not found their band, and were slowly returning along the same slope.

After hanging the skin, we drank some tea and set out for the dead rams, toiling slowly up the slope I had descended the night before. Old bear diggings were everywhere, but the bear which had been seen on the snow-bank was the only one observed in the Pelly Mountains. Looking up we saw two golden eagles circling in the air above the carcasses.

Reaching the dead rams we learned the cause of the shattering of the lower jaw of the last ram killed the day before—a fact that had puzzled me. When I fired the first shot, the three large rams were lying close together, and the sun, shining directly in my eyes, had so confused my vision that, in aiming at the shoulder of the first ram, I had not perceived that the muzzle of another ram intervened. The bullet, passing through the lower jaw, had split in nine fragments, all of which penetrated the shoulder region of the ram at which I was aiming. Three of the pieces had passed through the heart and lungs, tearing large holes, and were lodged under the skin on the other side. At some time during its life that ram had broken a foreleg, and I noticed that it had been well joined and healed, though a large bunch remained about the fracture.

It was after seven in the evening when the last skin was off. Jefferies having tied both skins and heads in a pack, shouldered them, while I carried the hind quarters of another. It required three hours to stagger down the mountains and reach camp.

July 31.—The next day was spent preparing the skins and skulls and constructing a suitable framework under the trees, on which they could be hung to dry. The horns of all were of the narrow type, the widest not spreading over nineteen inches, and in the order killed their ages were seven, nine, and ten years, respectively. The food contents of their stomachs were the same as those of all the sheep I have ever killed in subarctic regions during the summer—a variety of young, tender weeds, particularly those of Dryas and mountain cranberry, scarcely any grass, and bits of lichens taken incidentally when cropping deep for the tender growth.

That day Alaska jays visited our camp for the first time, and after picking up a few pieces of meat, departed. During the three weeks we remained there, this was the only time when the jays, which were as abundant in that locality as elsewhere in the north, came about the camp. I have camped in other places, in both Yukon Territory and Alaska, where jays did not come to camp, but such absences are most exceptional. We had set out numbers of traps for mice, both in the woods and in the higher country, but not a mouse did we catch during all the time we were there, nor did I see any fresh signs. It was a season when nearly all the mice in that locality had disappeared.

In those happy days among the Pelly Mountains, a shadow was constantly playing over my exuberant spirits, the thought of the inevitable fate of the good horse *Danger*. Gentle, strong, and of good sense, he was naturally dependent on some kind of companionship. Far in the wilds, surrounded by woods, where the breezes often wafted to his delicate nostrils the air tainted with the odor of animals terrifying to him, he had become completely dependent on our near presence, except when he was obliged to stray off to feed. At intervals through the day he would wander about in search of good grass, but immediately after satisfying his hunger he would hasten back to camp, and after standing in the smoke of the fire to rid himself of flies would lie down in his hollow, three feet to the right of the shelter front. Although he continually begged for bits of bread and sugar, he developed none of those thieving habits so common among horses living in that country. Whenever I met him in the woods, after satisfying himself of my reality, he would trot up and follow me back to camp. He had become like an affectionate dog.

I was much interested to observe his keen senses of hearing and smell, which were fully as acute as those of the wild animals of the woods. When at a distance from camp he was as alert as any of them. Many times, when from an elevation I saw him feeding, I would try to approach unheard, but not even a moose could have detected me sooner than he did. When in a favorable wind he always scented me from a long distance, and Jefferies used to know of my approach to camp wholly by *Danger's* actions long before human ears could hear any

Camp in the Pellys, Tom Jefferies, July 28.

Standing in the smoke of the fire to rid himself of flies. Jefferies under the shelter, August 1.

sounds of footsteps. If one loves a horse, there is no situation where that affection can be so intensely bestowed as on the single animal far off in the wilderness where it seeks companionship in its master more dependently than anywhere else. After the trip, *Danger* must be shot—the only alternative was starvation.

August 1.—Very early the next morning I was pushing through willows on my way to climb the east part of the mountain behind camp, hoping that other rams might be found there. No clouds were in the sky, but a haze hung over the mountains and the wind was strongly blowing. In that direction a succession of spurs extended out from the mountains, enclosing large areas where rams might be feeding. One of the spurs sloped down to a high dome-shaped ridge, which I ascended nearly to the top, and keeping below the sky-line went around the dome to get a look on the other side.

The two stray rams I had seen before were lying down near the top, about two hundred yards to the left. Crawling behind some dwarf-birch bushes, I watched them through my field-glasses. Both were very light colored. The wind was blowing directly from me to them and although I was smoking my pipe, they showed no signs of alarm. After half an hour they rose and passed over the top. Then I went forward to photograph them, but just before arriving on the summit, expecting to see them at any moment below it, I heard sounds of their running and saw them fifty yards away rushing up toward the spur. At a hundred yards they stopped and gazed at me and then slowly walked upward, continually pausing to turn and look, until reaching the sky-line, where they followed the crest and were soon lost to sight. Were those rams frightened by my scent? It is possible. There was also no reason why they should not have been frightened by it long before. The sun was behind me and, standing my rifle upright on the surface, I went back and noticed its shadow extending down the slope. I had been careless about my shadow, and it is quite possible that they had been scared by it when I was moving.

I made a long, arduous ascent of the spur and toiled upward to the crest. Near that end, ice had once carved the mountain more irregularly than it had toward the west. The rock had been sculptured in rougher fashion, the cliffs being all splintered and buttressed by narrow walls hewn in fantastic shapes while the jagged crest was battlemented with imposing pinnacles. After reaching the crest, I seated myself and scanned the country through my field-glasses. The next spur to the east projected from the crest in a narrow, vertically inclined wall extending five hundred feet to a short, smooth, grassy saddle, which connected it to the mountain. The spur had a ragged crest topping rough, steep slopes fluted by cañons almost as deep as those of the big mountain. In fact, that spur was more like a separate independent mountain. As the saddle came into the field of my glasses, three sheep suddenly appeared, one very dark, the other two much lighter. I watched them closely until the dark one threw up its head and displayed curling horns, apparently very large. Big rams again!

It was not possible to go around the crest and descend along the ridge without being seen by them. The only alternative was to descend to the foot of the mountain, cross the basin below, and then climb the spur on its south slope. But then my approach might be announced by the wind, which would be blowing directly from me to the rams. Without hesitation I chose to face their noses rather than their eyes, and began the long zigzag descent, which was not accomplished until noon. Thoroughly concealed at the foot of the spur, half a mile south of the rams, I sought the bottom of a cañon falling down the slope, found a clump of willows, made a small fire, and after refreshing myself with tea and bread climbed directly up the bottom of the canon. Several times while descending the other mountain I had watched the rams, and at each view the horns of the dark ram appeared bigger. Once a golden eagle circled around them. How many times have I envied the eagle as it soared along the crests and above the woods and valleys, observing the animal life below from near or far!

It was a long, difficult climb, now clambering over huge boulders, now scaling little cliffs, again toiling on over the loose, broken rock; but at last I was near the crest, where a small spur jutted out. I was on a level with the rams, less than a third of a mile away, and a strong wind blew directly toward them. Going below the ridge of the spur, I looked over and saw the two large ones feeding in the same place and the other lying down, his head stretched out on the ground like that of a dog. After looking through my field-glasses, my eagerness became intense, for the dark ram had magnificent horns, appearing black and large. His companion also had fine horns, but those of the other were smaller. Intervening ridges jutting out from the spur made it impossible to form from my position any plan of approaching within shot. Dropping back below the sky-line, I climbed to the crest and slowly advanced, taking great care to observe as much of the area on the other side as possible, so that other rams which might be feeding there would not see me and give the alarm. Keeping a sharp lookout on all sides, I gradually came near enough to be convinced that no other rams were about and that the only remaining problem was to find a method of approaching close enough for a reasonable shot. Taking advantage of another favorable projecting ridge, I crept forward and looked over. All were still feeding and the heavy, wrinkled horns of the dark ram, then seen plainly, made me realize more fully the prize I was stalking. After another slow advance along the crest, I went out some distance on the roof of a ridge, broken on one side by a precipice, and looked once more. I had to take chances, since not yet had I found a method of approach. As I was proceeding, the dark ram suddenly appeared, feeding upward beyond the saddle, head to the ground, and my return to the crest was cut off unless attempted in plain sight. I noticed, however, a way to stalk close enough. Two hundred yards ahead, another ridge jutting out at right angles extended far enough to bring me opposite the rams if I could succeed in reaching it without disturbing them.

From the time the rams had first been seen, not once, when I could see them, did one raise his head to look, a most exceptional thing. Lying flat on my stomach, I had to risk working back to the crest, and, foot by foot, all the time closely watching the ram, I wormed along and at last, to my great relief, succeeded in reaching a rock behind which I could keep out of sight until the crest was gained.

Then began the increasing excitement of the final advance. Ahead, the buttressed cliffs lifted up to the spired crest; on either side below were desolate, rock-filled basins and deep canons from whose depths sounded the subdued roar of the creeks; to my left, a rugged mountain reached twenty miles to the valley of the Lapie, and to my right continued a few miles to the smoother ranges around the basin; while behind, filling the horizon, were the Pelly ranges. All the colors were deepened under the soft haze which the sunlight tinted blue, and which gave to the mountain world a distant, mysterious grandeur.

As I carefully walked ahead, the strong wind blowing from behind caused much anxiety. Then the loud, shrill whistle of a marmot made me shudder as I looked ahead and saw a mother and three young, sitting on a rock at the point where I was to turn off on the ridge. Twice they whistled before I reached the rock, when the mother plunged down in a hole at the foot, giving at the same time a final, loud whistle. The young quickly followed and I waited, fearing that the rams would appear running up the mountain-side. For a few moments all was silence except the whistling of the wind around the rocks and the faint roar of the cascades in the canons below.

As I edged over on the ridge, other ground-squirrels began to chatter, still more increasing my excitement. Creeping on a steep slope just below the top, I slowly advanced to a point which seemed to be opposite the rams. The wind was then blowing without obstruction directly toward them, and holding my rifle cocked, I momentarily expected to see them dashing up in sight. Not twenty feet beyond them the spur connection was broken by a deep hollow, so that a few jumps upward would take them out of sight, where they could descend the slope and cross to the side of the mountain in safety. Crawling forward on my stomach, inch by inch, I raised my head and some distance to the left saw the lighter ram with good horns, feeding downward—a beautiful shot. The other two were not in sight. Dropping back and slowly worming along for fifty feet, I crawled forward and was carefully raising my head, when I suddenly saw the smallest ram, who was lying down on the opposite slope of the saddle, looking directly at me. By the alertness of his gaze I instantly recognized that, though uncertain as to the nature of the object, he had seen me. At the same time I saw the horns of the two others who were lying down below facing me, the dark one with black, curling horns to the right.

Almost instinctively I lowered my head, and turning on my back revolved in pivotal motion until my feet were ahead. Then quickly rising in sitting posture, elbows on knees, my rifle was pointed at the dark ram as it appeared in the line of vision. All three quickly elevated their heads with a jerk, but it was too late. Before they could rise I had aimed at the breast of the dark ram and the report echoed among the rocks as they all sprang to their feet. The responding whack of the bullet sounded before they began to dash upward, and I knew that it had gone true. The dark one attempted to follow but after five jumps fell dead. The others disappeared in the break, but soon reappeared on the opposite slope, which was one mass of protruding rocks and almost vertical. I sat motionless and watched them. While still within range of a long shot, they stopped and looked back, as if wondering why the leader did not follow. Then they ran upward in a series of jumps for a hundred feet and stopped again. This method of ascending was continued until they reached the crest, when again I had before me that wonderful sight of the mountain ram walking on the sky-line. I had noticed particularly their attitudes. The large one seemed to be all elasticity. His head was held straight up, his neck swelled out, his back straight, his legs rigid. He reminded me of a strutting cock. Thus appears the mountain ram under excitement. But I made an interesting discovery. The other ram was three or four years old and his horns curving behind did not curl upward. When he reached the skyline and came under a certain angle with the sun, I beheld the famous "*ibex*," often reported to have been seen on the far northern summits of Alaska. The horns appeared to be magnified to a long sweep of three or four feet, curving behind exactly like those of an ibex. So complete was the deception, that had I not been certain of the animal, I would have been deluded into the belief that an ibex stood before me. I have many times witnessed similar delusions and have thus learned to give more credit to the good faith of those who report having seen an ibex. Also, I know that they have not been so fortunate as to have had experiences similar to my own.

It was just a year, lacking one day, since a veteran ram had been stretched out before me on a high mountain in the Ogilvie range at the head of Coal Creek, a veteran ram, the prize of many days of tramping over the mountains. Now, stretched before me, was another veteran ram, the prize of my trip among the Pelly ranges.

The dead ram was a hundred and fifty yards distant, and I was interested to test the wind by throwing up pieces of paper which were blown directly toward him, near enough to prove that no eddying of the air currents had deflected my scent. Going forward when the papers fell, I tossed up others and they were carried in the same direction. It was clear that my scent had not frightened these rams. I went over to the dead ram and found him lighter in color than the typical Stone sheep, and darker than Fannin sheep. He was so old that I could not count the rings on his wrinkled horns. They were blunted at the tips, and his teeth were badly worn. Though not large in circumference or unusually long, I class them as the most impressive type of wild sheep horns—massive, well-curled, and more than all, thoroughly and deeply *wrinkled.* After taking some photographs I measured him—I never measure a mountain sheep unless it falls on fairly level ground smooth enough to insure accuracy, and just after killing, before it has stiffened or become swollen. All the conditions were favorable and my steel tape recorded his length as fifty-nine inches, height forty inches, and girth behind shoulders (a measurement which varies according to the condition of the animal, and doubtful to get twice alike under any conditions) forty-eight inches. His weight, so near as I could estimate it, was about two hundred and forty pounds.

The ram was lying at an altitude of six thousand seven hundred feet. It was then nearly six in the afternoon, and after resting awhile to smoke my pipe and behold the glorified landscape, I took off the skin and cleaned the skull.

At nine I reached camp; the air was frosty and the warmth of the crackling fire congenial.

August 2.—The next morning I prepared the skin of the

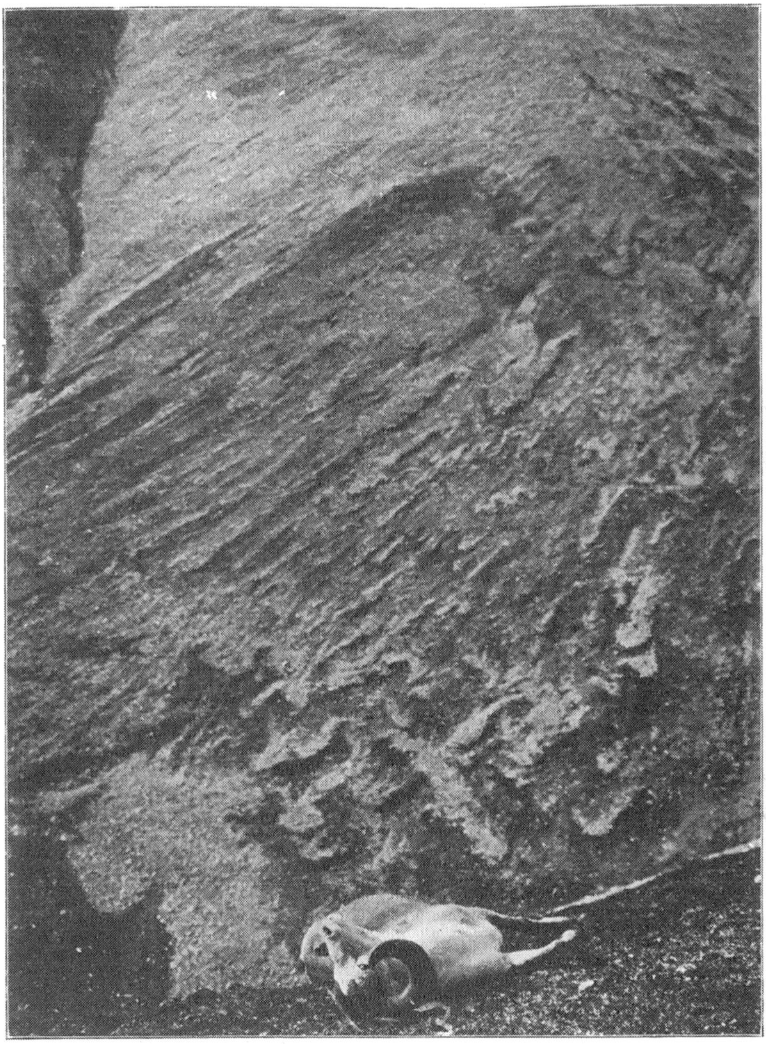

After five jumps, fell dead, August 2.

ram, and also those of several ground-squirrels. In the afternoon I took the mouse-traps and set them high on a mountain in front of camp. Now and then I had seen a chipmunk in the woods, but red squirrels were entirely absent from the locality near camp. Of all my camps in spruce woods in the interior of Yukon Territory and Alaska, including even those in the timber-line spruces, this was the only one where I did not see or hear red squirrels. Rabbits were very numerous.

CHAPTER XV

THE FINAL HUNT FOR RAMS – 1905

AUGUST 3.—THE following day, though it was so hazy that I could not see from mountain to mountain, or from ridge to ridge, if separated by any distance, I started to climb the spur where the ram had been killed, and to ascend to the crest of the main mountain, on the chance of seeing more rams on the other side. Reaching the crest, and walking in a westerly direction I had not advanced far before I saw an old ewe with her lamb, together with two small rams, each about three years old. They were feeding below at the head of a spur which divided two basins. Concealing myself, I watched them. After awhile they began to ascend toward a part of the crest which was three hundred yards ahead of me. Their gait was typical, like that of all mountain-sheep when travelling undisturbed. They usually walk up smooth places, and run up the steep rocky slopes. Their ascent or descent is a succession of walks, runs, and jumps. But on a smooth, easy incline or on the level, except when encountering rocks, they always walk. The head is usually carried forward at an angle, and the necks of ewes as well as of rams are straight, or sometimes swelled when the head is held back.

The old ewe was extremely watchful and distinctly the leader. Taking out my Kodak, I remained flat on my back, hoping that after reaching the crest they would turn and come in my direction. But they passed directly over and disappeared on the other side. The wind was blowing from me to them. Holding my Kodak ready, I slowly followed the sheep-trail on the crest, toward the point where they had disappeared. When within fifty yards, I passed around a high, protruding rock and saw them lying down just below the sky-line. Instantly dropping back and preparing the Kodak, I suddenly stepped forward in plain sight and pressed the bulb as the old ewe jumped up. All had begun to run across the curving slope as I snapped another exposure. It was hazy, and their color blended so perfectly with the rock that they appear but indistinctly in the negative. I saw them again after they had crossed a cañon and were beginning to ascend the slope toward that part of the crest where the two large rams had gone the day before.

Proceeding in that direction, I looked over all the country that I had not previously seen, until about the middle of the afternoon when I observed some sheep feeding in a basin below me. There were two ewes, each followed by two lambs, and five mature ewes without lambs. All, including the lambs, were very dark, and the neck of one ewe was distinctly gray. I watched them for some time until they lay down to rest without a "sentinel." Like other ewes they fed much more actively than rams; were more nervous, and oftener threw up their heads to look; and they also maintained a more constant watch on the slopes above them. All the sheep I had seen up to that time in the Pelly Mountains were continually tormented about the lips and nose by insects. They were constantly shaking their heads or rubbing them along the ground, and striking the ground with their horns. No mosquitoes were there and some of the varieties of small flies must have been worrying them.

Later I returned to the carcass of the ram I had killed the day before, and rested for half an hour. Looking up at the crest

I suddenly stepped forward… and pressed the bulb, August 3.

of the mountain I saw the sheep which I had photographed in the morning walking along the sky-line. They evidently had been resting there all the afternoon. The angle of the sun was again just right to transform the three-year olds into "ibexes." Then, instead of *leading*, as she did in the morning before they were disturbed, the wily old ewe was walking in the rear, and pausing every few moments to stop and look behind. The small rams walked somewhat indifferently ahead of her. Cutting off the hind quarters of the ram, I shouldered them and returned to camp.

August 4.—The only territory available to hunt from that camp, which I had not already investigated, was that west of the south basin. Early in the morning, I tramped three miles up toward the basin, and arriving at the foot of the range waited for the atmosphere to clear. Heavy mists obscured all the mountains and I did not want to attempt the long climb unless the nearer mountains could be distinctly seen. Instead of lifting the fog increased, and by the time I had eaten lunch mists had filled all the basins. I returned and the next day was so foggy and rainy that I remained in camp. It was the first bad day experienced up to that time on the trip.

August 6.—The following morning I started before five. During the night heavy frost had whitened the mountains, and the little pools of water were frozen. The sky was perfectly clear, a light wind was blowing from the south, and weather conditions were perfect to start the day. Arriving at the foot of the mountain, I began to ascend a steep, smooth slope, and soon found extreme difficulty in keeping my footing on the slippery ground. I should have waited for the frost to melt, for while wearing leather moccasins it was dangerous to climb under those conditions. But with my rifle as a staff I gradually zigzagged upward until reaching the last twenty feet below the crest. That part of the slope was smooth rock and very steep, the slippery surface relieved here and there by loose pieces of stone lodged in cracks and indentations of the surface. There I paused for awhile and considered the chances, for up to that point the climb had been trying to my courage. Eagerness to gain the crest spurred me on to attempt it, and after feeling among some of the loose rocks, I thought they were lodged securely. After a step or two it was clear that my moccasins would not hold; so, taking them off, I was encouraged by finding more friction in my socks, and, with rifle slung on my back and clinging with hands and toes, I began to crawl upward. Three thousand feet of slope, sharply inclined and slippery, was below, and one slip, a slight momentum gained, and I would have dashed downward.

After six feet, the loose rocks were scarcer and my position was becoming doubtful. Four feet more and I realized extreme danger, since I could scarcely hold to the slope and could not retreat. Three more steps and I began to go backward, but held myself in time. Another attempt and I gained six feet, when a small rock, which was all that held my left foot, as I was reaching above for a handhold, gave way and I began to slide quickly. Before it was too late, my knee caught a rock and held me. I could not even look back, but feeling with my hand another rock above, I pulled myself upward and made a vigorous scramble, trusting all to the result. It was successful, for I caught a secure rock on the edge at the top and pulled myself up. Only those who have had a similar experience can realize my relief.

A new panorama burst into view; below were three exquisite Alpine lakes nestled high in the mountains at the head of a cañon, through which they drained to Teslin waters on the other side of the divide, while to the south-west, endless ranges and ranks of peaks extended toward the horizon. Clouds began to gather as I started to walk along the crest.

Nothing is more fascinating than to roam along the crest of the higher ranges in that far northern country. You feel that the whole country below is yours—in it you are supreme. In the vast wilderness unfolded around you, you feel a wild, unfettered freedom; you follow the sheep-trail, always a good path, leading you securely around the pinnacles; with strained excitement you walk slowly along, every step bringing new pictures in view; you look off over a vast bewildering landscape of lofty ranges rich in color, abounding in sculptured crags, deep cañons, and green basins, the desolation relieved by the chatter of the ground-squirrel, the bleat of the coney, or the whistle of the marmot, while you are ever alert for larger game—the noble ram or the shaggy grizzly.

By noon the wind from the south had increased, bringing dark clouds, mists, and a heavy shower. I had noticed among the Pelly Mountains, that whenever the wind came from the south, it brought heavy mists and showers. Sitting under a shelving rock, I ate some bread and remained for an hour until the sky was again clear. Looking westward across the valley to another range, I saw a band of eighty ewes and lambs feeding and resting on the slope. The variations in color were the same as in the case of the sheep already observed in the Pelly Mountains. As they rested, I watched them and noticed at times an apparent sentinel, but at other times all rested without one.

I then continued along the crest toward the amphitheatre of mountains surrounding the head of the basin. Their north slopes, then fronting me, were covered in places with much snow, and iron-stained rock imparted to them a rich, red color. At three in the afternoon, when nearer the head of the basin, I seated myself for the purpose of looking through my field-glasses at a very high mountain farther to the west. This was connected by a high saddle to another mountain which was joined to the basin ranges by a ridge. A large bank of snow extended down the slope of the saddle, two miles distant.

On the snow I saw a three-year-old ram, which soon left it, and was joined by two others of the same age. It was interesting to observe how extremely conspicuous a sheep of that dark color was when on the snow. They walked upward in single file along the sky-line to the crest, when the sun magnified their horns to the ibex transformation. They were apparently very suspicious and as they proceeded, kept looking down. When I saw another small ram appear above the snow-bank and lie down, I concluded that there were more rams below on the other side. Not being able to pass around the precipitous sides of two peaks near me, I had to climb over them and this required some effort and crag work. Proceeding, I was in plain sight of the ram which stood above the snow, and my progress, between pauses to watch him or to observe others that might appear near him, was, therefore, slow and careful. The other two rams soon appeared on the top of the mountain and lay down facing me. They must have seen me, for several times I saw them rise and look suspiciously in my direction, although they were fifteen hundred feet above me and more than a mile distant. At length I reached the foot of the intervening mountain, and, thoroughly concealed, slowly made the ascent. Reaching the apex I looked over. Below, on the other side, was a small circular basin of broken rock alternating with grassy areas, almost completely enclosed by surrounding rock walls. In the bottom was a gleaming crystal lakelet, strongly reflecting the peaks. To my right, between the two mountains, was a deep gorge.

Circling to the right, I saw three small rams lying above the snow, two of them facing me, the other looking toward the north-west. The rams on the peak above had risen and were looking at me. I felt sure there were rams below, and began to descend toward the gorge. After I had gone a short distance, a large band of rams, feeding just above the edge of the gorge, suddenly came into view. Instantly I withdrew from sight, since it was impossible to approach them from the mountain I was on. Retreating upward around the slope, I descended to the top of the connecting ridge, observing everywhere numerous fresh sheep tracks indicating that this band of rams had been occupying the areas about this basin for a long time. It was after five when I began to advance directly toward the gorge, hoping to come near enough for a good shot before the rams below would come in sight. Having studied the ground, I knew that a successful approach was doubtful, and I had been obliged to take the one possible way—to advance along the rolling slopes in plain sight of the three rams above the snow. The rams on the summit were already standing and watching me.

Keeping my eyes on the lower rams and stooping low, I slowly advanced, but they soon saw me and at once rose and stood looking at me. As I progressed, they remained motionless and I could almost feel their penetrating gaze. When the band below was not more than three or four hundred yards distant, I came to a swell in the ground and knew that from the top of it I could see them. But I could not get nearer. The slope on the other side fell almost vertically to the gorge. Creeping upward, I looked over. Twenty-five rams were below, some lying down facing in all directions, some lazily feeding. They seemed to feel perfect security in the secluded basin where probably during the whole summer, they had lived undisturbed. All were dark in color except three, which appeared almost white. Most of them were five or six years old, but the darkest one, then lying down, had particularly fine horns. Only two of the others had large horns. I wanted that dark ram.

The most noticeable feature of that band was the appearance of their horns. All were amber-like, and seemed almost transparent. The horns of the rams I had previously seen behind the camp were in color almost exactly like those of the Rocky Mountain sheep. Future investigations enlightened me on these facts. The differences in color are due partly to the amount of rain which washes them, and still more to the composition of the soil and rocks among which they feed. Rams in the fly season are continually striking their horns in the ground, and at all seasons are poking them among rocks when they feed, thus discoloring them in different degrees. After heavy rains, horns always appear cleaner and more yellow, and in winter they are much cleaner than at other times of the year.

There was no sentinel among these rams, unless the three small ones, five hundred yards above, could be considered as serving that duty. In spite of the lazy comfort which they seemed to be enjoying, I noticed that individuals kept up an alert watch in all directions, turning their gaze up as well as down. While I was watching them, well concealed behind some low rocks, a large mass of rock broke away from the top of the mountain behind them, and thundering down the slope landed about fifty yards to their right. During the crashing descent I observed them very closely. They remained absolutely indifferent to the small avalanche, only one of them turning his head in that direction. Three single rocks fell at later intervals, but they took no notice of them. After awhile in seeking a different position so that I could better hold my glasses, I dislodged a small stone not three inches in diameter, which went rolling down the slope. Up to that time I could not see that any of the rams had suspected my presence, except the three small ones above, two of which were then lying down. These small rams evidently trusted the larger ones, and even after having seen me approach, they were indifferently awaiting some warning of alarm from the leaders below. At the sound of that small rock, the whole band jumped up at once and started to walk up the slope. It was perfectly calm and I could feel no currents of air. The rams were suspicious and I knew that in a moment they would see me. Being so far from camp, I realized that an opportunity might be lost and that after seeing me they might leave the locality before I could return. So resting my rifle on a rock, I aimed at the largest and fired. All suddenly ran to the right, while the young rams above dashed down the slope to join them. My bullet struck the ground three feet below the big ram. I fired twice more as he ran. Both shots missed and the sheep disappeared around the slope.

Hurrying down, I found a way to cross the gorge and ascended to the saddle. All were standing six hundred yards away, low down on the slopes of the mountain on the crest of which I had travelled all day, and were looking up in my direction. Returning through the gorge, I again climbed to the connecting ridge, circled around, and saw the rams travelling low on the slopes in a northerly direction—that from which I had come in the morning. They passed out of sight around the end of a spur half a mile ahead. I climbed to the crest, reached the spur, and descended along its ridge almost to the foot, before I saw them travelling well ahead, still lower on the slopes. Looking back, some of them saw me and all broke into a run, still keeping the same course. I watched them through my field-glasses as they passed over spur after spur for two miles, until, reaching the foot of some high cliffs, they bunched and stood in hiding.

It required more than an hour to climb back again to the crest, cross over the two pyramid peaks, and travel along until I reached the spur at the foot of which I thought they were hiding. Descending its acute ridge for half a mile, I looked over and did not see them. A succession of spurs projected out from the mountain, and by that time I was utterly confused as to which one sheltered the rams. I had taken landmarks, but from

The big dark one was leading. He fell dead to my shot, August 6.

He was the whitest of all and I killed him in his tracks, August 6.

the crest above could not recognize them. Again ascending to the crest and advancing to the next spur, I slowly descended and looked over the cliffs at its foot. No sheep were there. But looking across a wide cañon, at the foot of the next spur, under the cliffs, I saw the whole band, all its members lying down and looking only upward. There was nothing to do but again to climb up on the crest; but I had studied the ground and knew just how to approach them and also the point on the spur from which to get a shot. Reaching the spur I began to descend, and the stalk was on in earnest. When I started downward the sun was just above the horizon and threw long shadows. Cañons were on both sides of me, and my shadow fell far out down the slope. I waited, therefore, until the sun went down, and again started. There was not a breath of wind, the sky above was clear, the whole landscape was hushed and still. Peace breathed over the mountain; the peace of approaching twilight. Directly below were the three Alpine lakes, their surfaces like glass and burnished with the reflection of the colored sky. So calm was the water that the delicate ripples made by insects could be plainly seen. Three teals were gently floating on the lower one. To the west ranks of bewildering peaks lifted up in a sky of gorgeous crimson, gradually shading into the cool gray above. A golden tinge haunted the crests, while pyramids, spires, and domes were rosy yellow above the blue cast of the slopes which led down to the shadowy purple of the valleys.

The ridge-top of the spur was steep. Step by step I advanced downward, now over a little grass, now over broken rock, often letting myself down low ledges. It was already so dark that I felt doubtful of seeing my rifle sights. It was so still that I crept for a hundred yards before coming to the two rocks from where I expected to get a shot. Nearer I came, my noiseless moccasins answering well to the occasion, until, with rifle cocked, I was ready to attempt a running shot if the rams should suddenly dash in sight. Reaching the rocks I looked over. I was not quite far enough, and before me was a steep incline of ten feet, all loose, broken rock. Sitting down, I carefully prepared each step by arranging the rocks with my hand. Then with rifle at my shoulder, I slowly rose.

In spite of my caution the rams had heard something suspicious. Four were standing just below the cliffs and, as my head came in sight, were looking directly at me. They were a hundred yards away. The dark one with big horns was still hidden with the rest of the band nearer to the foot of the cliff. One of the rams looking at me had large horns. While the four were standing still, a clatter of hoofs sounded. Off-hand, I quickly shot at the largest one in sight, and saw him fall as the whole band dashed diagonally up the cañon on my left. There was no time to rest my rifle. Four rams were running together up the opposite slope, the big dark one leading. He fell dead to my shot. Another large one ran up the bottom and, firing, I heard the bullet strike him. One that was running more to the left suddenly turned and came running toward me. He was the whitest of all, and I killed him in his tracks. By that time all were running well up the slope, and a wounded ram followed fast enough to gain on them. I fired once more at him, but he kept on with the others and went over the crest.

Darkness was rapidly descending. Passing the white ram curled up among the rocks, I had started for the big ram which was lying dead in the bottom of the cañon, when a noise below caused me to turn my head, and I saw the first one I had fired at rolling and bounding down the slope until he disappeared in the dusk. Following as rapidly as I could, I almost reached the foot, but it was so dark that I could not find him. Fog began to settle, and I hurried back to the crest. It was nearly ten in the night when I reached it, and a dense fog enveloped the whole mountain. It was dark and the descent over an unknown slope was before me. I was at an altitude of seven thousand four hundred feet, and it was very cold. Feeling my way with the butt of my rifle, hour after hour I descended, step by step, always in danger, and twice falling.

August 7.—It was two in the morning when I reached the foot near the creek coming from the basin. There I kindled a fire and made tea, which together with a small piece of bread refreshed me. Dawn was beginning as I started down the creek, and a heavy rain began to fall. The drenching received while walking through the last two miles of willows was equivalent to complete immersion.

At 4:30 in the morning I reached camp. A big fire, a plate of rice soup, and some boiled mutton invigorated me before writing in my journal the events and details of the day. After three hours of sleep, I breakfasted with Jefferies and we started for the carcasses, hoping also to recover the wounded ram. The day was over-cast, but the clouds were high and it did not rain. We cut long willow staffs, climbed the mountain, and having travelled for five and a half hours, reached the dead rams. I had noticed on the crest the tracks of the frightened band of sheep, which had followed it almost to the end of the mountain before descending the west slope and crossing the valley to a high mountain beyond, but I did not see a sign of the wounded ram.

From the spot where the first ram that had been shot began to roll we descended just two thousand feet, according to my barometer, before finding him among the willows, almost at the foot. He was not badly bruised, and had fine, large horns. After taking off the skin, we went up to the big one, which had beautiful horns, shapely and well curled. We took off his skin, and later that of the light-colored ram, and brought them up to the crest. It was then 9:30 in the night and a fine half-moon was shining in a clear sky. The lakes gleamed below and the distant peaks were suffused with a mysterious, shadowy light.

There was more light than the night before, and the descent was less hazardous, even though we were burdened with awkward loads. The staffs were of great assistance. Reaching the basin, we made tea, and later, at 2:30 in the morning, arrived at camp. That day I had seen a rough-legged hawk on the crest; and had also heard conies, the second time I had noticed them during the trip. They were scarce in the Pelly Mountains.

August 8.—I rose at eight the next morning. The pure mountain air had put me in such good physical condition that I felt thoroughly refreshed even after the short hours of sleep and the strain of the two previous days. New fields of exploration were to be undertaken and I resolved to return to the Pelly River as soon as the skins should be dried enough for packing. It required all day to prepare them, and I wanted good clear weather for their drying, but was disappointed.

August 9-12.—The next three days were damp; mists, showers, and clear sky alternating. The fourth was clear, and a large fire near the skins dried them sufficiently for packing. During those four days I occupied myself with unsuccessful efforts at catching mice.

The bird life at timber-line was limited. Along the creeks I had heard the tinkling notes of the water-ousel. An occasional spotted sandpiper had skipped along the bars, or a harlequin duck had dodged among the rocks. The golden eagle was always in sight. Ravens were entirely absent, having gone to the salmon rivers to feast on dead salmon. I did not hear the hoot of an owl. Several pigeon-hawks were in the woods near camp, and once I saw two of them following an eagle, darting at it again and again. Rough-legged hawks were about the high mountains. Juncos, and Alaska jays were abundant. The last did not come near the camp but once, and then only for a few moments. Rock ptarmigan were on the mountains, but nearly all the willow ptarmigan were below with their young in the brush. I did not see a grouse until returning along the Lapie River. An occasional marsh-hawk appeared there as everywhere else in the Territory; chickadees were always present, usually in small flocks. The Western tree sparrow and the Gambel's sparrow were common. Occasionally a kingfisher would fly up the creek.

I was always interested in testing the acute senses of the ground-squirrels. Though I could approach close to them before they plunged into their holes, they always detected my approach long before. Their sense of hearing is exceedingly keen, and at any suspicious sound they sit up to look and their sight is as sharp as their hearing. The senses of marmots are equally keen. They have their homes high in the mountains and well up near the heads of the basins.

In the fall and winter, moose are very abundant among the willows above timber. After a great deal of observation I came to the conclusion that they seldom feed on dwarf-birch, *Betula glandulosa*. This conclusion I verified by numerous subsequent observations. The willow flats in the draws among the Pelly Mountains are well situated for hunting moose in the fall. These draws are always bordered by clear slopes above, from which the hunter can see the animals. At that time, however, pack-horses, necessary to the transport of their heads, could not subsist, and the hunter would have to remain until November and bring his trophies out with dogsleds.

I saw no signs of caribou in those parts of the Pelly Mountains I had tramped over, and the Indians informed me that they do not range anywhere in the Pellys. I did, however, see one old track on a bar near the lower end of the Lapie. An occasional caribou must at times stray across the country.

Wolves must be abundant, for I saw great quantities of their old dung everywhere. Much of it contained rabbit hair, and some of it moose hair, but in none of it could I find sheep hair.

Finding him among the willows, almost at the foot, August 7.

The diggings and trails showed that grizzly bears are abundant there in the spring. The fact that I saw only one does not indicate that others were not about, for in the summer the sight of grizzlies is always uncertain. When we reached the Lapie on returning, I saw numerous fresh signs where grizzlies had been digging the root of the wild pea vine. Although huckleberries were very abundant where I found the diggings, no berries or seeds were in the fresh dung which contained only grass and roots.

August 14-16.—Dried sheepskins are somewhat delicate, and it was a problem to make a pack of seven, including some of the skulls and our equipment. I loaded my rucksack with forty pounds and tied a skull on top. Jefferies was to carry two skulls, and we succeeded in putting the rest of the material on *Danger*, and started. *Danger* had been going lame in his right foreleg for a week, and by the end of the day he was so lame that the following morning we ourselves had to carry in relays all the material for two miles over a ridge, when we again loaded the horse, who limped along for the rest of the day. For the next two days we proceeded, the lame horse keeping up nobly, down grade and over a route then well known to us. When trophies are carried on a pack-horse, travelling through swamps, brush, and timber, it is excruciating agony to follow. Smash, bang, tear, rip, crash, are the sounds all day as the pack is pushed through stiff willows and spruces, each jar causing an anxious shudder to the owner of the precious stuff.

On the return trip, the big horse-flies, which had before tormented the horse, were absent, but the small black flies made him bleed. It was the season for sand-flies, small creatures like midges, but slightly larger. They appeared in swarms in the afternoon and retired at night, and while active attacked both man and horse.

Aside from rough travelling and tired shoulders, which ached under the loads, no incident occurred on the return trip. We saw no animals except red squirrels which were abundant the last day we were on the Lapie, and a few more varieties of birds. We reached the Pelly August 16, having made about the same time from camp on the return as on the trip in. None of the skulls or skins were damaged, and all were stowed safely in an abandoned cabin. Lewis not having returned, all the Indians were still there. On seeing my sheep horns they became very much excited. They had previously doubted my ability to kill sheep.

Dan McKinnon's trade had been that of a blacksmith and at once he offered to take *Danger*, a suggestion which I accepted on condition that he would gather sufficient grass to keep the horse through the winter. This was intended as an indirect refusal, for *Danger* was lame, and I knew that it was best to end his life rather than leave him subjected to the cruel conditions of the wilderness. McKinnon, however, accepted my condition, and soon had the barrel of a .22 rifle red hot in a fire. By noon the next day he had hammered out a scythe, which was sharpened on a grindstone. He immediately began to cut the long nutritious grass growing abundantly on the banks, and old *Danger's* lease of life was prolonged.

THE ROSS RIVER COUNTRY

MOUNTAINS BORDERING THE PELLY RIVER

CHAPTER XVI

THE TRIP UP ROSS RIVER – 1905

AUGUST 17 AND 18 were spent in storing the skins, sorting out provisions, and preparing the canoe. The following morning we started up Ross River. I wanted to investigate the mountain ranges adjacent to it, and examine the sheep if any could be found. The Indians had told me that no sheep existed west of the Mackenzie divide, but knowing that they did not like to have anybody hunt in their territory, I realized that I must personally explore the mountains.

The volume of Ross River at its confluence with the Pelly is slightly less than that of the latter. It was discovered by Campbell during his trip down the Pelly in 1843, and named by him after Duncan Ross, chief factor of the Hudson Bay Company. Its source is near the divide of land separating the Mackenzie River water-shed from that of the Yukon, about latitude 63°. The sources of the Pelly River and the South Branch of the MacMillan on the west side of the divide, and those of the Gravel River on the east side, are within a few miles of those of the Ross, which latter meanders for a distance not far from two hundred miles in a south-westerly direction to the Pelly. Several lakes, situated at intervals in the upper reaches of its main drainage channel, are features not possessed by the other rivers. It flows through the hunting territory of the Pelly Indians.

Four years before I arrived at Nahanni House two French Canadians, Cassat and Dumas, had ascended the river to a point just above Prevost Canon, where they constructed a cabin and passed the winter trapping. The following year Lewis and his partner ascended a short distance, but returned. At the same time, two other trappers continued still farther and trapped through the winter, while the same two Frenchmen trapped up the East Branch, later called the Prevost River. A Russian went up to the first lake and trapped that same winter. The following winter Lewis and his partner trapped at Lewis Lake, while La Croix and Prevost trapped on the Prevost River. The winter before my arrival at Nahanni House, a trapper had trapped around Lewis Lake. According to information given to me by Lewis, these were the only white men who had ever ascended the river. No information about it had been brought to the outside world, and I was about to explore new territory.

Two years after my trip, Joseph Keele, of the Canadian Geological Survey, was detailed to explore the mountain region between the upper Pelly and Mackenzie Rivers. After spending the summer of 1907 in ascending the Pelly River to a point one hundred and forty miles above its confluence with Ross River, he returned and ascended the Ross River, wintered on Sheldon Lake, and in the spring crossed the divide, conveying his canoe and equipment by means of dog sleds to a navigable point on the Gravel River. When the ice went out later, he descended to the Mackenzie. His report was published in 1910. With the report, which discusses topography, drainage, climate, and general geology of the regions, is an excellent map on which names are given to lakes, tributaries and mountains.

August 19.—While flocks of geese were flying south overhead Jefferies started with the rope over his shoulder, dragging the canoe, which contained a load of five hundred pounds. I followed and after awhile relieved him. The first six miles we towed through a wide canon of broken water, and after emerging at the head, poled for over three hours and camped in some spruces on the bank.

For the next three days we ascended without an incident. The river was five feet below high-water mark, and favorable for poling. I poled from the bow, while Jefferies poled from the stern. The river followed a serpentine course through a low, rolling country which was very monotonous as compared with either that of the Pelly or of the MacMillan. The current was not swifter than three miles an hour, and we resorted to tracking only through the riffles and some of the longer reaches of broken water. The character of the river is very much like that of the MacMillan, but it lacks the scenery. There are the same wide bars, the same spruces, poplars, willows and alders along the banks; similar areas of burnt country; innumerable curves and numerous cut and scarped banks—all reminding me of the MacMillan. The fall colors had just begun to appear, though the nights were quite warm.

The second day some dome-shaped mountains of subdued type loomed up ahead in the distance west of the river. Dead king-salmon were on the bars, and all the ravens in the country seemed to be congregated along the river for the purpose of feeding on them. The farther up we went, the more salmon we saw spawning in the pools. Thousands were dead on the bars or dying in the water, and equal numbers were still spawning or struggling up against the current; hundreds, too weakened to remain, were drifting down, many striving to swim against the current, but without strength left to do so. We were there during the end of the spawning season, the last stage in the life of those noble fish. Observing that enormous sacrifice of life, I reflected on it without discovering the

Ewes seeking shelter from approaching storm.

From a painting by Carl Rungius.

Beneficent Law of nature or Goodness of Design, by virtue of which countless millions of these magnificent fish are annually sacrificed in the full flush of life, for the sake of propagating their race. Battered, bruised, and torn by their long journey of nearly twenty-three hundred miles from Bering Sea, stemming the sweeping current, forcing their way through dashing rapids, they finally deposit and fertilize their eggs as their life ebbs away.

I noticed the same birds that were seen on the MacMillan River, but fish-hawks were very abundant, and bald eagles were present—the only place I have ever seen them in the interior of either the Yukon Territory or Alaska. Rabbits and red squirrels were numerous, but the little beaver cutting that I noticed was very old, the Indians having practically exterminated the beavers long before. On the lower parts of the river moose tracks were not nearly so abundant as on the MacMillan. When we reached the part of the river where salmon first appeared, fresh tracks of the black bear were very numerous, and still farther up were abundant tracks of the grizzly. Well-worn bear-trails extended along the edge of the woods, usually through the grass bordering the bars. This greatly interested me, for it showed the extreme caution of bears. There was no reason, except for purposes of concealment, why they should not have made trails through the grass well out near the bars. I particularly observed the fresh dung. That of the black bears always contained berries, but no signs of berries were observed in that of grizzlies. Often, sections of tapeworm, still living when I saw them, appeared in the dung of both.

Some impressions of my camps along the banks of Ross River are still vivid in my memory—the moaning of the sweeping current, the numerous dying salmon drifting down on top; the continual quarrelling of the ravens gathered on the bars; the chattering of the red squirrels in the trees. The nights were perfectly calm, and during the late hours the sky colors were gorgeous. A waste of dreary wooded wilderness surrounded me. But every scene of desolation in that wild northern country has its beauties. Along the Ross River it was the fringe of spruce-tops against the sky. I have not elsewhere enjoyed the charm of it so continuously, for the reason that near the other rivers much less of the country is flat. In the evening, when the sky is golden, when deep pink clouds are floating high above the woods, a long line of graceful spired spruce-tops, delicate in texture, varying in forms, fringes the gilded horizon, while all is dimly reflected in the gliding sweep of the current below.

August 24.—On the night of August 23 there was a heavy frost and the next day was perfect—cloudless and calm. We divided the time all day between poling and tracking. In the morning I saw a flock of geese, which kept alighting and flying ahead of us all day. Two more bald eagles appeared, and for the second time I saw a goshawk chasing a kingfisher. Both lynx and wolf tracks were abundant on the bars. I noticed that the bears, after catching salmon, had always taken them into the woods or brush to eat. The water of the river was more broken, and the wading reminded me of my arduous trip up the North Fork of the MacMillan River. Old Indian camps and caches were often seen on the bank.

After six in the evening we reached a part of the river where it was confined to a short, narrow canon between ridges on both sides. The bottom was filled with huge boulders and big rocks. The rapids surged over the rocks and whirled around the boulders, eddying among the deep pools below them. When I was hauling the boat, with Jefferies in the stern guiding it with the paddle, and we were well inside of the canon, I saw a black bear rapidly approaching along the bank three hundred yards ahead on our side of the river. Beckoning to Jefferies, I pulled the boat to the shore, and taking out my rifle told him to hold the canoe. He was greatly excited, having seen the bear just before it went out of sight behind a jutting cliff. I seated myself facing in the direction of the bear, which I knew would soon come in sight, since the wind was blowing down the river. The bear suddenly appeared swimming out in the rapids, and when in the middle, turned and came directly down, dodging around the rocks and keeping as much as possible in the deeper pools. Before witnessing that feat of swimming, I had believed that any kind of a bear would have avoided such dangerous water. It would have been very easy to kill it when swimming by, but the current would have carried it down and I did not care to take the canoe down river and lose the distance gained by so much hard work. It was heading for the opposite side, so I waited for it to arrive on the bank. When it landed, I could scarcely see it, so perfectly did it blend with the dark rocks. My shot missed, and the bear gave a spring and stood looking. I was again aiming, when Jefferies suddenly fired and followed his first by three more shots, all missing, while the bear ran back and forth in complete bewilderment. I had not noticed that he had taken his rifle out of the boat, nor did he pay any heed to my protests. He was so excited that he was really in a state of frenzy. After his last shot the bear stopped a moment on a hummock rising above some brush, even then not having detected the direction of the shots. I fired and it fell in the brush, but immediately jumped up and ran over the ridge. That was the last time I ever allowed a man employed by me to carry a rifle. I had never done so before and this time had made the mistake of yielding to Jefferies's promises that he would not use it unless in case of accident. Crossing over, I saw blood and followed it for a mile in the woods and over ridges until no more could be found. Returning to the river, camp was made there, and, later, we slept in spite of the roar of the rapids.

Towing up the Ross River, August 23.

Head of Provost Canon. Big Rock at right where accident happened.

August 25.—From there on the water was broken, the tangents were longer, the bottom rocky, and the river was bordered by low ridges. We were then in the moose country, for the abundant willows were everywhere cropped, and moose tracks were numerous. In two and a half hours we reached the *Skookum Rapids* (so called by the trappers), eighty-one miles up the river. Over a precipitous descent for five hundred yards the river rushes in a succession of white combers. Because of the low stage of water, we succeeded in lining the boat up the west side, and successfully passed through some similar rapids of shorter length, two miles farther up. We then poled for several miles to Prevost Cañon. This cañon, several hundred yards long, is enclosed between high cliffs which are so close together that the river is swelled and forced through in a succession of cataracts. We were obliged to unload and portage around to a favorable place, and then carry the boat to the smoother water of an eddy just at the head of the cañon.

Having again loaded it we crossed to another eddy on the opposite side where a rocky shore gave a good foothold for lining. This eddy was formed by a big boulder standing out in the riffle where the river curves into the canon. Jefferies put the rope over his shoulders and throwing it around the boulder walked on the other side, while I held the bow. After taking up the slack of the rope he told me to push the bow out in the current.

What followed shows that one of the best rivermen in the North will sometimes err in judgment. He did not realize the strength of the current. I could not see Jefferies as I slowly moved the bow out until the current caught it, but noticed that the canoe was rapidly being carried diagonally across the riffle instead of being pulled to head directly up against it. Then I heard Jefferies shout: "Everything is lost," and the canoe rapidly swung out broadside to the current and started down the canon. He had not been able to pull the bow up into the riffle, and to save himself from being pulled in had cast the rope loose.

My rifle was on the shore. In the rucksack on my shoulders were my Kodak, field-glasses, and instruments All the provisions were in the bottom of the canoe. On top of them were three or four canvas sacks containing our sleeping robe, clothes, gill-net, matches, cartridges, a small tent I had brought for the purpose of protecting trophies, and a few plain cooking utensils and other things. An extra rifle and the axe were fastened to a sack. A canvas had been placed over all and roped down tightly.

The canoe was rapidly carried down ten feet and lodged broadside for a moment against a large rock projecting out of the water. It was tipped at once and the current rushed through, sweeping all the provisions below into the canon. The canoe then slipped off the rock, swung around and was caught by the eddy which whirled it within my reach as I stood breast deep in the water. The fates were not entirely against us, for the canvas sacks were not forced out during the first rush of the water, the rope holding them secure until the provisions were swept from the bottom. As the eddy caught the boat, the sacks began to float toward the bank and Jefferies was on hand to save them. The axe and the extra rifle dropped in four feet of water close to the bank. There was nothing to do but to make camp and pass the night.

August 26.—The whole of the next day was devoted to walking down the river in the hope of finding some of the provisions, many of which were in small bags. We found only one bag of rice and it was thoroughly soaked. But we spread out the rice, dried it near the fire, and boiled enough for a good meal.

August 27.—We knew that some lakes were not far ahead, and then the gill-net could be set with a good chance of catching fish. Early in the morning we started, and in a little over seven and a half hours reached Lewis Lake. The Prevost River enters the Ross about half a mile below the outlet of the lake. For that distance from the outlet the water is broken by shoals and riffles, while ledges of rock occur along the bank. Thousands of dead salmon were on the rocky bars, and fifty or sixty ravens and two bald eagles were there to en joy the feast. I was towing the boat and the wind was blowing down river. A ledge jutted out into the water and I had to wade well out in order to pass around it, while Jefferies was pushing the canoe from behind. Heaving on the rope I rounded the rocks and saw on the bar a hundred and fifty feet ahead a magnificent male grizzly standing, head up, one forepaw raised from the ground, ears cocked straight up, looking at me. Quickly stooping low, I beckoned to Jefferies to bring my rifle, but it was too late. Before he could act the bear turned and two bounds carried him into the woods. I found his trail as it emerged from the fringe of woods bordering a swamp. It showed that he had continued to run. That was the last grizzly I saw in the Yukon Territory. The experience reminded me of other chances lost, for there is no doubt whatever that the noise of poling and tracking as we ascended the river had frightened off several bears which I might have shot, had I been walking quietly a sufficient distance ahead.

It had been a cold, bleak day with a strong head-wind against us, and the night before snow had fallen on the mountains. After reaching the lake, we paddled against a head-wind to the upper end and found the old cabin that had been occupied by Lewis. Immediately after unloading the canoe, we set the net and returned to await results. After two hours we visited it and found it empty. We slept under the stars, hoping to appease our hunger in the morning.

August 28.—It was very cold that night and in the morning the robe was white with frost. Finding a large pike and two large white fish in the net, we ate a hearty breakfast. No fish of the fresh water is more delicious than the white fish of subarctic lakes and rivers. Hard, very fat, of delicious flavor, one large fish will provide two hearty meals. The pike is almost as good.

By the course of the Ross, Lewis Lake is one hundred and one miles from the Pelly. Our canoe was about twenty-one feet long and weighed a hundred and fifty pounds. Until the last day it had carried a load of about five hundred pounds. The water was low and very favorable for both poling and tracking. Our actual travelling time, after deducting all stops, from the Pelly River to Lewis Lake was sixty-six hours and five minutes. Of this time, we poled the boat for forty-one hours and fifteen minutes, and towed it for twenty-four hours and fifty minutes. This included forty-five minutes in going through the *Skookum Rapids*, twenty-five minutes the heavy rapids two miles above, and one hour and fifty minutes in portaging around Prevost Canon.

A few words about poling up the swift tributaries of the Yukon. Jefferies called poling "bucking the current," and I have not heard it better expressed. The river glides and races steadily, strongly, resistlessly. Even when two men are using poles, one in the stern, the other in the bow, they simply push against it. It is continuous, downright hard labor, with only slow progress as a reward, for the boat creeps slowly upward, and when overcoming the numerous riffles it barely moves under exhausting effort. Like any other hard physical labor, you soon become accustomed to it and acquire a swing, but the expenditure of muscular energy is none the less fatiguing. There is, however, one satisfaction. After you have settled down to the continuous strain all day, now going faster in the eddies and slower reaches of the current, now going slower in the swifter water, and again barely moving as you rapidly chug your poles on the rocky bottom and pull with heart-breaking effort, you finally go on the bank to camp, and looking down the river realize that you are putting a long stretch of country behind you for delightful days to come, when you will be paddling down with the current.

It was quite necessary to kill game as quickly as possible for a food supply. We spent the morning erecting the tent and drying everything at had been soaked in the wreck, and after eating another fish for lunch, poled two miles up the river to Field Lake. Thousands of ducks and geese were floating on its glassy surface, its shores were fringed with thick spruce timber, and all its numerous beaches were bordered by tall green grass. We paddled around the shores in the hope of seeing a moose until nearly dark, but were disappointed. When we reached camp, half a dozen white fish were in the net. Salmon were running up the river between the two lakes, but the net was too light to hold them.

August 29.—In the morning the net had yielded four or five white fish and I found in the traps, which had been set the day before, four red-back mice, *Evotomys dawsoni*. Crossing the river I started up toward some fairly high plateau-shaped mountains east of the lake, hoping to find a moose at the head of the draws. For three hours I toiled through thick woods and brush to timber-line, and then climbed the highest point of the mountain, from which I could command a view of the whole country south and east. Moose signs were abundant below, but above the timber there was no sign of sheep or caribou.

The three lakes were directly below me—beautiful lakes, each somewhat circular and about two miles in diameter, all buried between mountains. On the east is a range of rounded mountains of a subdued type, three and four thousand feet high, quickly falling away both north and south of the lakes. That range is isolated and on the east slopes to a rolling wilderness below. West of Lewis and Field Lakes, irregular ridges rise

Lewis Lake. Direction—South-West, August 29.

Field Lake, Mount Sheldon, August 29.

continuously for three miles back to Mount Riddell, a series of dome-shaped crests, sixty-eight hundred feet in altitude. A low depression separates this mountain from Mount Sheldon—the mountains and lakes were so named by Joseph Keele, the Canadian geologist—which is seventy-two hundred and fifty feet high, and rises almost from the shores of Sheldon Lake.

Mount Sheldon, a massive granite mountain completely isolated in that section of the country, towers up like a majestic sentinel guarding the lakes below. Owing to its isolation it has a stern, impressive grandeur more imposing than any mountain I have seen east of the Yukon River.

To the south I could see the whole course of the Ross as far as the Pelly River, and dimly discern the summits of the Pelly Mountains beyond. The country between the Ross and the Pelly, and that to the south-east is low and rolling—a vast timber-clad area. Three or four fairly large lakes glistened in the forests.

Far to the east are the ranges across the Mackenzie divide—ranks of snow-white peaks.

Mount Sheldon, Mount Riddell, and the single range east of the lakes compose an isolated group, separated from other mountains by many miles of low timbered country. Sheldon Lake is at the end of canoe navigation, and I realized that the only chance of finding sheep was to climb the slopes of Mount Sheldon.

Late in the afternoon, after having taken compass directions and having made sketch maps of the surrounding country, I turned my field-glasses toward Lewis Lake to look over the shores, and saw near the lower end a cow moose with her calf, both well out from the shore and repeatedly plunging their heads under water to pull up some succulent weeds growing below the surface. It was absolutely calm and the lake was like glass; the sun was low in a sky of gold and crimson; Mount

Sheldon, grim and desolate, towered over the wild regions below; the silence pervading the landscape was unbroken. But the wilderness depths revealed a scene of life—the calf moose and its mother separated from the recesses of their forest abode, and feeding in the dimly shining water of the lake. I had to hasten down to reach camp before dark. Ptarmigan were abundant, but I saw no signs of ground-squirrels to remind me of past days spent in other mountains.

CHAPTER XVII

THE SHEEP OF MOUNT SHELDON - 1905

THE FOLLOWING MORNING a white fish and an "inconnu" were taken from the net. The latter I found similar in flavor and almost as good as the former. A salmon enmeshed in the net had torn it so badly that part of it was ruined. Red-backed mice were very abundant, their intersecting trails spreading all over the surface of the woods. I prepared several that had been taken in the traps, and waited until nearly four in the afternoon before we started out in the canoe, hoping to find the cow and calf feeding in the same place in the lake where I had seen them the previous day.

A strong head-wind was blowing and both of us had to use the paddles, as we went toward the middle of the lake so that I could see, from a distance, around the point where the moose had been feeding. When we were out far enough, I saw both the mother and calf feeding in the water exactly where they had been before. Dropping back, we paddled the canoe close in shore, and then along it until within three hundred yards of the point. After landing I followed the beach, intending to creep through the woods across the point, and was about to enter the woods, when the cow suddenly emerged not a hundred feet from me, and stepping without hesitation into the water began to wade out on the sandy bottom. The calf then appeared and followed. I shot the calf through the neck, and it instantly dropped dead. Jefferies, evidently excited, jumped into the boat as the calf fell, and the cow at first stood looking at him. Then she looked at the dead calf and, turning, trotted into the woods for a few feet and stopped; then trotted a few feet more and stopped again and looked back. Then she disappeared. As Jefferies, with shouts of glee, came paddling the boat, the cow came trotting back, looked at the approaching canoe for a moment and again trotted off, not to reappear.

After we had dressed the calf and loaded it into the boat, a large flock of short-billed gulls surrounded us and followed all the way to camp. Their plaintive cries reminded me of coasting along the Inland Passage to Alaska. We now had a supply of food, and not being dependent on the net, could devote time to looking for sheep.

August 31.—The next morning we poled up to Field Lake, and paddled the boat across it and through the narrow channel to Sheldon Lake at the foot of Mount Sheldon which towers up from its shore. There we pitched the tent among some scattered spruces and constructed a cache to hold the meat. Along the shores and on the island I noticed many shed horns of moose, showing that they had been there in January. That night as I sat in the frosty air before the fire, while sparks were shooting up among the tree tops and the sky was studded with stars brightly twinkling above Mount Sheldon, over the water sounded the call of the loon. I have never heard it before or since in the interior of Yukon Territory or Alaska.

September 1.—Early the next morning I started up through the woods, and fighting my way for three hours through the willows and dwarf-birch, emerged above timber on the slopes of Mount Sheldon, which was covered with a few inches of snow. Looking up through my field-glasses I saw near the crest three young sheep which were very uneasy and kept nervously looking about. One was a three-year-old ram, the others two-year-olds. They acted in the way characteristic of young rams when separated from their band. They would lie down for a few moments, and then get up and look, until they moved a short distance to feed. After feeding a few moments they would become restless, and after looking about lie down again. But they would soon rise up and move nervously around. At last they went up near some cliffs and lay down facing up, but they still remained nervous and kept jerking their heads in all directions to maintain the watch. One was quite dark in color, the other two almost white.

Circling around the slope so as not to disturb them, I ascended for some distance. Ptarmigan were very abundant, and the holes of ground-squirrels were everywhere, though some of the squirrels had retired to hibernate. A few greeted me with familiar chatter. To the south of the mountain was a vast level meadow swamp extending to the lower slopes of Mount Riddell. Moose signs were abundant, and I decided to move the camp up to timber-line, since the long climb up through the woods from the shore of the lake consumed so much time that little remained for hunting.

September 2.—In the morning, each with a pack of sixty pounds, we slowly toiled upward, fighting the dense willows at every step. In the afternoon, timber-line was reached and the tent pitched among scattered balsams festooned with exquisite black moss hanging like silken cobwebs from the branches. We could look down on the lake below and command views to the north, east, and south. Behind was a long fringe of spruce tops adorning the golden horizon, while the peak of Mount Sheldon glistened under the rays of the setting sun.

September 3.—Three inches of snow fell during the night and the wet willows gave me a drenching before reaching the

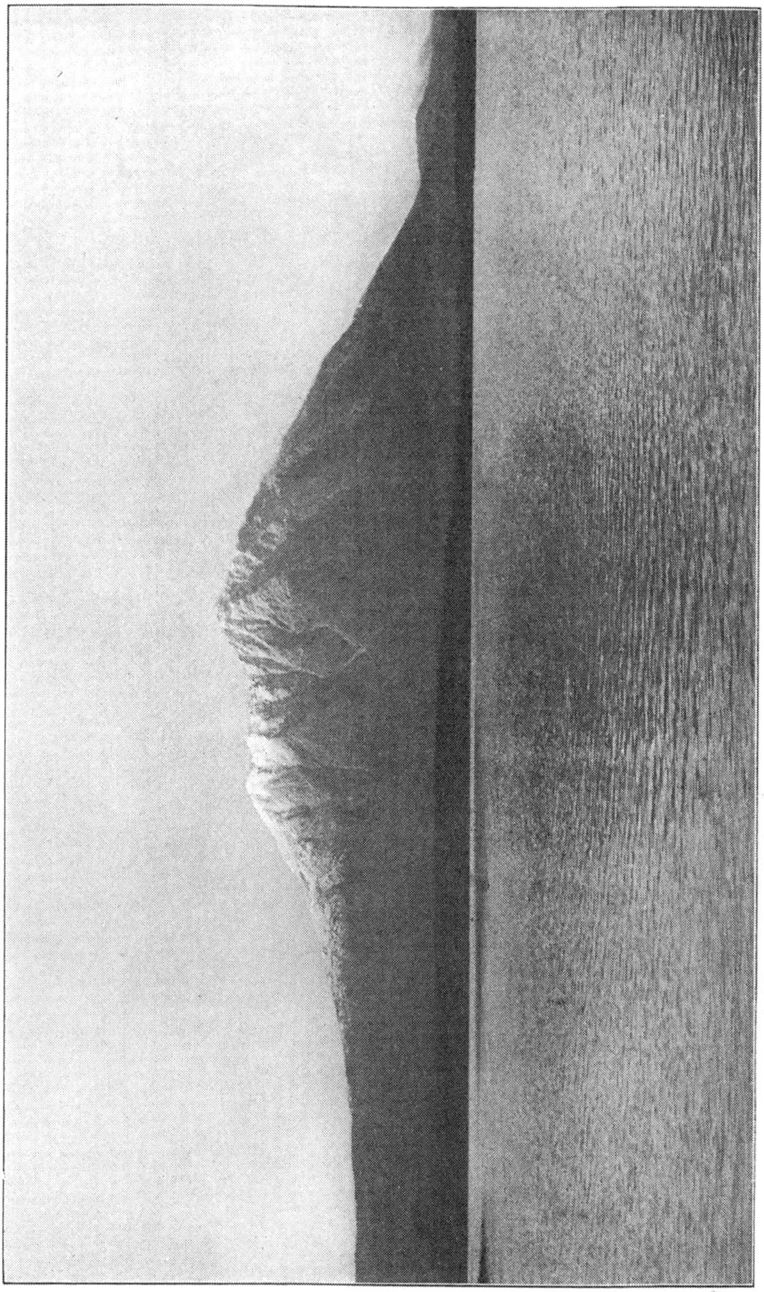

Sheldon Lake at the foot of Mount Sheldon which towers up from its shore, August 31.

south slope of the mountain, which I began to climb. A strong, cold wind bringing snow and hail came from the west and I was obliged to descend to the timber and make a fire to dry my clothes. It cleared at noon, and starting up the slope I had not gone far before seeing a bull moose just inside some scattered timber a mile distant at the west of the swamp meadow, where the waters drain to the South Fork of MacMillan River.

His horns were of fair size and he was rubbing them against a tree to clear them of the velvet. He would either butt the tree or rub vigorously, and continued these operations for some time. Then, after feeding for awhile, he would begin rubbing on some other tree. Once, pushing his horns into the branches of a fallen dead tree, as if in a frenzy, he kept tossing it. I watched him through my field-glasses for an hour, until he was in a place favorable to approach. Then after circling to a point where the wind was right I started toward him. The moose, feeding in some willows near a clump of spruce trees, was soon out of sight, and I went rapidly toward the spot, until within five hundred yards, when he suddenly appeared in an opening, and I dropped low. He again passed out of sight, and I advanced. Finally, I saw him through the spruces a hundred and fifty yards away, but the trees were too densely clustered to try a shot. Again he disappeared, and going to the left, step by step, I approached until soon I could see all of the clear area where he had last been feeding, but he was not in sight and I knew he was lying down.

Advancing fifty yards, I saw the tips of his horns. He was lying facing me, near a clump of willows. Lying on my stomach I crawled along and with rifle at my shoulder, suddenly rose and fired full into his chest. He stiffened out, trembling, and I walked toward him, but to my surprise he suddenly struggled to his feet and trotted fifty yards ahead before he fell dead. After taking the scalp and cutting off the head, I cut out fifteen pounds of fat and opened his stomach. It contained only willow leaves. His horns were shapely and had a spread of forty-eight inches; the velvet was entirely off one, and some was hanging in strips on the other, where one point was still soft. He had a fine bell sixteen inches long. Shouldering all, I struggled back to camp. Jefferies shouted with enthusiasm when he saw the fat, for the meat of the calf was lean and we both craved fat. We then sat before a fire of balsam wood which burns beautifully, without sparking.

September 4.—It began to snow, and the next morning four inches covered the ground. It was a beautiful clear day and I was soon on the slopes of Mount Sheldon. After ascending diagonally in a north-west direction, I saw eight sheep three hundred yards beyond—two rams, each six years old, one dark, the other light, together with three ewes and three lambs—all quietly feeding. Two of the ewes were dark, the other almost white. The white ewe had a very dark Iamb, while one of the dark ewes had two nearly white lambs. I watched them for a long time, but did not care to kill one. In color they agreed strictly with the sheep found near the MacMillan River.

Seeing a possible route to the peak of the mountain, I began to ascend. Though leather moccasins were dangerous, I had chosen a path among protruding rocks where I hoped to find footing. Step by step I struggled upward, often slipping and falling, and after reaching the top made up my mind never to attempt another snow-covered mountain unless with suitable footgear. When I reached the crest of that stupendous granite mountain and looked over, instead of seeing rough slopes, I looked down into the depths of a magnificent cirque—a vast amphitheatre of perpendicular walls falling more than three thousand feet to a lake of sapphire blue. Ancient ice had carved out a great circular pit resembling a huge, deep volcanic crater, the circle of cliffs almost meeting toward the north-west, not three hundred feet apart. Through this opening a stream trickled out from a lake. Time had fashioned the precipice, walls in thousands of fantastic shapes, the upper cliffs projecting in pillars, turrets, cones and rough-hewn crags. Scarred, seamed, and shattered, cliff upon cliff, ledge upon ledge, the great walls reared straight up from the *débris* below.

Neither before nor since have I commanded at one view such vast areas of forest on all sides. I could see both forks of the MacMillan, the Selwyn ranges, the smoother plateau mountains between the MacMillan and the Pelly, the Itsi Mountains, and the distant peaks of the Mackenzie ranges across the divide.

The impression felt when standing on the summit of that lone, massive mountain peak, isolated from other high ranges by miles of intervening wilderness was not that caused by silence and grim desolation, although they reigned supreme. It was a profound sense of loneliness—a loneliness caused by the vacancy of uninterrupted space. Never had I felt it in a similar way before. My nature was compelled to a stern accord with the upper world of sky, rock, and snow. But when I gazed down upon the great stretches of wilderness below, the impressions of the world above were transformed into those produced by the beauty and grandeur of the surrounding landscape.

Walking around the crest I could see no more sheep except those below which were peacefully resting. I made the descent without disturbing them and returned to camp.

September 5-6.—I had seen a few old caribou tracks on the mountain and the next day we took the sleeping robe, a piece of canvas, and some meat, and crossed four miles through the woods to timber-line at Mount Riddell, which appeared to be a better range for caribou. There we threw the canvas on some inclined poles and filled the sides with brush. In the morning I ascended the smooth slopes of the mountain, which was of the

Time had fashioned the precipice walls in thousands of fantastic shapes, September 4.

A vast amphitheatre of perpendicular walls falling more than 3,000 feet to a lake of sapphire blue, September 4.

type that caribou prefer for their range. In two hours I was on the crest, and after circling all around it, returned to camp by noon. I had observed only a few old caribou tracks, and an old, abandoned sheep-trail almost obliterated by grass and weeds.

It was clear that a few sheep had once been accustomed to feed there. It was also clear to me that the only sheep in that section of the country were on Mount Sheldon, and even there the band was very small, as indicated by the fact that the larger rams were with the ewes. I had, however, learned the character of the sheep in that part of the country, and that was the object of my exploration of the Ross. Therefore, I decided to go back to the Pelly as quickly as possible, and devote the remainder of my time to examining the sheep on the mountains bordering both sides of the river, between the mouth of the Ross and that of the MacMillan River. In the afternoon we carried all our material to the shore of the lake and there passed the night.

The Ross River country offers no good hunting, except for moose, which near the lakes are as abundant as on the MacMillan. But since the mountain area is so limited that few draws are favorable for finding them, the topography of the country, compared with that of the MacMillan, makes it most inferior as a place for successful moose hunting. I saw a few old bear diggings, demonstrating that grizzlies are there, but the lack of more open country would be unfavorable for seeing them in the spring. Keele, who spent the winter on Sheldon Lake in 1907-1908, found moose very abundant everywhere, but saw only five or six caribou near Mount Riddell. He observed no sheep on Mount Sheldon, and probably the small band I had seen there will decrease to the point of extinction, if any still exist. Keele does not think that there are any other sheep in any of the mountains bordering the Ross River.

I observed the same varieties of birds as on the MacMillan. In the Yukon territory bird-life in the summer and fall is not

Camp at foot of Mount Riddell, September 6.

Indian cache near a bar of the Ross River, September 8.

great in variety and birds are not observed so often as in the spring. On the Ross and at the lakes Alaska jays were about camp all the time. Rabbits, red squirrels, ground-squirrels, marmots, and red-backed mice were the common small mammals. The vast spruce forests yielded to former trappers abundant martens, lynxes, and some minks, but foxes are rather scarce. During the winter Keele saw a great many wolves, which usually were gathered in bands to hunt moose.

September 7-9.—As we paddled through the lakes early in the morning, numerous whistling swans were floating on the surface. Later, Lewis told me that thousands came to these lakes in October. We paddled down the river for three days. The whole country was aflame with brilliant fall colors. The areas covered by huckleberry bushes were deep carmine in contrast to the bright-red leaves of the currant bushes along the river banks; yellow and gold streamed out from the poplars and willows, while the scattered birches reflected charming tints of green, delicately shading into the others; splashes of crimson among the dry, gray tufts of the burnt spruce timber glowed in the sun, while the network of leafless branches assumed an exquisite blue.

Smoothly and rapidly we glided down the river among the gay colors under sunny skies. An occasional mink slipped along the bank and once I saw a black bear, but it went in the woods before I could stop the canoe. Another time, as we were silently gliding by a dead log, not ten feet away, my eye caught a female lynx stretched at length on it, trusting to her color blending with the log to hide her. But as we floated by, I saw her in time and killed her. From the outlet of Lewis Lake we had paddled twenty hours and twenty-five minutes to reach the Pelly. We accepted the chances and ran through both Prevost Canon and the heavy rapids below, and continued paddling until September 9, when we reached Nahanni

House and found that all the Indians had departed and were scattered to hunt moose, Lewis having arrived with ammunition a few days before.

Old *Danger*, still lame, was peacefully feeding on the other side of the river. But later in the fall he was killed for dog food.

On reaching Nahanni House we craved, first *sugar*, and then bread and tea. After our meat diet, these provided a feast more delicate to the palate than the choicest viands served to the gourmandizing man of the city. We rested for a day and then started down the Pelly River.

CHAPTER XVIII

THE ROSE MOUNTAINS – 1905

SEPTEMBER 11.—UNDER the azure sky of a calm Indian summer day, surrounded by gorgeous color, the broad surface of the charming Pelly floated our canoe along, as the swift current, assisted by our paddles, bore us rapidly around the sweeping curves and along the wide bars and fantastically escarped banks. The mountains above were white with snow, the terraces below them brilliant in contrast. As the Pelly range faded from sight, the Glenlyons came into view. Goshawks were then very numerous along the river and I saw two different ones, each at a different place, chasing a kingfisher. Once I saw one chasing a herring gull, and, another time, one chasing a raven. Different flocks of red-breasted mergansers scurried down the current ahead of us all day.

September 12.—We camped just before dark, and in the morning, after paddling forty minutes, reached Rose's cabin. As we landed, he stepped out on the bank to welcome us, with that taciturnity and lack of demonstration always acquired by those who habitually live alone in the woods. He had been there two years and had constructed a V-shaped cabin without even a window. It was banked with earth from the ridgepole to the ground and hence, though gloomy, was very warm in the winter. He was an old man about sixty, who, after having spent several years without success in locating a mining claim, had come up on the Pelly, "to trap and prospect," as he said. "To trap and prospect!" the final stage in the career of numerous unsuccessful prospectors in that northern country. It means coming to the country full of hope and ambition, lured to endure its hardships by a burning desire of finding the gold where nature has milled it into dust and nuggets, so that the individual miner has only to dig out the gravel and wash it. After a year or two of hard work, in the midst of other men more successful, the grubstake becomes exhausted before anything is found, but the golden flame burns even brighter than before. The prospector must then build his cabin far off in the woods and trap through the winter in order to secure enough fur to exchange for supplies sufficient to enable him to work his claim during the summer. It may not produce, and then he must try another. Repeated failures dim the flame and deaden the ambition, and new country is sought where animals may be trapped to exchange for a new grubstake with which to prospect for a new discovery. By this time the man has become accustomed to a life of mere existence and is unfitted for anything else. Still, for some time he calls himself a "trapper and prospector." After this stage, he soon acquires the habit of living entirely alone, which often marks the beginning of hallucinations, sooner or later, usually, developing into insanity. In proportion to the population of white men, there is more insanity in those far northern countries than in any other part of our continent.

We pitched our tent near his cabin and made up the packs which would cause our shoulders to ache the next day. In the afternoon I took a walk through the woods and circled around to the shore of a long slough, half a mile below the cabin, which I named Rose Slough. The shore was hard clay and contained the tracks of a moose which looked so fresh that I concluded they had been made the night before. But Rose told me that they had been there for eighteen days—which only goes to show how easily one can be deceived as to the age of the tracks of hoofed animals.

The day before, Rose had constructed a set-gun two miles below on the river, for a bear, and that evening asked Jefferies' advice as to his method of constructing it. "Absolutely wrong!" was Jefferies' verdict. "Impossible for the bear to set it off." My own judgment seconded his opinion. Then it was explained how a set-gun should be arranged, and Rose decided to go down river the next morning and reconstruct it according to expert advice.

September 13.—As he left, we burdened our shoulders with the packs and struggled upward through the brushy woods. Behind a succession of benches and terraced ridges the range of mountains rises, rugged and bold, to a crest culminating in peaks from five thousand eight hundred feet to six thousand two hundred feet in height. I named this range the Rose Mountains, as a tribute to the old man, who will probably spend his last days beneath them on the banks of the Pelly. For five hours we climbed up through a deep draw, and emerged at timber-line on the north side of the range. There we constructed a canvas shelter and made camp. Later, before we slept, the moon shed its glory on the snow-covered mountains enclosing us.

September 14.—Early the next morning I climbed one of the smooth, dome-shaped mountains to the north, and spent the whole day travelling over their summits. To the north, I could see the whole country between the Pelly, MacMillan, and Ross Rivers—a country different in character from any other draining to the Pelly. It has more the character of a vast, uneven plateau eroded into wide, basin-shaped valleys, with

The Rose Mountains, July 20.

Mr. Rose and his cabin, September 12.

high, dome-like mountains grouped without any regular trend. Most of them rise above timber, some are very massive, others extremely subdued. They are, first of all, caribou ranges, and the extensive willow growth marks a fine country for moose. It is quite probable that here and there on the summits small bands of sheep may range, but it is also doubtful if they wander far from the Rose Mountains.

While scanning the valleys beyond, I saw smoke curling up one of the slopes far to the north-east. It undoubtedly came .from a camp of the Pelly Indians who were hunting moose and caribou. There were no sheep tracks in those smooth mountains, but caribou tracks were everywhere, none of them very fresh. Ground-squirrels were still out, and great flocks of ptarmigan were flying about the slopes. Late in the afternoon as I was looking through my field-glasses over on the Rose Mountains, sixteen or seventeen sheep appeared, but they were too far away to observe their color or sex. I reached camp at dark when the air was crisp and frosty.

September 15.—Early in the morning I was high on the slopes of Rose Mountain, and after reaching the crest saw eleven ewes and lambs lying down two hundred yards below me. A heavy snow blizzard suddenly descended and lasted for an hour, while I sat sheltered from the wind by a rock. The sky cleared as quickly as it had darkened, and moving to a point where I could get a good view of the sheep, I watched them. All were of the same color as the sheep in the Pelly Mountains—bodies and legs gray and necks and heads light or white. They were browsing and one continued to rub her body against a stiff willow. The lambs also browsed like the ewes.

Without molesting them, I climbed the peak and could look across the Pelly and see both the Pelly and the Glenlyon Mountains. The crest of Rose Mountain is about five miles long and culminates at an altitude of six thousand two hundred feet. The slopes are steep, with a series of jutting crags extending far down, enclosing troughs between them. These troughs are grassy, and favorite feeding-places for sheep.

By noting the more densely wooded character of the slopes on the north side of the Pelly River east of Rose Mountain, Dr. Dawson had inferred that this increased growth was owing to greater humidity—because of a probable gap existing between the western end of the Pelly range and the Glenlyons. This inference was correct, for I could plainly see the gap, and Rose told me that the Little Salmon River headed there, not far from the Pelly.

I went along the crest to the west end of the range, and there had to endure another snow blizzard which lasted two hours. Then I saw about seventeen ewes and Iambs not a hundred and fifty yards away. All were of the same varying color as the others seen on the same mountain. None of the sheep observed in Rose Mountain acted as "sentinels," but they were as restless and active as ewes generally are. After watching them for an hour, I left without disturbing them and returned to camp. I had seen two fresh caribou tracks on the mountain, great quantities of ptarmigan, a few ground-squirrels and marmots.

That night, as I was lying under the shelter and looking down the basin, then filled with mist, while the surrounding mountain-crests were bathed in a ghastly light shed by the moon, and complete silence reigned over the weird scene, the grunting of a bull moose sounded a hundred yards behind me. Nearer and nearer out of the gloom came the sound, but not a stick cracked, not a footstep was heard. Still nearer it came, until only forty feet away, but although I strained my eyes to penetrate the dimly lighted mist, I could see nothing. Not a sound was audible except the regular grunting, which now began to grow more distant and finally ceased, on the opposite side of the basin.

September 16.—The next morning we returned to the Pelly and found that Rose had the skin of a small female black bear stretched on a frame. Not even a humorous twinkle beamed in his eyes when he told us that when he had arrived to reconstruct the set-gun, he found that the bear had already discharged it and killed herself.

September 17.—The last three frosty nights and the cold winds had done their cruel work and killed the foliage. Snow covered the slopes, the willow leaves near the river were brown, the golden glow of the poplars had gone, and the leaves were falling fast. From a landscape of brilliant color to one of brown and gray the transition had been abrupt.

We were again gliding down the Pelly under an overcast sky, in a raw, cold wind, bringing at intervals flurries of rain. Twenty-five miles below we passed a large creek coming from the north. I had seen it flowing through a fine valley north of Rose Mountain. It had not been named, so I called it Rose Creek.

As the afternoon hours pass by when one is sitting in the bow of a canoe, silently paddling, with rifle ready by his side, a deep fascination is added to the charm of gliding down those parts of the rivers where game is abundant. At any moment, a moose—that monarch of the northern forest—may appear on the bars; a bear may be seen swimming or moving among the willows; a lynx may be observed sitting on the bank; a fox playing on the shore, or a wolf skulking in the shadows. On the tangents, the eyes are continually strained to detect an animal far ahead, and when going around the curves the eagerness becomes intense. Later, as the sun goes low, the aspect of every inanimate thing changes, and from a distance many objects so resemble an animal as to impel the eyes to a close scrutiny.

About four in the afternoon, just before reaching the Tay River, where the Pelly curves sharply around a bar bordering

Dropped almost at my feet, September 17.

Jefferies cabin, September 19.

a flat of fine poplar trees, we heard a loud crack back in the woods. As we rapidly glided around the curve and approached a favorable wind, another crack sounded, and then another. The moose were rutting, and I thought that the noise was made by a bull knocking his horns against a tree. We dropped down to the lower end of the bar, quietly paddled to the shore, and I stepped into the woods. Fortunately the wind came from the direction of the noise, and I was wearing moose-hide moccasins—the best of all footgear to muffle the footsteps. The undergrowth was not dense and I could see well ahead through a fine poplar grove.

As I entered the woods a rabbit ran away, thumping the ground to the right. I paused some time to listen, but not a sound was audible, except the rustling of the leaves on the trees. Then, step by step, I cautiously advanced, and, nearing the spot where the noise had sounded, saw another rabbit skipping away to the left. I stood for several minutes and listened, but could not hear a sound. Just as I was about to return I saw the dusky form of a lynx, fifty feet ahead, apparently following with noiseless tread the trail of the rabbit. Its grayish color blended so perfectly with the fallen leaves and poplar trunks that I could scarcely distinguish it as it glided along. Raising my rifle and following the lynx as best I could, a favorable opportunity was presented as it passed through the dense poplar growth, and I fired, knocking it down. But it jumped up and was running in zigzag leaps as I fired three more shots, each missing. By that time it had circled to a point fifty feet ahead of me, and after the last shot it squatted down. I could see blood streaming from its chest, and holding the rifle to my shoulder I covered it, but did not fire the last cartridge, thinking that the lynx would expire.

A sudden rustling of the leaves caused me to turn my head, and I was startled to see a large black bear walking not ten feet away, and apparently looking at the wounded lynx. It stopped just as I saw it, and with one foot raised and head held high, it seemed to watch the lynx. Quickly swinging my rifle, I fired full into its chest. It gave a great spring, and, clutching its chest, reeled, half running in a short circle, and dropped almost at my feet. It kicked twice and died just six feet in front of me. The lynx was in the same position. Quickly reloading, I whistled for Jefferies, who came running into the woods. As he approached, the lynx began to move off in awkward leaps and we followed. After a short distance it again lay down and I killed it with a club. Jefferies went for my Kodak as I brought the lynx to the bear, and after photographing both, we carried them to the canoe, and an hour later reached Jefferies' old cabin opposite the Glenlyon range, where he had spent the winter two years before.

September 18-21.—The black bear was a mature male, five feet one and a half inches long. In the afternoon, while we were fleshing the skin, Jefferies saw two wolves about four hundred yards above on a bar. I hurried through the woods, but before I could come near enough for a reasonable shot, they were swimming the river and soon a third one followed them. Arriving on the opposite bank, all three trotted along until lost to sight.

During the day thousands of little brown cranes, in large flocks, passed over, all going south. I noticed that each flock on arriving at a point just below us, became confused and paused in its flight, circling higher and higher, until at last, when high in the heavens, almost lost to sight, it found its course and filed away in a V-shaped wedge to the south-west. Large flocks of geese also passed over, and several flocks of ducks.

We dragged the carcass of the bear well below the cabin in the hope of later finding a wolf feeding upon it. All along close to the Pelly great horned owls were very common, and rabbits were at their maximum of abundance. The next three days were boisterous, the equinoctial storm having descended, and we could not start for the mountains; fog, snow, and rain held us prisoners in the cabin. We craved meat, and, walking through the dripping brush in the morning, killed six rabbits. In September rabbits are very fat, and after hanging for a few days are excellent to eat. Ravens, gulls, and Alaska jays feasted on the bear carcass, but no larger animal came to it while we were there. The ravens first picked holes through the belly and pulled out the entrails to get at the fat attached to them. Several large flocks of herring gulls were seen flying down the river, and numerous flocks of migrating birds passed through the fog and rain.

CHAPTER XIX

THE GLENLYON MOUNTAINS – 1905

SEPTEMBER 22.—WITH heavy packs we started on the morning of September 22 for the Glenlyon Mountains, and after fighting through willows and travelling over benches, reached a creek flowing through a draw which extended well up in the ranges. After five hours we had ascended two thousand feet, from the river to timber-line, and were well within the outside range. A broad, rolling mountain valley spread out on both sides of a fine willow draw, and camp was made among some scattered spruces. Two pieces of canvas were tied together and thrown over inclined poles in the form of a shelter, from which we had an outlook over the whole valley.

September 23.—It was near zero in the night, and the following day was calm, cloudless, and mild. I climbed to the crest of the mountain north-east of camp and was then almost directly above the Pelly River, which wound in a wide curve below me. I could see all the mountains along the MacMillan River, the Kalzas range, Plateau Mountain, the Dromedary Mountain, the Russell Mountains, and more dimly the peaks of those between the Forks. All were covered with snow.

The Glenlyons, trending in ranks, stretched away to the south-west. They are rugged and bold, like the Pelly range, but with more dome-shaped tops, the peaks reared up from five to seven thousand feet. The Glenlyons are mostly granite, and the width of the ranges is about ten miles.

The wind had not yet swept off any of the snow that had fallen during the storm, and walking along the top was tedious. I noticed rabbit tracks on the very top, and a few ground-squirrels were still out. I travelled all day along the summits and over the peaks without seeing a sign of sheep until five in the afternoon, when I saw nine ewes and lambs, half a mile away walking along a crest extending in a north direction. While watching them as they kept pausing to paw out the snow, sixteen others suddenly came in sight, crossing a saddle toward the south side of the mountain I was on.

Wading through deep snow I climbed over the top and going down on the other side to a point where I could see the sheep found myself in plain sight as they were approaching. It was too late to return, so I found some rocks near, and crawling to them concealed myself and watched the sheep. All were of the same color as the sheep in the Pelly Mountains. They kept advancing, now and then stopping to feed, until reaching the crest they passed above me and soon were out of sight. They crossed my trail without noticing it. After allowing time for them to gain sufficient distance, I ascended to the crest and observed their trail on the snow. The tracks followed the crest two hundred yards and then led down the mountain-side, almost directly above our camp. I decided to kill, if possible, two two-year-old rams which were with the ewes, and a ewe which I intended to bring back to Skagway for my friend Newell, Vice-President of the White Pass Railway.

While the dark, wide valley of the Pelly River, stretching away to the white mountains beyond, was before me on one side, and the snow fields and peaks of the Glenlyons merged into a golden horizon below a gorgeous crimson sky on the

Looking down on "Detour" of Pelly—ranges along MacMillan in distance, September 23.

Glenlyons toward south-west—Tay River Mountains in the distant, September 23.

other, I slowly walked along the crest, fearful that the grating noise of my footsteps breaking through the crust would alarm the sheep. Reaching the point where the tracks led down the slope, I saw all of them two hundred yards below, about to cross a deep canon which furrowed the mountain-side. It was 6.30 in the evening and rapidly getting dark. At the first shot a small ram fell dead. The band rushed closely together and paused to look. A second shot killed the other ram. One ewe still stood and looked, while the rest of the band dashed down into the canon. As I fired she fell, but rose and began to run diagonally up the slope. My next two shots missed and after putting in a clip of cartridges, I fired again and she fell and rolled.

Quickly going down to the first one killed, I skinned the hind quarters and cut them off. It was then dark and I had before me the dangerous task of carrying them down the steep, slippery slope. It was finally accomplished and that night we again feasted on mutton.

September 24.—The next morning Jefferies went to bring back the dead sheep, which could be seen from camp. We intended to take off their skins later. I started toward the southeast mountains, but after having crossed the valley, a snow storm descended and I was obliged to return to camp. Foxes had completely eaten up the remainder of the ram I had first killed. The two others were in camp.

September 25-26.—The next day a heavy snow fell all the morning and a dense fog settled in the afternoon, so I could not go out. This fog continued also through the following day. We spent most of the time sitting before the fire. There was a fine grove of dry burnt spruces near the shelter. Dry spruce is the main fuel supply of northern camps. If thoroughly hard and dry it does not spark, though it is quickly consumed. After a grove of spruce is burned over, at least two years are required before the charred trunks dry to perfection for burning. Dry

Highest peaks of Glenlyons, opposite Tay River, September 23.

Glenlyons looking south from same point, September 23.

balsam makes a much better fire, burning steadily without a spark, and is not consumed so quickly. Not often, however, is the camp pitched where balsam is abundant. Dry poplar makes a beautiful fire, very hot, no sparks, and steadily burning. It is the best of all fires for baking bread. But it smothers in its own ashes, which quickly accumulate, and for that reason it is not used in a stove if other wood can be found. Dry willow makes a hot fire, but the smoke is unendurable. Alder, like poplar, accumulates ash, but it is the best of all the northern fuel-wood to burn when green. The most perfect wood is, of course, white birch, but it is so scarce that it can be eliminated from the fuel used by the camper in Yukon Territory and Alaska.

September 27.—The fog did not lift until the third day at noon and I was soon climbing a low mountain southwest of camp. There was not a track of any kind on the snow in the valley, except that of the fox and the rabbit. Late in the afternoon I saw seven ewes and lambs lying on the snow on a slope of an adjacent mountain. They were colored like the others and, after resting, they started single file for a new feeding-ground, walking, running, and jumping over the rocks and rough places.

September 28.—I started early and toiled upward to reach the peak of a high mountain south-east of camp, hoping finally to find the larger rams, for I wanted a big one from the Glenlyons. Just before noon I stood on the apex, fifty-two hundred feet above the river. A violent storm suddenly descended—a raging snow blizzard—and I had to hold on to a projecting rock to keep from being blown off. Fog settled around, and the blasts of wind whirled the snow in violent eddies about me, filling my neck and even blowing up the inside of my trousers. It lasted three hours and I was so cold it did not seem possible to endure it much longer. The wild desolation of that blizzard, shutting everything from sight and suspending me in tumultuous clouds, produced a feeling of profound loneliness. During the storm I heard flocks of ptarmigan going by, and now and then a croaking raven. After it cleared, I went down from the peak to the crest and walked along it all the rest of the day, but saw no animals. When about to return I started to cross a steep slope of hard snow lying solid for two hundred yards, and after going well out in it, it proved steeper than I had thought and I could look two thousand feet almost directly down. Without axe or staff, and wearing rubber shoes with small hobnails, my situation soon became alarming. Taking out my knife I had to cut steps through a crust too hard to break with my feet, and my anxiety was only relieved when I finally stepped upon the rocks of a ridge I had to cross in order to shorten the descent to the valley.

September 29.—The next day, the last that I could spare for hunting in the Glenlyon Mountains, was clear and cold. Starting early, I walked rapidly up the valley to the forks of the creek. On a mountain beyond the forks I saw a single ewe with a lamb, both travelling rapidly; the ewe was especially alert and watchful. Often I have seen these single ewes, detached for one reason or another from their band, hastening to find it. When alone they always suffer from intensified sense of danger.

I then climbed a high mountain to the east, and, passing over its crest, saw on the other side a mountainous country of rolling slopes filled with canons and ravines, all leading up to a rough range beyond. Three hundred yards below me were two ewes, each with .a lamb, and a small ram. Carefully concealing myself among some rocks, I was interested in testing their sense of hearing. Several marmots, nearer to them than I was, had been whistling. The sheep were quite indifferent to the sound. If there is any animal sound in the Northern wilderness that can be easily imitated, it is the whistle of the marmot, and I thought that my whistle was a perfect reproduction of the original. But when I gave it the sheep at once threw up their heads and looked. After a few moments they began to feed. Not fifty yards to my right a marmot again whistled. They were utterly indifferent. But at my second whistle, shortly after, they ran about for a few feet and looked above and below in anxiety. They were able to distinguish instantly between the genuine and the imitation. It must not be inferred, however, that the marmot's whistle does not alarm sheep, for often they receive the sound as a warning and become nervous and watchful. Then I began to drop pebbles. It was absolutely still and as I threw a small stone on some rocks a few feet below the sheep at once ran down the slope and disappeared.

A quarter of a mile beyond were twelve ewes and lambs and I could trace their tracks coming down from the high crest beyond. Along their trails the slope, in places where they had pawed away the snow, had the appearance of a checker-board. Though keeping a careful lookout in all directions, no one of them acted the part of a sentinel. The ewes with lambs would butt the lambs away if they approached too close to them when they were feeding. The lambs were pawing away snow just like the ewes. All were of the color of the other sheep I had seen in the Glenlyon Mountains. I withdrew without disturbing them and returned to camp.

September 30.—The next morning we each brought a load to Jefferies' cabin.

Sheep are abundant in the Glenlyon Mountains, which are the most accessible for sheep hunting of any of the ranges near the Pelly River. But no other kinds of game were observed, and, except in the spring for bears (whose old diggings were abundant), the hunting must be limited to sheep. Fine large willow draws exist everywhere among the ranges and willow is abundant on all the slopes. All the Glenlyons are fine ranges for moose, but I did not see even an old track, nor were any of the willows mutilated by their browsing. In the lower country

Camp in Glenlyons, September 29.

Ready to load the canoe. Glenlyons across river, October 2.

outside of the range, moose signs were abundant.

No signs of caribou were observed. It is strange that when wolves were so near, no tracks appeared in the snow above near the sheep. Foxes were more abundant in the Glenlyons than in any of the country near the Pelly where I had been.

October 1.—Jefferies went up to the camp the next day to bring back the rest of the meat, and I tramped five miles north of the river to a fair-sized lake, more to see the country than anything else. It had all been burned over and was full of tangled, fallen timber. While returning late in the afternoon I must have seen several hundred rabbits. That year was the period of maximum abundance of the rabbits, but the following year they were scarce.

October 2-3.—The river had fallen several inches during the time we had been up in the Glenlyons, and all the trees were bare. The whole country was ready and waiting for winter to seal it up. For the next two days we paddled without incident, except the sight of two lynxes at different places on the bank of the river. My bullets failed to hit them. Lynxes do not appear to be frightened by a canoe floating by. I have seen many sitting indifferently on the bank and watching the canoe if it is near the middle of the river, or crouching in a hiding attitude if it is close to the bank. That year when rabbits were so abundant, we must have passed numerous lynxes without seeing them. So well do they blend with the color of the rocks on the bars, or with the trunks of the trees or faded leaves, that it is difficult to detect them.

The second evening we reached the cabin at the mouth of the MacMillan River, and later Hosfall arrived, having come from Kalzas Creek for the purpose of waiting for me and of delivering some skulls of sheep and caribou which had been killed in the Kalzas Mountains. From his description of the color of the sheep there, I knew they varied exactly like those in the mountains near the North Fork of the MacMillan. A fine large skull of a male otter with a note from Mrs. Hosfall, was found in the cabin. Her experience in killing that otter, whose skull is now in the Biological Survey in Washington, merits description.

While occupying the cabin in the latter part of July, she had a net for salmon stretched across an eddy in the river. One morning, when her husband was back in the woods, she saw an otter swimming across the river in the: direction of the net. At the same time, one of her large dogs noticed it and immediately jumped in and swam to intercept it. She thought that the otter would get caught in the net and quickly jumped in her canoe and began poling toward it. She was not mistaken, for the otter became entangled in the meshes and was struggling to get loose when the dog arrived and grabbed it, both going under the water and struggling in the net. Mrs. Hosfall quickly arrived, and while one hand held the canoe steady with the pole, with the other she grasped the dog's tail and pulled him into the canoe. His jaws were closed on the otter, which was hauled in with him, together with part of the net.

Then dog and otter, both entangled in the net, began to struggle in the cranky canoe which Mrs. Hosfall had to balance with nothing but a pole. But she was equal to it. In some way pulling off the dog, she grasped the hind leg of the otter and killed it with the pole. Few men could have successfully accomplished such a feat, and may this record of it stand as a suggestion of her skill!

October 4-5.—The next day a rain storm prevented my setting out to climb the MacMillan Mountains, but the day after it was clear, and after following for some distance a trapper's blazed trail, I struggled through the timber and began the ascent of the slopes. It was a climb of three and a half hours from the river to the top, which was buried under deep snow.

The highest peak of the MacMillan Mountains, an irregular, dome-shaped crest extending three or more miles in a semicircle, curving north at its west end, culminates at the extreme western extension of the range. I found it heart-breaking to wade through the deep snow, but finally reaching the highest point rested and looked over the country. All the Kalzas mountains seemed close on the north-east—rugged granite ranges with serried, battlemented peaks. I could see Kalzas Lake and the mountains along the MacMillan River for a long distance. Broad, deep valleys separated the Kalzas range from the MacMillan Mountains, and judging by the appearance of the country, it must be a fine range for moose. A beautiful view of the junction of the Pelly and MacMillan Rivers was below me, and the subdued rolling wilderness stretched out in the distance to the south and west. Still farther to the west I could faintly see the bluffs near Pelly Road Crossing, six miles from the Yukon River.

Tramping about I saw no signs of sheep, but caribou tracks were abundant. A bull moose had crossed over the mountain that morning or the night before. His deep trail along the side of the mountain, winding up over the crest, and continuing down to the timber on the other side indicated his search for a cow. A wolverine's tracks followed the crest for some distance until lost among the wind-swept rocks. Flocks of ptarmigan were flying about, but all ground-squirrels were asleep, and I returned to camp.

October 6-7.—We resumed the canoe trip down the river, and two days of steady paddling brought us to Selkirk on October 7.

When the Selkirk Indians saw the sheep skins as I unloaded them, they told me that many of the sheep in the mountains near the head of Selwyn River were of a similar color. One of the Indians had in his cabin two skins of sheep

Indian grave on bank of Pelly, 25 miles above mouth of MacMillan, October 3.

Trappers' line cabin on MacMillan Mountain, October 5.

Moose trail on top of the MacMillan Mountains, October 5.

that he had killed there, and I went to look at them. They were much lighter in color than the lightest Pelly Mountain sheep, but intermediate between the types of *Ovis fannini* and *Ovis dalli*, approximating the latter. Since the Selkirk Indians find sheep within the limits of their hunting territory only to the west of the Yukon River, I regard their statements as to the color of the sheep near the Selwyn River as reliable, and I so obtained a most interesting record.

October 9—The steamer *Selkirk* whistled and I had to part from Jefferies. It was with deep regret that I grasped his hand and said good-by. He had been efficient in every way, and, what counts more than anything else, he had always been cheerful and willing to undertake the hard work of that eventful summer. During all the days that I had been hunting, he had been content to remain in camp while I was getting the sport. I am glad to record his good qualities.

Travelling without stopping longer than necessary to make connections by boat and rail, I reached New York October 24th.

I had established the fact that nearly all sheep on the mountains adjacent to the. Pelly River are of approximately the same color. Also that those near the Ross are of the same color as those near the MacMillan. The Pelly sheep, though variable, are intermediate between *Ovis fannini* and *Ovis stonei*, approaching more nearly the color of the latter. The sheep near the MacMillan and Ross Rivers throughout the Selwyn Rockies are so variable that as a whole their color cannot be defined. The variation continues on the Stewart River, where lighter shades begin to predominate farther north. In the Ogilvies, the intermediate color between *Ovis fannini* and *Ovis dalli* is common, though variations range between the two, and the majority of the sheep can be referred to dalli. Not much farther north, all the sheep are white.

Junction of MacMillan and Pelly Rivers as seen from top of MacMillan Mountains, October 5.

MacMillan Mountains, October 5.

The type color of *Ovis fannini* is so rare, even in the mountains from which the type came, that numerous sheep might be killed before one could be found to coincide with the description. Now and then it exists among the variables.

I have learned from sources which I accept as reliable, that the sheep in the Teslin and Atlin Lakes districts are in color like those on the MacMillan, more variables occurring among them. Nearer the Yukon, lighter colored sheep predominate, and among the white sheep north of the Yukon a few intermediates are exceptionally found in the Watson River country, and perhaps easterly, wherever sheep exist, as far as the mountains near the head of Selwyn River. Farther north, west of the Yukon River, all are white, except for a few gray hairs in the sheep in the Tanana Hills.

The variation in the color of the sheep in the Yukon Territory having, therefore, been settled, I resolved to make future explorations in the far interior of Alaska.

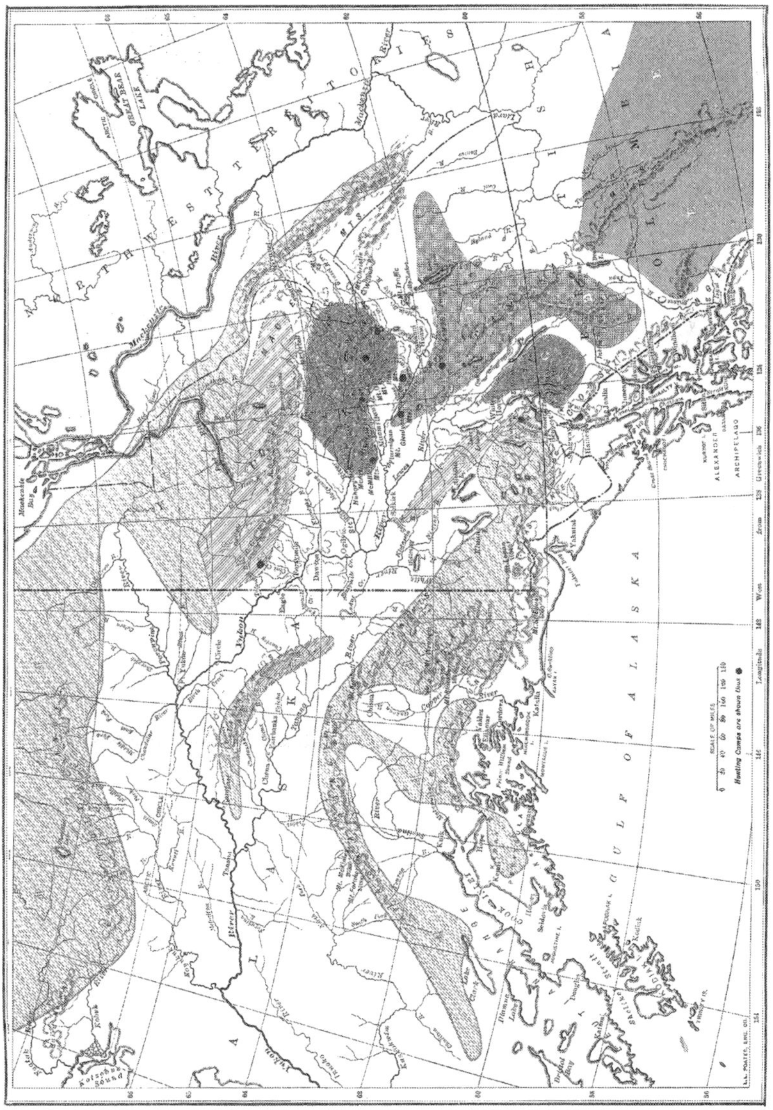

Map of Yukon Territory, adjacent portions of Alaska, British Columbia, and North-west Territories, showing distribution of sheep according to their colors.

Fig. 1. *Ovis dalli*, Type.

Fig. 5. *Ovis fannini*, Type.

Fig. 9. *Ovis stonei*, Type.

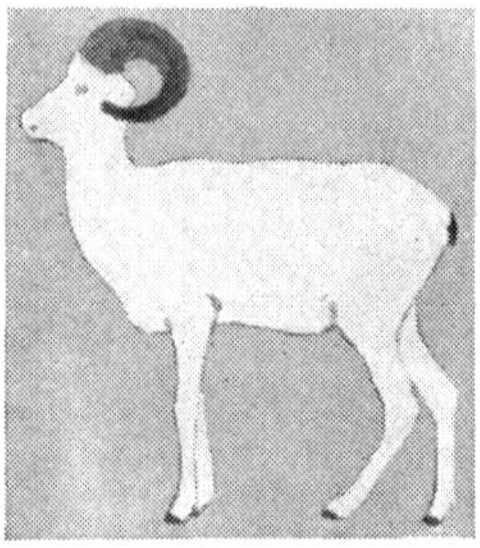

Fig. 2.

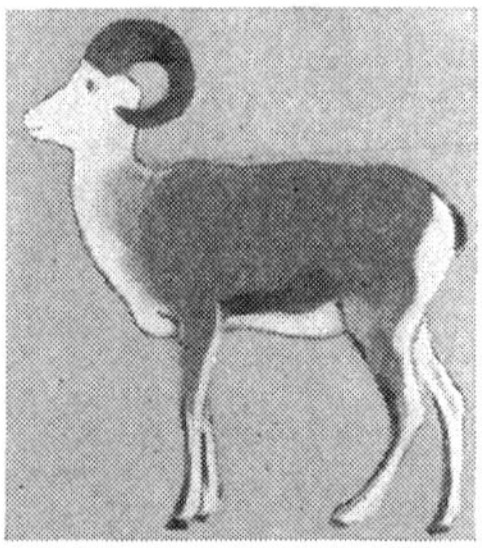

Fig. 6.

Fig. 3.

Fig. 7.

Fig. 4.

Fig. 8.

Distribution Areas.

A—Occupied by Fig. 1 (*Ovis dalli*) exclusively.

B—*Ogilvie Rockies* occupied by Figs. 2-3-4, exceptionally Fig. 5 in eastern section. Figs. 2 and 3 greatly in the majority. *Between Yukon and Tanana Rivers* occupied mostly by Fig. 2 with much less black on tail, occasionally Fig. 1. *West of Lewes River* occupied by Figs. 1 and 2 in the majority. Figs. 2-3-4-5 exceptionally.

C—Occupied by Figs. 2-3-4-5-6-7. Figs. 3-4-5-6 most common. Intermediate colors between 2 and 3 equally common.

D—Occupied by Figs. 4-5-6-7-8. Figs. 5-6-7 in the majority. Tendency toward lighter colors in the north. Fig. 4 exceptional in the north, still more so toward the south. Fig. 9 occasionally in the south.

E—Occupied by Fig. 9 (*Ovis stonei*). Rarely Figs. 6 and 7 are found in this area.

Plate illustrating distribution of sheep in areas indicated on map.

Figures 1–5–9 were drawn from the Types. The other figures are from specimens illustrating the average colors, but actually every intermediate graduation of color occurs respectively between each.

CHAPTER XX

REMARKS ON SOME OF THE ANIMALS OF YUKON TERRITORY

THE PRECEDING NARRATIVE records accurately the animal life observed during my wanderings in Yukon Territory. In this chapter I have assembled not only some of the facts mentioned, but also those gained from other reliable sources.

SHEEP

(THE REMARKS IN THIS CHAPTER ARE PRELIMINARY TO A FULLER DISCUSSION OF HABITS IN A FUTURE PUBLICATION.)

The habits of all sheep on this continent, existing north of the range of the Rocky Mountain sheep *Ovis canadensis*, are the same except in so far as they are slightly varied by local topographic and food conditions and by the accumulation of snow on their ranges during the winter. The environment and the climatic conditions where they live are practically the same, their natural enemies are the same, and they select and eat the same food. All dwell above timber-line, and by nature are timid and wild.

Their body measurements, according to age and sex, allowing for slight individual variations in size, are practically the same.

The same statement applies to the size and character of

their horns. The first Stone sheep brought out from the Stikine River region had the diverging or "spread" type of horns, and this, therefore, was assigned to them as a definite *character*. But among the numerous specimens coming from the same region during subsequent years, the narrow type of horns has probably been more common.

The diverging type of horns is found in all localities where sheep exist, though in some districts it is more common than in others. I did not see the diverging type among the sheep on the Pelly River, though undoubtedly it exists there. It is common among those at the head of the MacMillan and Stewart Rivers, and in the Ogilvie Rockies. It is particularly common in that part of the Yukon Territory close to the coast ranges and directly east of them. But, everywhere, the narrow type of horns is more abundant; sometimes both types occur together in the same band; sometimes all the members of a band have one type of horns, while all the sheep of another band in the same locality have the other type.

What is true of the comparative divergence of the horns is equally true of their comparative length, circumference, and shape. In some districts, including the Pelly River and the Ogilvie Rockies, horns of large basal circumference (fifteen inches or more) are most exceptional. Big horns are more common in those districts where the diverging type is most abundant.

It thus appears that the northern sheep, wherever they live, are subject to essentially the same conditions of environment and climate; their food and enemies are essentially the same, and their natures, their habits, their horns, and their body measurements do not differ materially. It remains to examine their skulls and to study their variations in color.

Difference in skull *characters* have been detected among sheep in three widely separate areas: the Stikine River region, the east slope of the Mackenzie Rockies, the whole of the areas inhabited by sheep elsewhere; but as yet no satisfactory study has been made, since the available series of adult skulls from each locality have not been brought together for careful comparison. Such a comparison may result in the elimination of most of the supposed differences, and under any circumstances, by skull *characters* alone, the sheep could only be separated into weak subspecies. At the present time only one positive statement can be made. *The differences in skull characters are slight.*

The northern sheep do not undergo seasonal changes in color, but they do present marked individual and local color variations, the study of which is beset by perplexing problems. In this connection a few words on the distribution of sheep in the Yukon Territory will be helpful. A detailed description of distribution cannot be given in the space of this chapter, and besides, the exact topography in many areas and the occurrence of sheep in each are not known. Nevertheless, facts sufficient for a few generalizations have come under my observation.

Except within the humid belt of the Coast Ranges, sheep exist on nearly all the mountains which rise rough and rocky, well above timber-line. Sheep do not live on lower mountains, the areas of which above timber-line are smooth and unbroken. Sheep are most abundant in those regions where the mountains are continuous and connected. Hence they occur in greatest numbers on the ranges, including their direct lateral connections, east of the Alaska Coast Range—near the heads of the Slims, Donjek, and White Rivers. Next they are most abundant on the Pelly Mountains (including the Glenlyons), and those parts of the Ogilvies not hunted to supply meat for Dawson and miners in the same vicinity. Elsewhere in the Territory the high mountains are complex groups, rather than continuous ranges, and the number of sheep inhabiting regions of this character is comparatively more limited.

The regions where sheep exist are divided into "sheep ranges," each of which is very limited (only a few miles) in area, and occupied by a group of sheep which pass their lives on the same range, precisely as do cattle in the unfenced portions of the West. Except for some mingling at the borders between neighboring groups, each colony of sheep keeps to its own range. The sheep cling so tenaciously to their ranges, that a destructive enemy, like man, usually exterminates them before they will leave. If driven off temporarily, most of them soon return. It is a mistake to think that sheep are driven from one region to another. Aggressive hunting kills off most of the group, and only a very small proportion migrate to other ranges. This is particularly true in regions where the mountain ranges are not continuous. But when the number of sheep on a range increases and crowds the food supply, a gradual overflow to other regions takes place, and this overcrowding also causes an irregular migration of sheep over areas inhabited by them.

Therefore, all through the territory where sheep formerly existed near routes of travel or Indian villages, or where their ranges were easily accessible to Indian hunting or mining districts, they have become scarce or extinct. Such active hunting of them, however, has recruited adjacent regions only in a limited degree.

The *type* of *Ovis stonei* was killed in the Cheonee Mountains south of the Stikine River in British Columbia. These sheep have been traced south near the head of the South Fork of the Stikine to the Iskoot River, not far from the head of the Nass River. The extreme southern and eastern range is not known. It is probably between latitude 55 degrees and 56 degrees, and west of longitude 126 degrees.

The grayish color of the back and chest extends up the neck to the face, and nearly all the sheep in the regions south of the Stikine are uniformly colored. I know of two sheep, killed near the type locality, which had white necks and heads, and so much white hair intermixed with the gray of the back that they were similar in color to many of the sheep of the Pelly Mountains. Therefore, it is fair to infer that there must be other exceptional cases of light color among them. These sheep south of the Stikine extend their range northward along the main Cassiar range, probably crossing to it in the vicinity of the Dease River. It is possible that some cross the Stikine directly from the Cheonee Mountains, and reach the Sheslay River district on the north, although there is probably an overflow of migration southward to that region from the Cassiars near Dease River.

We are familiar with sheep directly north of the Stikine River, which come from the Sheslay River region. Here some have the typical color of Stone sheep, but many have so many white hairs intermingled with the gray on the neck that they resemble closely the sheep of the Pelly Mountains, and often very light-colored sheep are found among them. From this region the most uninterrupted mountain route for sheep to travel is north-east through the Cassiar range, on to the Pelly Mountains, Glenlyon Mountains, and across the Pelly River near the Tay River to the Rose Mountains.

Directly north of the Sheslay River district are serious barriers of lakes—Atlin, Teslin, the Taku Arm of Lake Bennet and numerous other small lakes. Also the mountains in that district are in groups, separated by wide valleys, rather than in continuous ranges. Here sheep are comparatively scarce, only small bands occurring in a few of the mountain groups. The last group of mountains, west of Atlin Lake, that are inhabited by enough sheep to be called "sheep mountains," are near Big

Horn Creek at the south end of the Taku arm of Lake Bennet. Between Teslin River and the Lewes, sheep are very scarce. Throughout this region the sheep vary in color exactly as they do in the Selwyn Rockies—presenting various degrees of color between white and dark gray. Between Big Horn Creek and the Watson River country north of Lake Bennet, the barriers of lakes and wide timbered valleys prevent continuous travel back and forth, and probably the few sheep that cross this area, either from the north or from the south, are scattered and driven from their ranges. Sheep do not enter the humid belt of the continuous Coast Ranges.

That sheep do cross the barriers is proved by the fact that occasionally one of intermediate color is found among the white Dall sheep on the Watson River, and Dall sheep are sometimes found among the variables near Big Horn Creek, and even farther south. In the Watson River country, some of the sheep are pure white with black tails, a very few have gray hairs mingled in the back, but most of them are pure white including the tails. Directly west of the Watson River region—west of longitude 136 degrees and south of latitude 62 degrees—all the sheep are pure white.

Just north of latitude 62 degrees, near the head of the Selwyn River, a few of the sheep have enough gray hairs on the back to suggest the pattern area of coloration. I have not been able to get many facts about the occurrence of sheep between the Selwyn River and the Watson River. Sheep, however, are known to cross the Thirty Mile River (that part of the Lewes River between Lake Le Barge and the mouth of the Teslin), and it is quite possible that some of the variables between the Teslin River and the Lewes mingle among the sheep west of Thirty Mile, and hence influence the colors northward to the Selwyn River. Sheep do not cross the Yukon River south of the vicinity of Eagle in Alaska.

The natural route of uninterrupted sheep travel northward from the Stikine River is directly through the Cassiar range, along and across the Pelly River to the Rose Mountains. The color of the sheep occupying the mountains parallel with the Pelly River is similar to that of the sheep in the Sheslay River region, except that more have white necks, and more have a larger proportion of white hairs mixed with the gray of the back. A series of skins from both regions would show a general similarity, more specimens with dark necks occurring among the sheep from the Sheslay River, and more with light necks among those from the Pelly River. Neither series would show uniform coloration, each varying between light and dark within narrow limits. Dark and light sheep occur exceptionally in both districts.

The only route of travel for sheep, between the Pelly River and the heads of the MacMillan and Ross Rivers, is through the mountainous region between the Pelly and the MacMillan (the southward extension of the Selwyn Rockies). Immediately north of Rose Mountains the country is so broken that few sheep inhabit the region. The mountains, mostly dome-shaped, are separated by wide valleys. In the main ranges, the Selwyns, the complex groups are more connected and rougher, and there sheep are more abundant. Throughout the Selwyns, the color of the sheep is extremely variable, the same bands containing sheep approximating the white *dalli*, and the dark *stonei*, and every degree of intermediate color, including the so-called *fannini*.

The topography of the country between the Selwyn Rockies and the Ogilvies is not accurately known, nor are exact limits assigned to each range, but sheep travel between the two ranges, probably in the water-shed between the Stewart and Peel Rivers. Owing to wide valleys and other features of topography, the travel back and forth is probably not extensive.

The Ogilvies, however, are continuous uninterrupted ranges like the Pelly Mountains, and toward the north the color of the sheep rapidly becomes white. At the head of Coal Creek the grayish pattern is faint and many of the sheep are pure white with black tails. The darkest sheep of the region are intermediate between *fannini* and *dalli*. The exact point north where none of the sheep show traces of gray is not determined, but it cannot be far, and we know that all sheep north and west of the Porcupine River are white.

The sheep west of Eagle and in the Tanana Hills, between the Yukon and Tanana Rivers, are mostly pure white, though some have enough dark hairs to suggest a pattern area. In the same region, along the ranges west of longitude 146 degrees, all the sheep are pure white. It is not known whether sheep from the Selwyn River have ever travelled northward to this region, or whether sheep from the Ogilvies have crossed the Yukon River. There are places below Eagle where sheep have been seen on the ridges bordering the Yukon River.

Now follows a most interesting and significant fact. That portion of the Mackenzie Rockies, extending parallel with the Mackenzie River water-shed, is an uninterrupted series of continuous ranges as far as the head of the Peel River. Sheep are abundant in all this area, including the Nahanni Mountains in the south, not only to the Peel River, but also continuously to the mountains west of the Mackenzie Delta on the north. All these sheep, including those ranging parallel with the sheep of variable colors in the Selwyn Rockies west of the divide, are *pure white*. Joseph Keele, who made a special study of the distribution of sheep at the head of the Ross and Stewart Rivers, and also of those east of the divide, asserts positively that in those regions, owing to climatic conditions and areas destitute of vegetation, sheep never cross the divide. It is probable that further investigations along the divide, both north and south, will show that sheep do not cross anywhere except, perhaps, far to the north. This view is supported by the fact that all sheep on the Mackenzie side are white, which would not be the case were there any intermingling.

Where gray, brown, or black hairs occur on the sheep, these hairs are within the pattern area emphasized in *Ovis stonei*. The dark hairs are most persistent in the tail and least persistent in the head and neck. Next they are most persistent on the mid-dorsal line directly above the tail; next on the back, ventral border extending to the chest, and on the front sides of all the legs. When I speak of sheep as pure white, it is never strictly true, since a careful search will always reveal a few dark hairs in the tail, and often above on the dorsal line, and more rarely on the back. This is true even of the sheep along the Arctic coast mountains, specimens of which I have recently examined.

Let us sum up the facts here presented.

All the sheep of Alaska are uniformly pure white, except occasional specimens between the Yukon and Tanana Rivers east of longitude 146 degrees. There are no other exceptions.

Throughout the Mackenzie Rockies, within the Mackenzie water-shed south farther than latitude 62 degrees, sheep are pure white.

In the Yukon Territory, all sheep north of latitude 66 degrees, south of latitude 62 degrees, and west of longitude 136 degrees, are pure white. Pure white sheep greatly preponderate west of the Lewes and Yukon Rivers.

The sheep south and east of the Stikine River in British Columbia are uniformly dark with occasional exceptions.

From the Sheslay River region north of the Stikine River, north along the uninterrupted area of travel through the Cassiar ranges and the Pelly River region, there is a more general uniformity of color, more lighter sheep occurring along the Pelly River.

In the Ogilvie Rockies the tendency toward white prevails increasingly toward the west and north.

Throughout the Selwyn Rockies, and in the region between the Sheslay River district and the Lewes River, the color of the sheep is extremely variable.

Generally, variation in color occurs in some of the regions west of the Yukon water-shed, east of longitude 136 degrees, between latitudes 58 degrees and 65 degrees.

The facts indicate that, within the areas of color variation, sheep inhabiting the continuous unbroken ranges have a tendency toward uniform colors, while those inhabiting regions where the mountain ranges are broken,. having the character of complex groups separated by wide valleys, tend to vary.

No positive conclusions can be drawn from the known facts about the colors of sheep until science has revealed more knowledge of the causes of color variation. I know of no case among the large mammals of this continent analogous to the colors of these sheep.

According to the theory *(I do not use the word theory as applicable to the facts of Mr. Thayer's analysis of animal colors in their relations to certain backgrounds. But, as a cardinal point, he insists that animal coloration is principally obliterative against the background when "animals are on the verge of catching or being caught." Since the exact conditions of attack, capture or escape between enemy and prey are in many cases unknown, many of the matching backgrounds, which Mr. Thayer describes as those in which the attack takes place, must be assumed. It is not, however, proved that such are the backgrounds which oppose the attack, and, therefore, I use the word "theory" to include the facts together with the unproved assumptions. Writing subsequently on the subject, Mr. Thayer observes that his book might have been called "An expert's presentation of examples of consummate resemblances between animals' costumes and certain of their backgrounds." To such a definition the word "theory" would not apply. C. SHELDON.)* of "Protective" or "Concealing" coloration, a theory developed and elaborated with great detail, and universally applied, by Abbott Thayer in his book on *Concealing Coloration in the Animal Kingdom*, the colors of sheep must result from Natural Selection acting through long periods of time, continually exterminating sheep possessing a color easily observed by their enemies, and preserving the sheep having colors which conceal them from their enemies. Mr. Thayer insists that this has resulted specially in animal coloration that is most obliterative, for enemy or prey, at the moment when the enemy is about to seize its victim, the last rush, the last spring, when sight alone is necessary for success.

With the eye of the artist, no doubt, Mr. Thayer has analyzed remarkably well the obliterative colors of the animal kingdom in their relations to lights and shades, and of blending under certain conditions with their background. His analysis reveals some important discoveries. His book presents an array of facts—animal coloration in relation to matching certain backgrounds, analyzed according to the laws of the science of optics—which I fully believe must revolutionize not only many of the preconceived notions on the subject, but must also destroy some of the theories which, in the attempt to determine the causes of animal coloration, have been widely accepted. It seems to be a necessary inference from Mr. Thayer's writings that concealing coloration has been exclusively produced by the relations between predatory animals and their prey. *(Mr. Thayer, while repeatedly asserting his own positive belief that the Concealing Colors of animals result exclusively from a process of Natural Selection which has established the most favorable balance of color between predatory animals and their prey, admits in at least two places in his book the possibility of other causes. In fact, he writes me that while he deeply believes the cause to be Natural Selection, he has given a wrong idea to any one who thinks that he lays stress on its being the modus operandi of all color matching. He emphasizes only the color matching itself.—C. SHELDON.)*

It may be granted (though by no means to the extent and under all the circumstances that Mr. Thayer asserts} that all animals more or less, according to certain conditions, blend with their background. The question is, What are the causes which produce such harmony?

Let us apply Mr. Thayer's theory to the sheep.

All the northern sheep live in regions where the snowfall is practically the same. Above timber-line, where they continually live, the country is in general the same, though in regions and localities the rock colors vary equally throughout their range in the north.

Owing to the character of the country in which these sheep live and to their habits, it is of the utmost importance to their enemies to detect them from a distance *by sight* before making an attempt to capture them. The following observations are based upon the angle of vision from which sheep are seen by man. The broken, mountainous country which sheep inhabit, however, is such that their enemies more often see them against a background of rock, slope, or ground surface (looking down on them from above), rather than against a background of cloud and sky. Hence for purposes of *detection*, these observations apply for the most part to all the enemies of sheep. For purposes of *capture*, they apply to all enemies of sheep except the wolf; but even to the wolf, they usually apply.

If the pelage of white sheep were to remain immaculate, the animal would be conspicuous in summer anywhere above timber. But, except for a short time during the month of November, the pelage is badly stained, and this staining causes the white sheep to become quite inconspicuous in some regions where the rock colors are in harmony with it—as in the Ogilvie Rockies, for example. But in other regions, where the rock colors are darker, the stained white sheep are so extremely conspicuous that on mountain-slopes they can be easily seen two and three miles distant, and nearer than half a mile they form a striking contrast to the background. This is true among the mountains bordering the coast ranges in Yukon Territory and Alaska, and in the whole of the Alaska Range. White sheep are always conspicuous on green slopes and pastures. They are inconspicuous on snow, although their stained coats, throughout all the winter, spring, and fall, except November, render a strong contrast against the white background.

The dark sheep, except against a background of sky, are never conspicuous in summer, their color blending well with rocks and green slopes. From a distance they are most easily detected by their light rumps. But in the snow, under nearly all circumstances, they are exceedingly conspicuous.

The sheep of variable color are still less conspicuous, except on snow where they are nearly as conspicuous as the dark sheep.

All the northern sheep, dark or white, are inconspicuous either when feeding among willows, or especially when the surface background is banded or striped with snow, or when bare areas are thickly patched with snow. This applies to the majority of the time in spring, fall, and winter when sheep always seek the wind-swept parts of the mountains to find their food.

When the dark of evening approaches, both white and dark sheep are usually conspicuous on the sky-line. In the twilight, during the darker hours of the night in summer, the white sheep are very much more conspicuous below the sky-line than the dark ones. During the night and all through the dark hours of fall and winter, sheep are lying down resting.

They move and feed only during the hours of daylight.

When travelling in winter with a dog team, my dogs repeatedly scented sheep on the mountain sides from a distance of more than two miles, and *always*, if the wind was favorable, saw the sheep long before I could detect them. The enemies of all the sheep are the same—the golden eagle, the wolf, lynx, wolverine, and possibly the fox. In the north, bears never hunt or prey upon sheep. Sheep have no other natural enemies.

The eagle preys only on the lambs and on them only until they are six weeks or two months old. After that, neither sheep nor eagles pay any attention to each other.

The wolf is not very persistent in hunting sheep, preferring rather the caribou and the moose. He catches sheep by chasing them on the smooth parts of their range, usually on the rolling hills of the basins, the pastures of the divides between mountains above timber-line, and sometimes on the level bars of a glacial river. He sometimes drives them off smooth mountains and catches them when they cross the low intervening country in their efforts to reach a high mountain beyond. The wolf, in his effort to detect sheep feeding or travelling in places favorable for catching them, roams on the ridges, lower mountain-slopes, and even the flat country above timber. He begins to run from a distance toward the sheep, in the hope of catching one. But if the sheep succeed in reaching a steep. mountain-slope or a ridge broken by rocks, the wolf never attempts to follow them upward. On smooth mountain-slopes the wolf always goes above the sheep and chases them downward, attempting to catch one before they can turn and go above the enemy. Wolves usually chase the youngest of the sheep—those which are less than three years old, but more often those which are less than two years old.

The lynx watches the sheep, for hours, if necessary, and after sneaking to a point toward which sheep are moving, crouches upon a rock and, as a sheep passes, attempts to leap upon its back.

I have no facts as to the method of the wolverine's attack, but, its gait being slow and awkward, the attack must be by concealment and pouncing from above. There is a positive record, reported by so reliable a man as Joseph Keele, of a wolverine concealing itself in the branches of a spruce tree and leaping on the back of a moose. *(Forest and Stream, Vol. LXXI, p. 971, December 19, 1908.)*

After observing foxes in the sheep country for several years, and after numerous examinations of their stomachs and the refuse about their dens, I have no evidence indicating that they attempt to prey upon sheep, old or young. During several months' observation where sheep were abundant and when the snow was on the ground, fox tracks never suggested that foxes hunt sheep. It may be possible that they sometimes take lambs.

It is doubtful if sheep are attacked in the dark, since at that time they are resting high on a mountain in rough places safe from their enemies.

Thus the eagle and the lynx attack sheep from above. The wolverine probably attacks in the same way. At the critical moment of capture, therefore, the sheep is seen, by his most persistent enemies, *from above.*

Mr. Thayer lays special stress on the angle of vision from which enemies see their prey at this crucial moment of catching it. He asserts that white top-patterns on animals (including sheep) have an obliterating effect when seen from below at such an angle as to bring the white against sky and cloud (and even snow). I think that finally it will be admitted that Mr. Thayer correctly states this optical principle. There may, however, be many cases of doubt as to its practical application.

It could only be of service to the sheep in escaping from a wolf, and only at times when the latter is trying to catch older sheep under conditions when the white is in such a position in the wolf's line of sight as to bring the white marking against a background of sky or snow. It would not apply when a wolf catches young sheep (which is usually the case) whose white patterns, unless the sheep were running upward, are below his line of vision. Nor would it always apply when sheep are seeking to escape by running downward. Therefore, though the advantages of these white-top patterns are true as a fact of optics, I have not observed that these white markings are of much practical advantage to sheep.

Nor do I believe that white top-markings on other animals have been developed because of their obliterative advantages to the animal. One of my reasons for this disbelief consists in the fact that such advantages, if they are practical, may endanger the young of animals inhabiting treeless plains (and also the young of sheep), and threaten the welfare of the race to an extent that offsets the advantages to the adults. The young of the animal as well as the enemy would see the white of the adult against the sky, and still more, the white markings on the young would be observed by the enemy from above rather than from below, and hence offer an effective target for attack. Not only would the attack be more apt to be directed against the young, but even when directed unsuccessfully at the adult (attacks fail far oftener than they succeed), during the immediate flight the white top-markings would deceive not only the enemy, but also the young who might lose their parents and remain unprotected against a pursuing enemy who could see the white marking of the young against a dark background.

The dark sheep have light rumps. Mr. Thayer would argue that these dark sheep have excellent concealing colors except sometimes on the snow, but even on the snow, at the final dash of the enemy, their backs would be turned in sudden flight and the rumps would blend with the sky or snow background and thus conceal them at the critical moment. But since there is fully as much snow on the mountains in the regions inhabited by dark sheep as in those inhabited by white sheep, and it remains on the surface practically as long, why has one species been developed white and the other with white only on the rump? If enemies cause the coloration, then the same enemies should act to develop the colors of all the northern sheep. Therefore, the same cause has produced not only two opposite colors, pure white and black, but also, and over vast areas, a variety of intermediate colors. Under numerous conditions the protective values of the opposite colors are contradictory.

As applicable to the northern sheep, therefore, we must dismiss theories suggesting that animal colors are caused by "Natural Selection" of their protective values.

The white rump patch on sheep has been called a directive marking, as it enables the members of a band quickly to recognize one another under varied conditions. If, owing to their natural color, the white sheep do not need a directive marking when they are so conspicuous for four months in summer, then likewise the dark sheep do not need a directive marking when they are so conspicuous during the eight months when the snow is on the ground. It is undoubtedly true that sheep take advantage of recognition marks, just as they take advantage of their color under conditions where it is protective. But I cannot believe that these recognition marks on the dark northern sheep have been developed by a process of Natural Selection favoring those which possess the white rump patch, since a vast majority of the sheep, being white, do not have a directive marking which would be advantageous to them for two-thirds of the year, while the dark sheep have need of one for only one-third of the year. Such a process of Natural Selection would not, under the similar conditions affecting all the northern sheep, produce contradictory color results.

The similarity of the sheep north of the range of *Ovis canadensis*, except in color, indicates that all came from a common ancestor. It's believed that originally American wild sheep migrated from Asia. The persistence of dark hairs in the pelage of all white sheep would suggest that the common ancestor was a dark animal. The close relation of these northern American sheep to those of Kamschatka, *Ovis nivicola*, suggests that all sheep from north-eastern Asia, and north-western America north of latitude 55 degrees, descended from the same parent type. Whether in past geologic ages sheep of a uniform dark color were separated by topographic and climatic barriers long enough to cause a differentiation in color; whether such a separation occurred before or after the migration; whether in later ages the barriers were lifted and a reversion in color progressed, or the sheep gradually intermingled—all such theories are in the field of speculation.

From my point of view, however, the facts indicate, during the present age, a gradual intermingling and interbreeding between the dark and white sheep, resulting in the variations in color. After studying for several years the nature and habits of these sheep, I am convinced that among all the color varieties there is no racial antagonism to interbreeding. Whenever, during the rut, a dark ram has strayed from its range and joined the white ewes, it has impregnated some of them. Likewise, white rams have impregnated dark ewes, and ewes straying among rams of a different color have been impregnated.

The colors are most variable where the routes of travel are interrupted by unfavorable topographical conditions—between the Pelly River and Ogilvie Rockies, and between Sheslay River district and Lewes River. In those regions limited bands of white and dark sheep met, interbred, and scattered throughout those sections of the country. Their offspring were of mixed colors, and they were continually receiving new accessions both from the white sheep on the north and the dark sheep on the south. Gradually these interbreeds extended their range (always in limited numbers, for the areas are not suitable for abundance of sheep) both toward the north where the dark colors are swamped by the preponderance of white sheep, and toward the south where dark sheep preponderate and swamp the light colors. Thus traces of the dark pattern exist, rapidly dying out, among the white sheep of the north, while the opposite is true in the south. As soon as the interbreeds reach the continuous ranges the variable colors are rapidly lost, and the result is a tendency toward uniformity in color within narrow limits. In the regions of uniform dark color, individuals are exceptionally found which have either reverted in color or have strayed there. Sheep do not cross the divide of the Mackenzie River water-shed, hence the sheep in the continuous ranges on the Mackenzie side remain pure white, notwithstanding the fact that they range parallel with the variables on the Yukon side.

Between the regions where typical *Ovis dalli* and typical *Ovis stonei* exist—a distance north and south of approximately six hundred and fifty miles, and of variable width east and west—there is no geographical area in which the color of the sheep is uniform. Within that intermediate region the uniformity of either species is destroyed, and the individuals must be referred to one or the other according to their color leanings.

It is the generally accepted view that all species are the products of evolution. True intergradation is so common that it is only necessary to mention it. As species of the same genera extend their ranges and reach different conditions of climate and environment, or become isolated, they tend to differentiate more or less according to their plasticity and the degree or character of the change in environment. As a result, geographical races are formed, gradually changing from one area to another, until the extremes may be widely different. Near the border-line between the geographical races there is an intermingling and—where two forms come close together—no doubt interbreeding, which results in intergrades referable to the race which they most closely resemble on either side of the border. But, within the geographical areas, the differing characters are sufficiently uniform to mark a race, though there may be individual variation. Where species of the same genera differ and intergrades are unknown, it is either because the intergrades have not been found or they have not survived.

Sometimes the difference in environment, physical and climatic, is so subtle as to be indeterminate. It is possible that the variation in the colors of the sheep is thus produced, by subtle and indeterminate changes of environment, to a much greater extent than the facts seem to me to indicate. A wider and more thorough familiarity with the facts of intergradation might cause me to change my present belief, that at some time in the past either the intergrading forms between the Dall and the Stone sheep disappeared, or that the extremes of dark and white were produced by long isolation, in different environments, owing to the interposition of barriers between sheep of similar color; or from some other cause and that the existing variations are the result of the gradual extension of the ranges of sheep of the two extreme types of color, with consequent interbreeding. At least, even if the different colors of sheep are caused by their environment, interbreeding must still be a factor in producing such irregular variations.

CARIBOU

Two well-marked species of caribou in Yukon Territory have been determined, the Barren Ground, *Rangifer arcticus*, and the woodland, so-called *Rangifer osborni.* At present there is not sufficient material in our public institutions to define accurately the exact relation between these two types and the other named species of caribou in British Columbia and Alaska. The life-history of no other large animal in the north is so difficult to observe as that of the caribou, and it would require special investigations extending over several years to determine accurately their distribution and habits.

The caribou in the Ogilvie Rockies is the true Barren Ground type. It is smaller in body and skull than the woodland type, its horns are less diverging and lighter in beam, although many of the horns of both types have *characters* so identical that the resemblance is complete. The only difference in the habits of the two types consists in the Barren Ground caribou's tendency to wander more restlessly over a wider area, and especially in its banding together in the fall and migrating. In Yukon Territory its habits are similar to those of its neighbor in the Barren Grounds of Canada, except in so far as the habits vary to suit the mountainous country in which the Yukon animal roams.

Scattered bands, always restless, travelling among mountains, always feeding and resting above timber-line, are found all summer throughout its range. In the fall large bands assemble far in the north and begin to migrate southward, passing through the Ogilvies in November and December. The main band, numbering between fifteen and twenty thousand—perhaps more—has provided the greater part of the winter supply of game meat for Dawson and the mining camps of the Klondike. After the winter hunters had disturbed this band for a few years, the caribou changed their route of migration farther to the east along the Peel River water-shed. In March the majority return northward. Numerous other small bands keep wandering about the Ogilvies during the fall and winter. Formerly, during the migrations, large bands of caribou crossed the Yukon River in the vicinity of Eagle, but at present this habit of crossing seems to have ceased.

I have been unable to determine the limits of the southern range of these caribou. Probably it does not pass from the Ogilvies to the Selwyn Rockies. The Barren Ground caribou range well to the south on the Mackenzie side of the divide, and Mr. Keele advises me that he has seen them near the head of the Pelly River. A few may cross the divide in that latitude. But none are found elsewhere in the Selwyns, unless very near the Ogilvies.

The woodland caribou, *Rangifer osborni*, exists throughout the Cassiars and the Selwyn Rockies. It does not occur in the Pelly Mountains or the Glenlyons. It is abundant in the mountain groups between the Pelly and the MacMillan and in the mountains near the South Fork of the MacMillan. It prefers mountains of a subdued type with smooth, dome-like summits free from too much erosion. Its favorite ranges are quite locally distributed in the regions it inhabits. It keeps within a definite habitat and, though restless and roaming in its habits, it does not gather in large bands and migrate. During the winter, however, scattered bands often gather to the number of two or three hundred and range in a well-defined route of travel over a limited area, usually less than a hundred miles.

A woodland type of caribou inhabits the Teslin Lake country, but no specimens have been examined. Also the same type inhabits locally many districts west of the Lewes River and becomes abundant near the coast ranges at the head of the Donjek and White Rivers. If specimens of these caribou could be compared, they would probably be referable to *Rangifer stonei* of Alaska which, when sufficient material has been secured, may prove to be identical with *Rangifer osborni*. It is my belief that greater series of specimens, brought together for comparison, will so resemble each other that it will be difficult to separate them, and perhaps all caribou of this woodland type may prove to be closely related to the Barren Ground type.

MOOSE

Moose, except in localities where they have been driven away from populous centres, exist throughout the timbered regions of the Territory. They are most abundant in the Selwyn Rockies, Pelly Mountains, and the region of the upper Liard River. They are almost equally abundant near the heads of the Donjek and White Rivers. They are very abundant in the Ogilvies, and less so in the forested country of low relief. I never heard of moose, caribou, sheep, or grizzly bears existing within the humid belt of the coast ranges. Moose have been seen at Log Cabin near the White Pass Railroad.

Their principal food is the willow. Notwithstanding much skepticism, they sometimes eat grass. I have killed moose when they were specially feeding on grass, and have found quantities of it in their stomachs. During the summer and fall they feed much in the lakes.

When their ranges are among high mountains, after August, when the flies are gone, their favorite haunts are near the heads of the draws. In winter their movements depend mostly on the condition of the snow. In spring and early summer they remain in the lower country among lakes and near rivers.

The rut begins in early September and ends in October. One or two calves at a birth are born in May or early June. In the winter they do not yard. Often from four to eight bulls feed together, though some bulls remain solitary. The cows remain solitary with their calves. Twin calves remain together a year or more after they leave the mother. The bulls shed their horns from the middle of December to the middle of January.

Moose are wary, after their kind, whether much hunted or not, but the bulls, during the early rut, come to the call of the birch-bark horn, or the scraping of a bone on a tree in imitation of a rival scraping his horns, and often to any unusual noise like the blows of an axe. Like caribou and bears, they desert settled districts, quite unlike sheep, which remain on their ranges almost to the point of extermination.

BEARS

The grizzly bear dwells among mountains rising well above timber-line and exists all over Yukon Territory. Except when it comes to the rivers for salmon, it roams near and above timber-line. It is most abundant west of the Lewes River, and north along the dry belt inside of the coast range. It is abundant in the Ogilvies, Selwyns, and Pellys. It never exists in large numbers anywhere. It hibernates, according to season, in October or November, and comes forth in May, when it immediately begins to eat the roots of the wild pea vine, and soon after digs mice and ground-squirrels. When the salmon begin to run up the rivers, the grizzlies begin to feed exclusively on them. Bears do not hunt moose, caribou, or sheep, though they will feed on a dead carcass. The females have from one to three cubs which remain with the mother for two years. Everywhere, the grizzly is wild and timid and flees from man.

The black bear dwells exclusively in the timbered areas of the Territory including the whole of the coast ranges. It is most common in Alaska on the west slopes nearer salt water. It does not regularly intrude in the haunts of the grizzly. The "cinnamon" or brown phase of color is found in the interior, but it is uncommon. I have never seen it among the bears on the west slopes of the coast range, though occasionally this color phase has been found there.

WOLVES

Wolves exist throughout the Territory, but are quite local in their haunts. The black phase of color is common. They tend to keep pretty close to caribou in localities where caribou are common. Their habits are similar to those of timber wolves elsewhere.

MOUNTAIN GOATS

Goats live exclusively in the humid belt of the coast range, seldom ranging far into the dry belt away from the east slopes. Where the goat ranges end, those of the sheep begin, though both are occasionally found quite close together. Goats are exceedingly abundant in the areas which they inhabit.

All the fur-bearing animals of the north are abundant in Yukon Territory. Many of them have diminished in number since the Klondike gold discoveries, when white men began to trap them. The smaller mammals and birds have been discussed in the published reports of W. H. Osgood.

APPENDIX A

LIST OF BOOKS RELATING TO SPORT, NATURAL HISTORY, AND EXPLORATION OF THE YUKON TERRITORY

SPORT

Pike, Warburton: *Through the Subarctic Forest.* A record of a canoe journey from Fort Wrangel to the Pelly Lakes and down the Yukon River to the Behring Sea. Illustrations and maps. (London: Edward Arnold, 1896.) Incidents of sport in Northern British Columbia and on the Pelly River.

Selous, F. C.: *Recent Hunting Trips in British North America.* Illustrated. (New York: Charles Scribner's Sons, 1907.) Contains narratives of hunting on both North and South Forks of the MacMillan River.

Schwatka, Frederick: *Along Alaska's Great River.* A popular account of the travels of the Alaska Exploring Expedition of 1883, along the great Yukon River from its source to its mouth in the British North-west Territory, and in the Territory of Alaska. Map. Illustrated. (New York: Cassell & Co., 1885.) Incidentally mentions the game observed along the upper Yukon waters.

NATURAL HISTORY

Osgood, Wilfred H.: *Results of a Biological Reconnoissance of the Yukon River Region*. Map. Illustrations. (United States Biological Survey, North American Fauna No. 19. Washington, D. C.: October, 1900.) Descriptive Natural History of Lewes and Yukon Rivers.

Osgood, Wilfred H.: *Biological Investigations in Alaska and Yukon Territory*. Map. Illustrations. (United States Biological Survey, North American Fauna No. 30. Washington, D. C.: October, 1909.) Includes descriptive Natural History of the Ogilvie Range and of the Macmillan River.

Ogilvie, William: The Klondike Official Guide. Maps. Illustrations. (Toronto: The Hunter, Rose Co., Limited; London: W. W. Smith & Sons, 1898.) Historical and descriptive; contains a short description of game and fur-bearing animals.

EXPLORATION, TOPOGRAPHY, AND GEOLOGY

Dawson, George M.: *Report of an Exploration in the Yukon District, N.W.T., and Adjacent Northern Portion of British Columbia*. Maps and illustrations. (Annual Report Geological Survey, Canada, 1887, Part B.) Includes Pelly and Lewes Rivers.

Ogilvie, William: *Exploratory Survey of Part of Lewes, T at-on-duc, Porcupine, Bell, Trout, Peel, and Mackenzie Rivers*. Maps. Illustrations. (Annual Report Department Interior, Canada, for year 1889, Part VIII.)

McConnell, R. G.: *Report of an Exploration of the Yukon and Mackenzie Basins, N.W.T.* Maps and illustrations. (Annual Report, Survey, Canada, IV, New Series, 1888-1889.) Includes Peel, Porcupine, and Yukon Rivers.

Keele, Joseph: *The Upper Stewart River Region.* Map. Illustrations. (Ottawa: Geological Survey of Canada, 1906.)

Camsell, C.: *Peel River and Tributaries.* Map. Illustrations. (Ottawa: Geological Survey of Canada, 1906.)

McConnell, R. G., and Keele, J.: *The MacMillan River.* (Annual Report Geological Survey, Canada, New Series, Part A, Vol. XV, 1902.)

Keele, Joseph: *A Reconnoissance Across the Mackenzie Mountains on the Pelly, Ross, and Gravel Rivers, Yukon and North-west Territories.* Maps. Illustrations. (Ottawa: Government Printing Bureau, 1910.)

APPENDIX B

SCIENTIFIC NAMES OF ANIMALS MENTIONED IN THE NARRATIVE

For a fuller list of mammals and birds of Yukon Territory the report of W. H. Osgood should be consulted (North American Fauna, No. 30, 1909).

MAMMALS

Bear, Black—*Ursus americanus.*
Bear, Grizzly—*Ursus horribilis* (subsp. ?).
Bear, Alaska Grizzly—*Ursus horribilis phoenix* (Ogilvies; Selwyn Rockies).
Beaver-*Castor canadensis.*
Caribou, Barren Ground—*Rangifer arcticus.*
Caribou, Osbom—*Rangifer osborni.*
Chipmunk, Gray-headed—*Eutamias caniceps.*
Cony or Pika—*Ochotona collaris.*
Fox—*Vulpes fulvus.*
Goat, Rocky Mountain—*Oreamnos montanos* (sub sp.*columbianus*?}.
Ground-squirrel—*Citellus pluius.*
Lynx, Canada—*Lynx canadensis.*

Marmot, Hoary—*Marmata caligata.*
Marten—*Mustela americana actuosa.*
Mink—*Lutreola vison.*
Mink, North-west—*Lutreola vison energumenos* (Pelly River).
Moose, Alaska—*Alecs americanus gigas.*
Mouse, Red-backed—*Evtomys dawsoni.*
Mouse, Meadow (Interior Vole)—*Microtus operarius endoecus.*
Muskrat, North-west—*Fiber zibethicus spatulatus.*
Otter—*Lutra canadensis.*
Porcupine, Alaska—*Erethizon epizanthum myops.*
Rabbit, White or Varying—*Lepus americanus macfarlani.*
Sheep, Dall—*Ovis dalli.*
Sheep, Fannin—*Ovis fannini.*
Sheep, Stone—*Ovis stonei.*
Squirrel, Red—*Sciurus hudsonicus.*
Weasel, Arctic—*Putorius arcticus.*
Wolf, Northern—*Canis albus.*
Wolverine—*Gulo luscus.*

BIRDS

Alaska Jay—*Perisoreus canadensis fumifrons.*
Bald Eagle, Northem—*Halioeetus leucocephalus alascanus.*
Bank Swallow—*Riparia riparia.*
Duck Hawk—*Falco peregrinus anatum.*
Gambel's Sparrow—*Zonotrichia leucophrys gambeli.*
Golden Eagle—*Aquila chysaëtos.*
Goose, Hutchins—*Branta canadensis hutchinsi.*
Goshawk—*Astur atricapillus.*
Great-horned Owl, Ogilvies—*Bubo virginianus* (subsp.?).
Great-horned Owl—*Pelly River drainage-Bubo virginianus* (subsp.?).

Grouse, Alaska Spruce—*Canachites canadensis osgoodi.*
Harlequin Duck—*Histrionicus histrionicus.*
Hawk Owl—*Surnia ululi caparoch.*
Herring Gull—*Larus argentatus.*
Hudsonian Chickadee—*Penthestes hudsonicus.*
Junco, Slate-colored—*Junco hyemalis.*
Kingfisher, Belted—*Cyrele alcyon.*
Little Brown Cran—*Grus canadensis.*
Loon, Red-throated—*Gavia stellata.*
Marsh Hawk—*Circus hudsonicus.*
Merganser, Red-breasted—*Mergus serrator.*
Northern Shrike—*Lanius borealis.*
Olive-backed Thrush—*Hylocichla ustulata swainsoni.*
Osprey—*Pandion halioetus carolinensis.*
Pigeon Hawk—*Falco columbarius.*
Ptarmigan, Northern White-tailed—*Lagopus leucurus peninsularis.*
Ptarmigan, Rock—*Lagopus rupestris.*
Ptarmigan, Willow—*Lagopus lagopus* (most commonly mentioned).
Raven, Northern—*Corous corax principalis.*
Robin—*Planesticus migratorius.*
Rough-legged Hawk—*Archibuteo lagopus sanctijohannis.*
Short-billed Gull—*Larus brachyrhynchus.*
Solitary Sandpiper, Western—*Helodromas solitarius cinnamomtus.*
Spotted Sandpiper—*Actitis macularia.*
Teal, Green-winged—*Nettion carolinense.*
Varied Thrush, Northern—*Ixoreus noevius meruloides.*
Whistling Swan—*Olor columbianus.*
Water Ousel—*Cinclus mexicanus unicolor.*
Western Tree Sparrow—*Spizella monticola ochracea.*

FISHES

Dog Salmon—*Onchorhynchus Keta.*
Grayling—*Thymallus signifer.*
Inconnu—*Stenodus mackenzii.*
King Salmon—*Onchorhynchus tochawytscha.*
Pike—*Esox lucius.*
Sucker—*Catostomus catostomus.*
Whitefish—*Cortgonus* (probably *Nelsoni).*

APPENDIX C

ORIGINAL DESCRIPTIONS OF NORTHERN SHEEP

From Proceedings United States National Museum, Vol. VII, pp. 12, 13, 1884

A New Geographical Race of the Mountain Sheep (Ovis Montana Dalli, var. nov .). From Alaska. By E. W. Nelson

This form can be recognized at once by its nearly uniform dirty-white color, the light-colored rump area seen in typical Montana being entirely uniform with the rest of the body in dalli. The dinginess of the white over the entire body and limbs appears to be almost entirely due to the ends of the hairs being commonly tipped with a dull, rusty speck. On close examination this tipping of the hairs makes the fur look as though it had been slightly singed. (*Later investigations proved the color to be pure white, the "dinginess" alluded to being merely discoloration absorbed from rocks and soil.-Charles Sheldon.) This form also has smaller horns than its southern relatives, but how the two compare in size and weight I am unable to say.

I name this form in honor of Mr. W. H. Dall, whose scientific work in Alaska is so well known.

Hamilton, New Mexico, *December* 22, 1883.

From Bulletin American Museum Natural History, New York, Vol. IX, pp. 111, 112, 1897
Preliminary Description of a New Mountain Sheep from the British Northwest Territory.(Measurements given in this original description have been omitted.-Charles Sheldon.) *By J. A. Allen*

Through the kindness of Mr. A. J. Stone, of Missoula, Montana, the Museum has received three mounted specimens of a Mountain Sheep, or Bighorn, quite unlike any heretofore described. They were collected by Mr. Stone on the headwaters of the Stickeen River British Northwest Territory, near the Alaskan boundary, at an altitude of about six thousand five hundred feet. The species may be described as follows:

Ovis stonei, sp. nov.

Male Adult.—Above gray, formed by an intimate mixture of whitish and blackish brown; face, ears, and sides of neck lighter and more whitish, being much Jess varied with blackish brown; whole posterior area and lower parts from hinder pan of back downward and forward, covering the posterior aspect of thighs, and the abdomen, white, the white area narrowing anteriorly and terminating in a V-shaped point on the middle of the chest; also a broad, sharply defined band of white on the posterior surface of both fore and hind limbs, extending from the body to the hoofs, and proximally including also the inner surface; front of neck, from base of lower jaw posteriorly to the white of the ventral surface, including the breast and greater pan of the chest, and thence along the sides to the thighs, nearly black; the lateral extension along the flanks becomes narrower posteriorly, and the neck is somewhat grizzled with white; outer surface of both fore and hind limbs blackish brown, either uniform or in some specimens varied with a slight mixture of whitish; back of head with a broad area of black, narrowing posteriorly and continuing to the tail as a well-defined blackish dorsal stripe; tail wholly deep black, except a few white hairs on the middle of its lower surface; a narrow blackish chin bar, varying in breadth and distinctness in different individuals; hoofs black; horns light brown.

This species is based on three males, of the ages, respectively, of two, five, and six years. The older specimen is taken as the type. On this the dark areas are blacker, and on some parts less varied with whitish tipped hairs than in the others, especially the two-year-old.

This species differs from *Ovis dalli* in the prevailing coloration, being either dark gray or blackish brown, according to the area in question, instead of being "a nearly uniform dirty-white color." In *O. stonei* the white is restricted to definite, sharply defined areas, in strong contrast with the adjoining parts. *O. stonei* and *O. dalli* apparently agree in size and in the character of the horns.

O. stonei agrees in a general way in pattern of coloration with *O. cervina* (Desm.), but the "umber-brown" or "wood-brown" of the latter is everywhere replaced in O. stonei with blackish brown or black. It is also a much smaller animal, and the horns are slenderer and have a more outward curvature at the tips.

From Fifth Annual Report New York Zoological Society, Appendix 1, pp. 1-4, 1901

Ovis fannini, sp. nov. Fannin's Mountain Sheep. Also,

"Saddle-backed" Sheep, or" Piebald" Sheep (Sheep of variable colors, including those of *Ovis fannini*, were well known to miners, prospectors, and traders along the Upper Yukon for many years. They were first recorded by R. G. McConnell, in his report of an exploration in the Yukon and Mackenzie Basins, in 1888. His Indians had killed a white sheep near the Peel River Portage, and commenting on the color he says: "The change in color and size toward the north is evidently a gradual one, as the saddle-backed sheep of the upper Yukon presents characters intermediate between the two extreme varieties." "Report on an Exploration in the Yukon District, N. W. T., etc., by George M. Dawson, with extracts from the report of R. G. McConnell." Geological Survey of Canada, Ottawa, 1898, page 210.—Charles Sheldon.) (Measurements given in this original description have been omitted.—Charles Sheldon.)

Type collected by Mr. Henry W. Brown at Dawson City, N. W. T., February, 1900, and presented to the Provincial Museum, Victoria, B. C.

DESCRIPTION OF AN ADULT MALE, NINE YEARS OLD, KILLED IN MIDWINTER.

Colors.—Entire head and neck, breast, abdomen, inside of forelegs, and rump patch for four inches above insertion of tail, snow white. Entire body, except as above, brownish gray, giving the appearance of a white animal covered by a gray blanket. This color is produced by a nearly even mixture of pure white and blackish-brown hairs. The gray color covers the shoulders from the insertion of the neck downward to the knee, where it fades out. On the outside of the thigh, the gray color grows paler as it descends, until at the hock joint it fades out entirely. The posterior edge of the thigh is white. The lower portion of the inner surface of the thigh partakes of the gray body color, but is somewhat paler.

On the front edge of the thigh, and extending down to the hoof, is a conspicuous band of dark brown, one and one-half inches wide, which, below the hock joint, joins rather abruptly the pure white hair which covers the sides and rear edge of the leg. A similar brown band extends down the front of the foreleg, from knee to hoof, similarly backed up posteriorly with white.

The tail is similar in color to the body, but much darker, and a thin line of dark-brown hair connects it with the gray mass of the body. The white rump patch is similar in form to that of *Ovis montana*, but covers a smaller area.

Pelage.—Thick and long; finer and softer than on *Ovis montana*. On the neck and abdomen it inclines to shagginess, like that of the mountain goat. The stiff, brittle quality is noticeably absent from all white parts of the animal. Everywhere the pelage is abundant and thick, as befits an Arctic animal. Because of this, the animal appears to be shorter in the legs and more stockily built than all other American species, save *Ovis dalli*.

Horns.—In color, clear, transparent, even amber-like, similar to the horns of *Ovis dalli* when clean. Annulations numerous and well defined. A slight groove under the superior angle, not so deep as that of *Ovis stonei*. In the type specimen the horns do not spread as in *Ovis stonei* and *dalli*; but this character is of little scientific value, because of the wide variations between individuals of the same species.

APPENDIX D

HORN MEASUREMENTS

Horn measurements in inches, taken with steel tape before shrinkage.
All horns perfect unless otherwise mentioned.

OGILVIE ROCKIES

Ram killed July 19, 1904
Number of age rings on horns — 7
Length on outside curve right horn — 30
Length on outside curve left horn — 30
Circumference at base of right horn — 12
Circumference at base of left horn — 12
Tip to tip — 23

Ram killed July 23, 1904
Number of age rings on horns — 7
Length on outside curve right horn — 29½
Length on outside curve left horn — 29½
Circumference at base of right horn — 13¼
Circumference at base of left horn — 13¼
Tip to tip — 25

First Ram killed August 2, 1904 (Big Ram)
Number of age rings on horns, more than — 13
Length on outside curve right horn — 36⅝
Length on outside curve left horn — 36⅝
Circumference at base of right horn — 13½
Circumference at base of left horn — 13½
Tip to tip — 17
Length from nose to end of vertebrae in straight line — 59
Standing height at shoulder — 40

Second Ram killed August 2, 1904
Number of age rings on horns — 8
Length on outside curve right horn — 32
Length on outside curve left horn — 32
Circumference at base of right horn — 13½
Circumference at base of left horn — 13½
Tip to tip — 17¾

Third Ram killed August 2, 1904
Number of age rings on horns — 5
Length on outside curve right horn — 27
Length on outside curve left horn — 27
Circumference at base of right horn — 13
Circumference at base of left horn — 13
Tip to tip — 17½

Fourth Ram killed August 2, 1904
Number of age rings on horns — 3
Length on outside curve right horn — 18
Length on outside curve left horn — 18
Circumference at base of right horn — 9½
Circumference at base of left horn — 9½
Tip to tip — 15⅜

PELLY MOUNTAINS

First Ram killed July 29, 1905
Number of age rings on horns — 6
Length on outside curve right horn — 31½
Length on outside curve left horn — 32
Circumference at base of right horn — 12 15/16
Circumference at base of left horn — 12 15/16
Tip to tip — 18 11/16
Weight of cleaned skull with horns — 11 lbs.
Weight of dried skin thoroughly fleshed — 5 lbs. 6 oz.

Second Ram killed July 29, 1905
Number of age rings on horns — 8
Length on outside curve right horn — 35⅛
Length on outside curve left horn — 35⅛
Circumference at base of right horn — 13 1/16
Circumference at base of left horn — 13 1/16
Tip to tip — 17¼
Weight of cleaned skull with horns — 14½ lbs.
Weight of dried skin thoroughly fleshed — 5 lbs. 3 oz.

Third Ram killed July 29, 1905
Number of age rings on horns — 9
Length on outside curve right horn — Broken at tip
Length on outside curve left horn — 36¾
Circumference at base of right horn — 13⅝
Circumference at base of left horn — 13⅝
Tip to tip — 17¼
Weight of cleaned skull with horns — 14½ lbs.
Weight of dried skin thoroughly fleshed — 5 lbs. 6 oz.

Ram killed August 1, 1905 (Big Ram)
Number of age rings on horns, more than — 13
Length on outside curve right horn — Broken at tip
Length on outside curve left horn, blunted at tip — 34⅝
Circumference at base of right horn — 12⅞
Circumference at base of left horn — 13¼
Tip to tip, about — 16
Weight of cleaned skull with horns — 17 lbs.
Weight of dried skin thoroughly fleshed — 5¾ lbs.
Length from nose to end of vertebrae in straight line — 59
Standing height at shoulder — 40

(It will be noticed that these body measurements are identical with those of the big ram killed in the Ogilvie Rockies, August 2, 1904.)

First Ram killed August 6, 1905
Number of age rings on horns — 6
Length on outside curve right horn — 32 9/16
Length on outside curve left horn — 31 15/16
Circumference at base of right horn — 14
Circumference at base of left horn — 14
Tip to tip — 17
Weight of cleaned skull with horns — 14¼ lbs.
Weight of dried skin thoroughly fleshed — 7 lbs. 5 oz.

Second Ram killed August 6, 1905
Number of age rings on horns — 9
Length on outside curve right horn — 37 1/16
Length on outside curve left horn — 38½
Circumference at base of right horn — 13⅝
Circumference at base of left horn — 13⅝
Tip to tip — 20¼
Weight of cleaned skull with horns — 16¼ lbs.
Weight of dried skin thoroughly fleshed — 7 lbs. 5 oz.

Third Ram killed August 6, 1905
Number of age rings on horns — 5
Length on outside curve right horn — 28½
Length on outside curve left horn — 28¾
Circumference at base of right horn — 12¼
Circumference at base of left horn — 12¼
Tip to tip — 17⅛
Weight of cleaned skull with horns — 9 lbs.
Weight of dried skin thoroughly fleshed — 5 lbs. 10 oz.

APPENDIX E

TIME SPENT IN PADDLING DOWN PELLY RIVER

From the mouth of the Ross River to the Lewes I had kept an accurate record of the time consumed paddling between well-known tributaries. All the time occupied during stops is deducted.

Strickland canoe, twenty-one feet long, weight one hundred and fifty pounds; weight of two men and materials an additional one thousand pounds; September stage of water; average September weather. Total distance two hundred and ninety miles (Dr. Dawson).

Ross River to Rose Creek — 13 hours and 45 minutes
Rose Creek to Glenlyon River — 1 hours and 20 minutes
Glenlyon River to Tay River — 2 hours and 15 minutes
Tay River to Harvey Creek — 2 hours and 25 minutes
Harvey Creek to Earn River — 1 hours and 25 minutes
Earn River to Tummel River — 3 hours and 15 minutes
Tummel River to MacMillan River — 7 hours and 5 minutes
MacMillan River to head of Granite Cañon — 2 hours and 5 minutes
Passing through Granite Cañon — 40 minutes
Foot of Granite Cañon to Mica Creek — 3 hours and 40 minutes
Mica Creek to Willow Creek — 50 minutes
Willow Creek to Grayling Creek — 1 hours and 10 minutes
Grayling Creek to the Lewes — 5 hours and 15 minutes
Total Time — 45 hours and 10 minutes